THE COMPLETE BOOK OF DRAWING
MANGA

DUDLEY BURNS

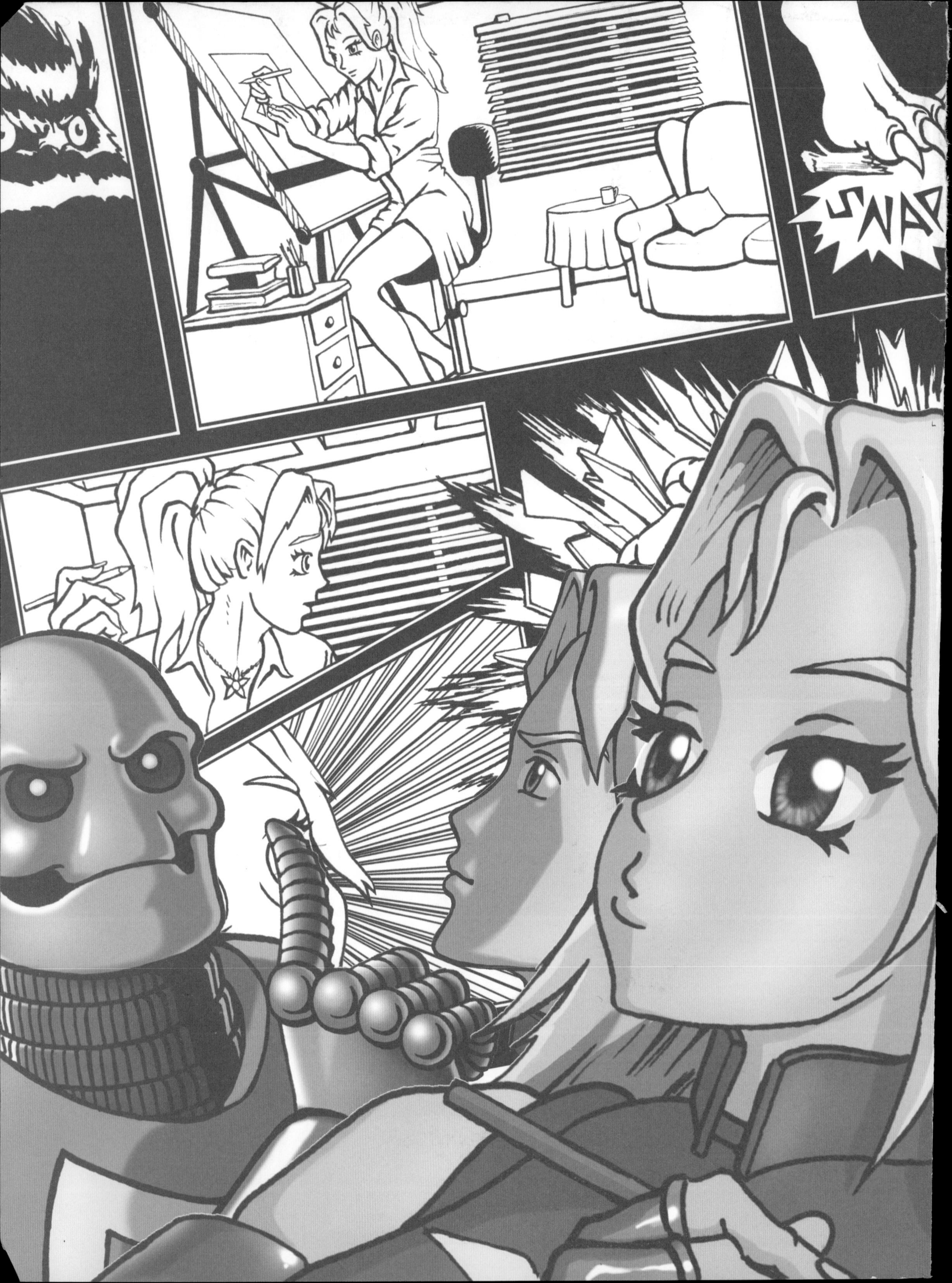
SNAP

THE COMPLETE BOOK OF DRAWING
MANGA

Peter Gray

ARCTURUS

CONTENTS

Much of the material used in this book was previously published in *The Art of Drawing and Creating Manga Action*, *The Art of Drawing and Creating Manga Women*, *The Art of Drawing and Creating Manga Mechas and Monsters* and *The Art of Drawing and Creating Manga Advanced Techniques*.

ARCTURUS

Arcturus Publishing Limited
26/27 Bickels Yard 151–153 Bermondsey Street London SE1 3HA

Published in association with
foulsham
W. Foulsham & Co. Ltd,
The Publishing House, Bennetts Close, Cippenham,
Slough, Berkshire SL1 5AP, England

ISBN-13: 978- 0-572-03307-1

This edition printed in 2007
Copyright © 2004, 2006 Arcturus Publishing Limited

British Library Cataloguing-in-Publication Data: a catalogue record for this book is available from the British Library

Printed in China

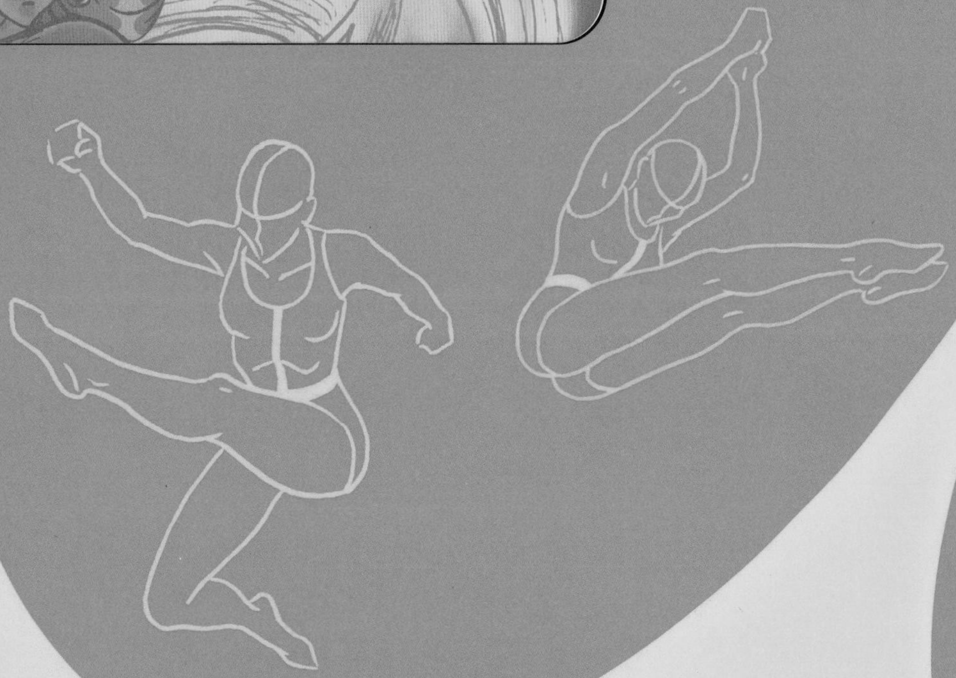

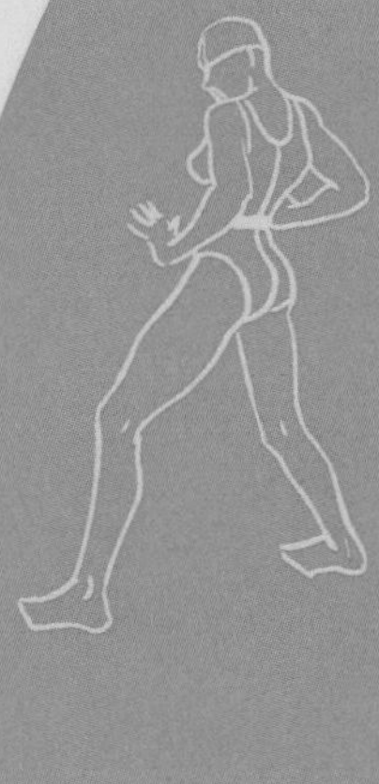

If you're into drawing manga, chances are you've already copied characters from your favorite comics or animations. You may also have created and developed characters of your own, or maybe you have already followed some of the step-by-step instructions to draw characters found in this book.

Interesting, dynamic, and glamorous characters are at the heart of what manga is about, so they are a logical starting point for drawing in the manga style. But at some point, you'll want to do more with your characters, so this book also tells you how to put characters into contexts that will show off their best attributes.

You'll learn how to design backgrounds, compose pictures, and tell stories with your characters. Whether you enjoy futuristic fantasies or gritty urban tales, romance or horror, the principles for making your characters come to life can be transferred from one genre to another.

So there's plenty you can learn from each and every one of the exercises provided in this book—even the ones that might not involve the types of characters or action that you are mainly interested in drawing.

This book also covers how to draw and create manga women, action heroes and heroines, as well as mechas and monsters. Here we'll look at some of the characters again and create environments for them.

Don't be afraid to be imaginative and make up worlds of your own devising—the characters are only used to demonstrate picture-making principles, and you can apply these principles to any characters and scenes you choose to create.

Although the main characters of manga comics and *animes* (the Japanese word for animations) are usually human, they are often supported by a cast of animals, robots, and monsters—from cuddly little four-legged sidekicks to enormous dinosaurs, robotic killing machines, and strange alien beasts. We'll also be focusing on these weird and wonderful creatures in this book. In many ways, they are the most interesting and enjoyable manga characters to draw. Many of them—good and bad—are based in some way on men, women, and children, so you'll need to know how to draw human beings and, most importantly, how to adapt their features.

Manga features in a huge range of magazines, computer games, and graphic novels. It is one of the most visible drawing styles in the world today, and very popular among comic-book fans.

Here, you'll find a wealth of exercises to get you started drawing in the style. There are easy-to-follow steps for you to create a range of characters, and you'll also find plenty of examples to help you develop your own cast of amazing beings.

Don't be put off by the slick look of the artwork produced by professional artists—it isn't that hard to emulate once you know some of the tricks of the trade. Nor do you need to own a computer to produce interesting color work.

The most important skill for any aspiring manga artist to develop is the ability to draw, and this will only come about if you keep practicing. Don't limit yourself to just drawing in the manga style—try a range of different approaches. All this effort will pay off eventually, and you will notice how much more inventive and interesting your drawings become.

THE TEAM

To help us through the challenges and to share in our triumphs as we make our way through the book, we'll be accompanied by this trio of friendly guides. They'll pose for some drawings and demonstrations and they'll also be popping up from time to time with hints and suggestions to help you on your way. They all know a lot about the world of manga and each is accomplished at drawing, so pay attention to their tips; they know what they are talking about. ***Let me introduce you to the team…***

DAISY

You can see that Daisy is a confident girl. She's 17 years old, and she's a pretty good manga artist herself—she's been drawing comics since she was 12.

Daisy is also good at defending herself—something she learned from growing up on the rough side of town. But she avoids fights when she can—she'd much rather be drawing or hanging out with her friends. She's a good and loyal friend and knows how to have fun.

DUKE

Duke, who is also 17, was brought up as Daisy's brother after he was orphaned as a small child. He has more muscle than most young men of his age because he is a black belt in Judo and trains every day. His other skills are in Kendo, playing guitar and, of course, drawing. Duke is a bit of a joker, but he knows when to stop playing around and be serious.

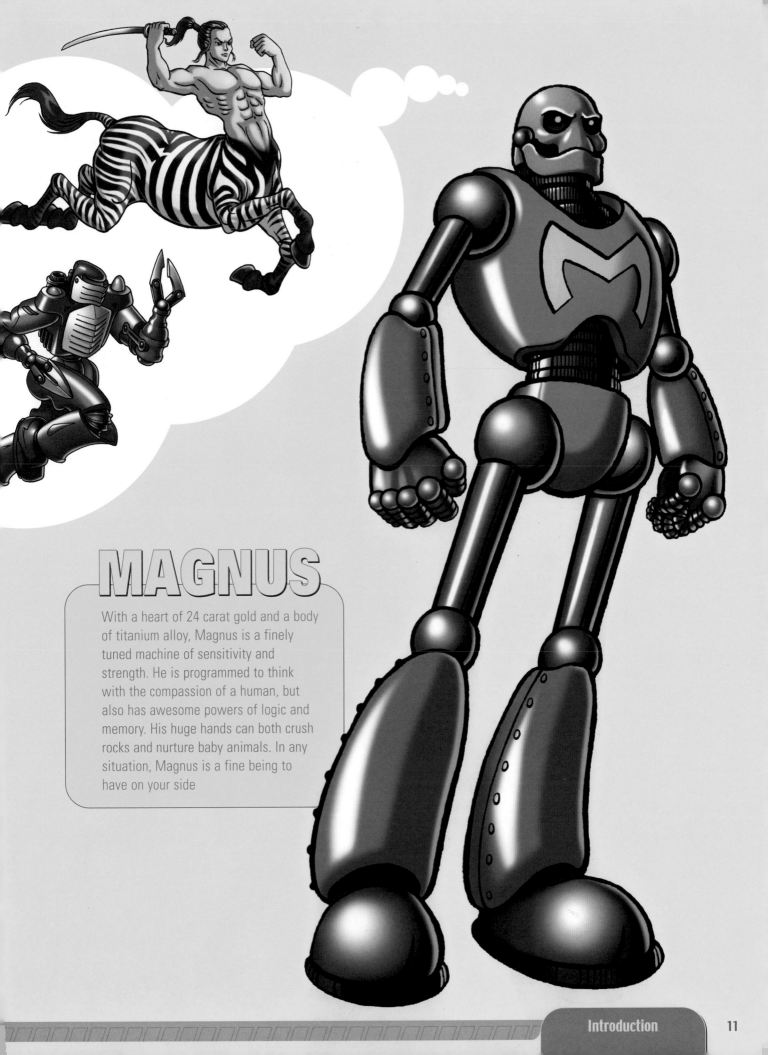

MAGNUS

With a heart of 24 carat gold and a body of titanium alloy, Magnus is a finely tuned machine of sensitivity and strength. He is programmed to think with the compassion of a human, but also has awesome powers of logic and memory. His huge hands can both crush rocks and nurture baby animals. In any situation, Magnus is a fine being to have on your side

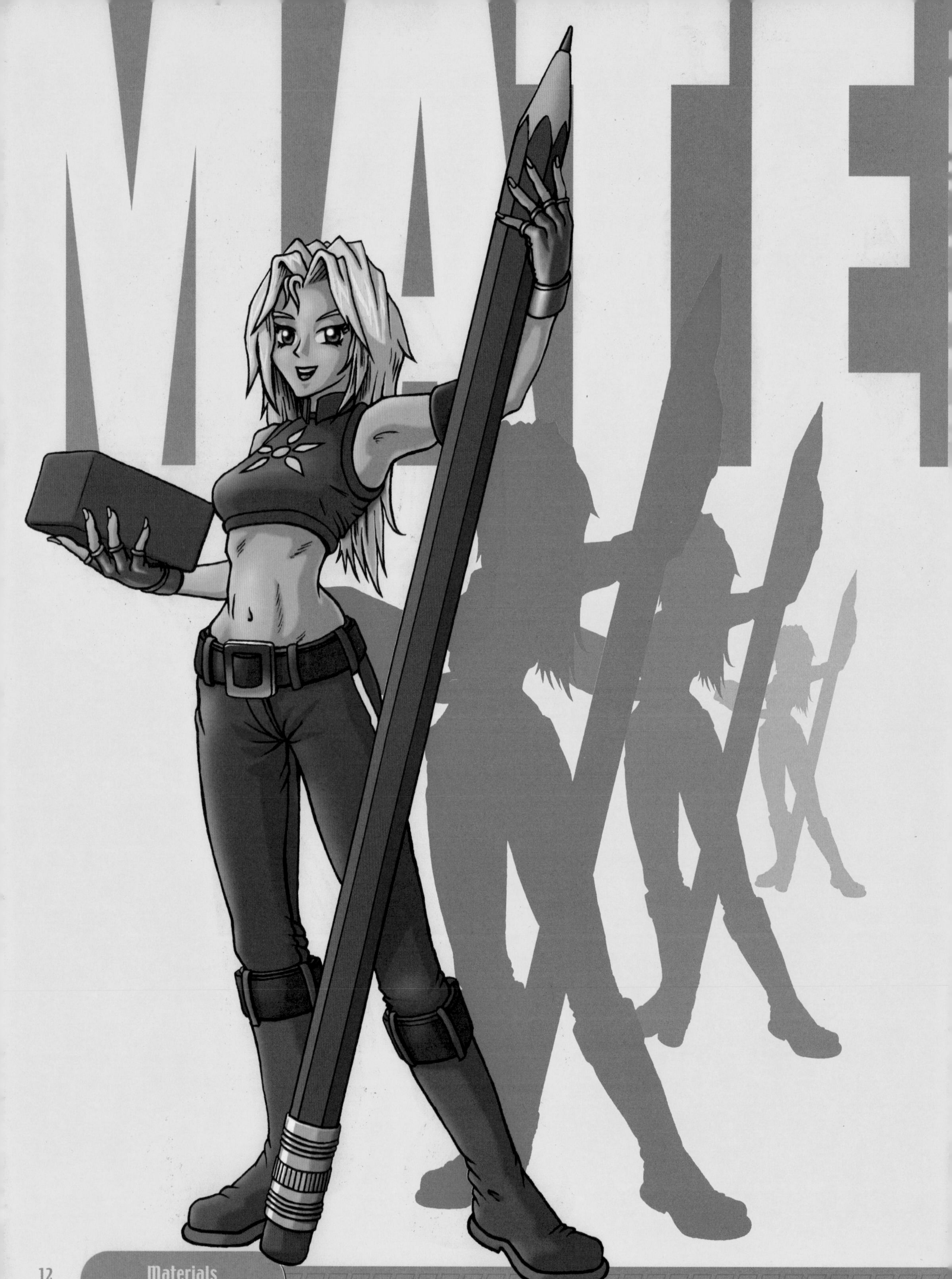

One of the biggest mistakes artists often make early in their development is to buy all kinds of materials, thinking these will make them a better artist. But you really don't need much at all.

Pencils

Pencils are graded from 3 to 1.
A number 3 pencil is hard, and a number 1 pencil is soft. Ordinary pencils used in schools and at home are number 2. They are good general-purpose pencils, but a harder pencil like a number 3 is more useful for sketching light guidelines. A softer pencil like a number 1 will help you darken your drawings. Using a number 2 mechanical pencil produces a constant fine line. Non-mechanical pencils will need sharpening regularly.

Eraser

You'll be drawing frameworks to help form your pictures, so these frameworks, and any mistakes you make along the way, will need to be erased. Any eraser should do the trick—just make sure it erases cleanly.

Paper

Most of the drawings in this book were done on cheap photocopier paper. You only need to worry about paper quality when you are using more advanced materials.

Pens

Traditional manga artists use a metal-tipped pen and black ink. The pen produces lines of varying thickness, depending on how hard it is pressed onto the paper. An easier alternative is to use good quality felt-tipped drawing pens.

Brushes and Ink

A brush and some black ink can produce a range of different effects. They are also useful for filling in large areas of solid black. Some manga artists use brushes for all their black line work. Choose good quality fine round-tipped watercolor brushes. White ink is useful for covering up mistakes and adding effects.

Color

Not long ago, manga artists did all their coloring by hand using watercolors or acrylic paints. Today, most manga artwork is colored on computer—most of the artwork in this book is colored that way. If you don't have access to a computer or the appropriate software, that's okay—the older methods can produce stunning effects.

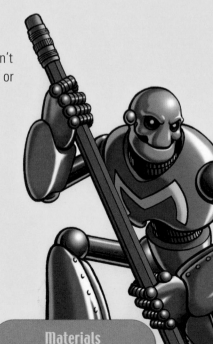

human HEADS

In manga-style drawings, female faces tend to be quite similar—even the bad girls are usually pretty and even-featured.

Male faces vary much more because for manga boys and men, the main emphasis is on character and action rather than beauty. Male faces can be fat or thin, long or round, square or heart-shaped, cheerful or sinister, handsome or downright ugly!

In this section, we'll be looking at a whole range of male faces and bodies. We'll start by focusing on Duke's face since drawing his face from a variety of angles will teach you the basic skills you need in order to draw all kinds of other manga characters.

For each drawing, we'll start by sketching some guidelines to form a framework for the head. We'll then add more guidelines for other features step by step. You'll want to erase most of these lines at some point, so don't make them too heavy. Use your hard pencil to draw them or, if you only have a soft pencil, press lightly so the lines are fainter.

My guidelines are dark in this book to make sure you can see them clearly to copy them. In each step, I've also made the new lines red so you know exactly what to do.

HEADS
HEADS
HEADS
HEADS
HEADS
HEADS
HEADS
HEADS
HEADS
HEADS
HEADS
HEADS
HEADS
HEADS
HEADS
HEADS

MANGA

Front View (male)

For each step, study the picture carefully to see all the lines that you need to draw.

Step 1

Start by making a basic framework. First draw a vertical line to help you make your picture symmetrical. Draw a circle over it and add four lines to form the sides of the face and jaw. Draw a horizontal line halfway down this whole shape. Add a short pencil stroke for the mouth.

Step 2

Eyes are roughly halfway down the head—Duke's irises are round, and the tops should touch the underside of the horizontal line. To draw the ears, start level with the tops of the eyes. The ears should finish level with where the bottom of the nose will be. Draw outline shapes for Duke's hair, neck, and collar too.

Step 3

Add the pupils, eyelids, and eyebrows, then use two long curved lines to mark the bangs.

Step 4

The main feature to work on here is the hair. Duke has a middle part, so the hair will hang symmetrically. It also has an angular look.

Step 5

A small circle in the top right of each eye makes the bright highlights that characterize manga artwork.

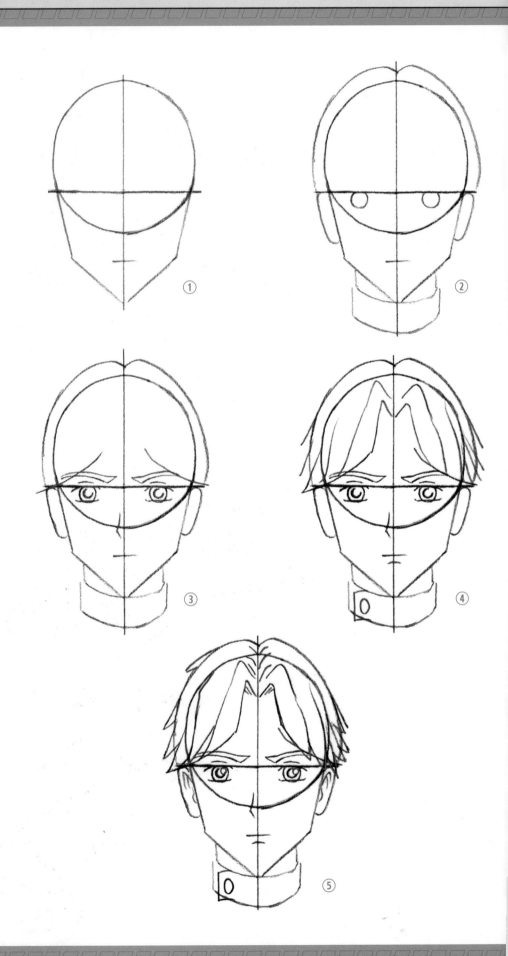

Step 6

Now ink over all your final pencil lines with a black ballpoint or felt-tip pen. Use long, confident pencil strokes for the pieces of hair that hang over Duke's forehead. Shade in Duke's pupils, but leave the bright highlights white. Once the ink is dry, erase the rest of the pencil marks—especially the ones that made up your original framework.

You can copy the colors I've used here or wait until you've worked through the Color section of this book so that you understand more about how to apply color.

The eyes of most manga characters are spaced more than a whole eye's distance apart. There's more information on drawing eyes later in this book.

Profile (male)

When seen from the side, Duke's skull is based on an oval-shape.

Step 1

Copy the framework for Duke's head. The vertical guideline drops down from the oval to form the front of the face. The horizontal guideline should sit halfway down the whole head shape again.

Step 2

Place Duke's eye and ear, starting on the horizontal guideline. From this angle, the eye takes the shape of a narrow oval, and sits near the front of the face; the ear is just over halfway back. The neck slopes backward slightly. To outline Duke's hair, roughly follow the shape of the top of the head, then curve your line in toward the back of the neck.

Step 3

You can see here how the vertical guideline helps you shape the front of Duke's face. Work on the eye and add the eyebrow. Draw a long curve to mark the length of the hair.

Step 4

Duke's hair is cropped close to the neck at the back. Copy its shape. A slight curve to the jaw makes for a much more pleasing profile.

Step 5

Add a few more lines to Duke's hair, particularly at the top to show how it hangs down from the parting. From this angle, Duke's pupil and the bright highlight should both be oval-shaped not round.

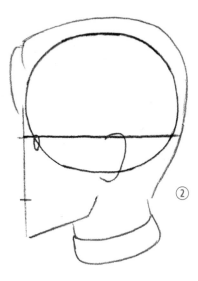

①

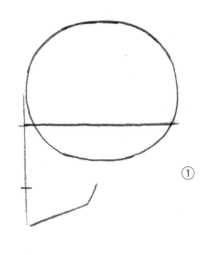

③

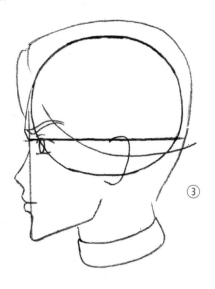

④

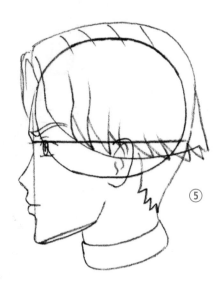

②

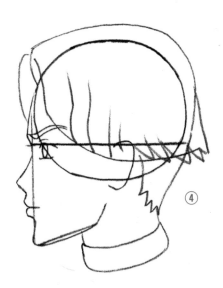

⑤

Step 6

When you're happy with your picture, go over your final lines again using a black ballpoint or felt-tip pen. Notice how while I was doing this, I decided to add a couple of tufts to the crown of Duke's hair. I also made the line of his neck more curved at the front. Let the ink dry, then erase the rest of the pencil marks to leave a clean drawing.

⑥

¾ View (male)

Duke has turned his head so that we can see both the front and side. This angle is slightly more complicated to draw, but mastering it is worth the effort.

Step 1

Copy the shapes that make up the framework of the head—start with a circle that's slightly elongated and tilted to the right. The vertical line marking the center of the face has moved in the same direction as the head and curves at the top. The horizontal guideline is still halfway down the whole shape.

Step 2

When you place Duke's eyes, notice that the iris of the one on the right of your picture is almost circular. The one turned farther away is slightly smaller and oval-shaped. It also sits closer to the vertical guideline.

Step 3

Add some detail to Duke's eyes and draw the eyebrows—we can't see all of the eyebrow on the left of the picture. Re-shape the jawline to make it less angular.

Step 4

To draw Duke's nose, start level with the bottom of the eyes. Don't forget the crease line on the chin.

Step 5

The main thing to notice here is that the bright highlight on the eye to the left of your picture is more of an oval shape, just like the iris.

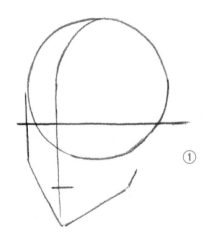

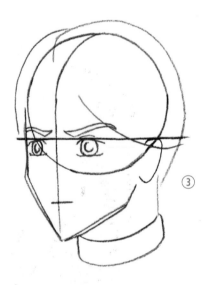

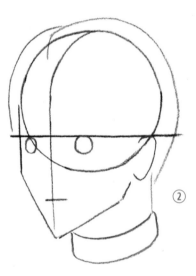

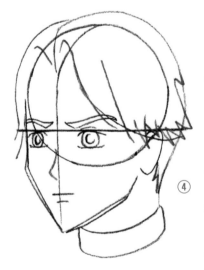

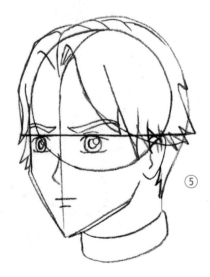

Step 6

Take another look at your picture. If the face seems crooked or squashed, look back over steps 1 to 5 and see if you can work out where it went wrong. If you need to start again, don't worry—remind yourself that practice makes perfect. Once your drawing looks similar to this one, go over your pencil lines with a black pen. Notice how I've added a few extra little lines to the hair and collar here to give them more definition. When the ink is dry, erase the rest of the pencil marks.

MANGA

Different Angles (male)

Like real people, manga characters move their heads in lots of different directions, so you need to be able to draw them from all angles. Some angles are trickier than others, but if you always use guidelines, you'll be much more successful at drawing well-proportioned faces. Look carefully at the way the guidelines curve in the next series of pictures.

① When Duke looks down, the top of the skull looks almost circular—its curve forms the guideline that helps you place the eyes and ears. We can see a lot of his hair and all the facial features are low down. The ears sit higher than the eyes.

② If Duke tilts his head up to one side, his hair becomes less prominent and we can see a lot of his face. Now the ears are lower than the eyes. The eye to the left of the picture is closer to the guideline running down the center of the face than the other eye.

③ If Duke is looking down at an angle, we can see a lot of one side of his hair and his face takes up a much smaller proportion of the picture.

④ The farther his head turns the less we can see of Duke's features.

⑤ Seen from this angle, all we get is a close-up of the cut of Duke's hair, his neck and ears. His features aren't visible.

①

②

③

④

Try drawing my head from the back or looking down on top of it. Study a friend's head from these angles to work out what features are visible and how they would look.

⑤

Proportions (male)

The pictures here show Duke at various ages. They demonstrate how the relative proportions of a face change as a person gets older. The horizontal lines will help you to see exactly how the proportions differ.

½

¼

At the age of nine, Duke's eyes were large in relation to his other features and sat below the center of his head.

Duke is 17 at the moment. His eyes appear smaller, and they are higher up on his head than when he was a boy.

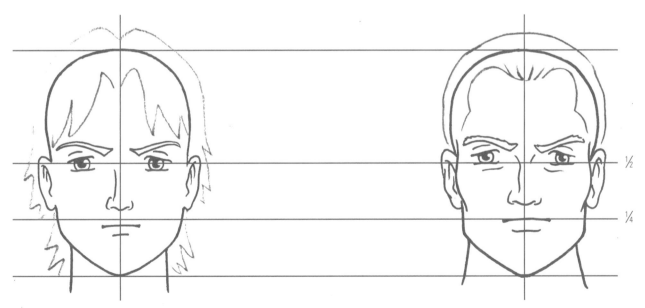

½

¼

By the time Duke is 25, his eyes will sit halfway up his head. His nose and mouth will have grown much bigger.

As Duke gets older, his eyes sit even higher on his head. The mouth and nose continue to grow.

MANGA

Front View (female)

Study each picture carefully to see what features you need to add.

Step 1
First draw a framework for Daisy's head. Start with a vertical line—this will help you make your picture symmetrical. Draw an upside-down egg shape over this, then draw four horizontal lines across it—the longest one sits halfway down the head and the others are evenly spaced around it. Add a short pencil stroke for Daisy's mouth.

Step 2
Eyes sit about halfway down the face. First draw two arches for Daisy's irises—use your framework to help you place them. Like most manga eyes, they are more than a whole eye's distance apart. The ears start level with the top of the eyes and finish level with where the nose will be. Add some guidelines for the hair and neck.

Step 3
Give the eyes and ears some more detail, then add a small upturned nose. Shape the chin to give it a gentle angular look.

Step 4
Sketch in the rough shapes of the hair and the direction in which it flows. Here Daisy's hair is tied back.

Step 5
Give the hair and face more detail. Add a small circle to each eye to make a bright highlight.

Step 6

Now go over your pencil lines with a black ballpoint or felt-tip pen. Use smooth, confident strokes. Shade in her pupils as well as the top half of each iris since this part is in the shadow of the eyelid. Leave the bright highlights white. Add the eyelashes, too. Once the ink is dry, rub out any remaining pencil marks, including the ones that made up your original framework.

Don't be overawed by the colored pictures at the end of drawing exercises like this one. We'll look at coloring later in the book. If you do want to add color, you might like to copy this color scheme.

The precise position and size of a person's eyes on the face change with age. There's more about this on page 23. You'll find more tips on drawing eyes on pages 34–37.

Profile (female)

Daisy's head looks more circular when it is drawn from the side.

Step 1

To make a framework, draw a circle, then attach a pointed shape to the bottom left of this to form the face and jaw. Draw a horizontal line across the center of the whole shape, then add three more horizontal lines as you did in the previous drawing. Make a short pencil stroke for the mouth.

Step 2

Use the guidelines to help you place Daisy's eye and ear. From this angle, the iris takes the shape of a narrow arch and sits close to the front of the face. The ear is just over halfway back on the side of the head. To draw the outline for the hair, it may help you to extend your main horizontal guideline. Notice how the neck slopes backward.

Step 3

Shape the front of Daisy's face, then soften the line forming the underpart of her chin. Now add some detail to the eye and ear.

Step 4

Study the picture to make sure your guidelines for the hair show the different directions in which it flows.

Step 5

Work on the hair to make it more angular—like the bright highlights on each eye, this is a key feature that distinguishes manga artwork.

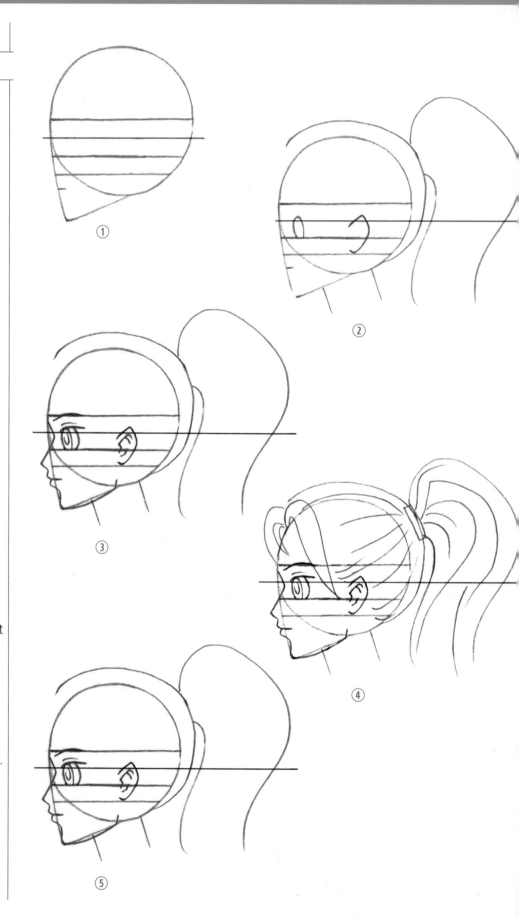

Step 6

When you're ready, go over your pencil lines in pen, as you did for the previous drawing. Let the ink dry, then erase all remaining pencil lines to leave a clean picture.

⑥

Outlining your drawing using black felt-tip pens of different thickness will allow you to make some lines heavier than others, adding solidity to your picture.

¾ View (female)

Daisy has turned her head so that we can see the front and the side.

Step 1

Draw a shape that's like a pointed egg standing upside down and tilting to the right slightly. Notice how the vertical guideline curves. Add four horizontal guidelines as before and a tiny one for the mouth.

Step 2

The eye on the left of the picture is slightly angled away from us, so make the arch of the iris narrower and place it closer to the vertical guideline than the other eye. Place the ear, hair, and neck.

Step 3

Add some detail to the eyes and ear. To draw the nose, start above the eyebrows and draw a long curve ending in a little point. Reshape the jawline to make it more angular.

Step 4

Draw the guidelines for Daisy's hair. Notice how one piece falls across the eyebrow. Don't worry that your pencil lines overlap each other, you'll erase unwanted lines later.

Step 5

Give the hair more shape, then work on the facial features again. When you mark the bright highlights on Daisy's eyes, make the one on the left oval-shaped rather than round.

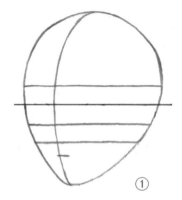

①

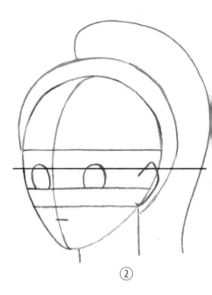

②

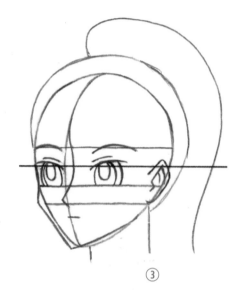

③

④

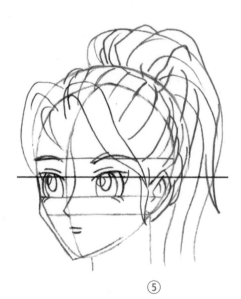

⑤

Step 6

Take another look at your picture—if the face looks odd, go back over all the steps so you can try to work out where you went wrong. Start again if you have to—it'll be worth it in the end. Once you're happy with your sketch, go over the lines that you want to form your final picture using a black felt-tip or ballpoint pen. Notice how I've changed the shape of Daisy's neck at this point by curving it to make it look softer. I've also used a smoother line to draw the side of the face to make the cheekbone less prominent. When the ink is dry, erase your pencil marks.

⑥

MANGA

Different Angles

Faces are rarely drawn from the front or side—like real people, manga characters move their heads in all directions. Some angles are trickier than others, but remembering to use guidelines will always help you.

① When Daisy turns away like this, her facial features almost disappear from view. Her hair becomes very prominent, as does the ear. Notice how the guidelines curve.

② When Daisy looks down, the horizontal guidelines curve up at the ends to make her ears sit higher up on the head. All the facial features sit toward the bottom of the egg shape.

③ If Daisy tilts her head down at an angle, we see more of the side of her head again.

④ When Daisy tilts her head upward, the horizontal guidelines should curve

downward at the ends to make the ears sit lower down on the head. Notice that we can see less of Daisy's hair from this angle.

⑤ If you look down on Daisy, the top of the head is circular. The face is hidden except for the eyebrows, the eyelashes, and the tip of the nose.

⑥ From the back, all you can see of the head is the hair, neck and ears.

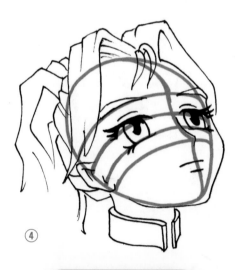

①

②

③

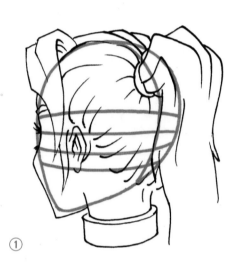

④

⑤

⑥

Proportions (female)

These pictures show Daisy at different ages. They demonstrate how the relative proportions of your facial features change as you get older. Try drawing all four pictures. Notice that the nose and mouth stay very similar at all ages.

A toddler's eyes are very large and sit low down on the head.

During childhood, the head grows to be larger in relation to the eyes, so the eyes look smaller and sit higher up on the head.

This is Daisy now—she is 17 and still has some growing to do. Her eyes appear even smaller and start to cross the halfway line of her head.

When Daisy is fully grown, her pupils will sit exactly halfway up.

Expressions

The human face is capable of revealing a very broad range of emotions. Good comic artists are able to show in their drawings different moods and reactions to help with telling a story and building character types.

Here Duke and Daisy are making some of the facial expressions that are common to manga characters. With the aid of a mirror, you can use your own face as a model for any expression you want to capture in your drawings.

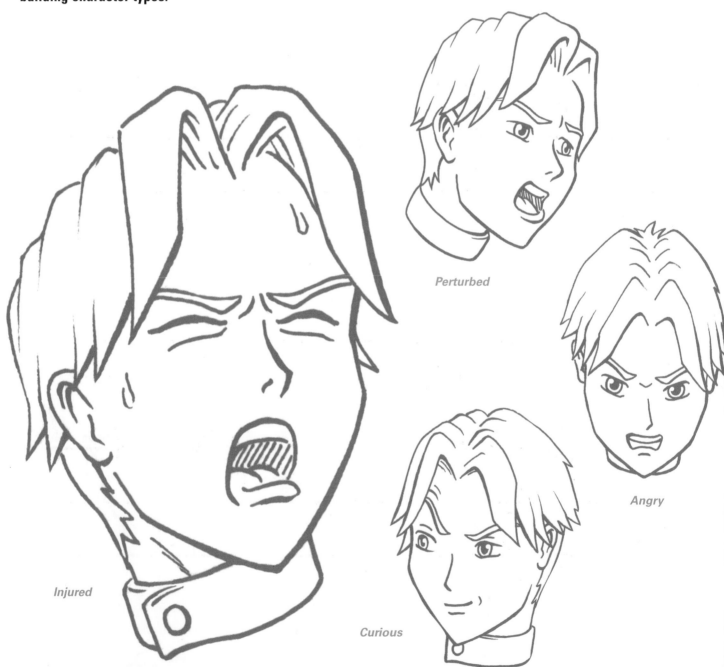

Perturbed

Angry

Injured

Curious

Relieved

Playful

Confrontational

Alarmed

Simple changes

Creating different expressions may seem complicated, but it's really about making very simple changes. Here are some dramatic expressions you can practice drawing—each one is made up of just a few simple lines and circles.

You should be able to tell what each of these faces is expressing right away, even though each picture is made up of only a few simple lines and circles. Now practice drawing them. Note how very simple changes—the tilt of an eyebrow or the drop of a lip—can bring about a complete change of mood.

Eyes

One of the most distinctive features of manga females is large, shiny eyes. When you draw them, bear in mind that the eyeball is round even if it doesn't look it because some parts are hidden by the eyelids.

① Daisy's eyes

Her iris (the colored part) and pupil (the black part in the middle) are both oval-shaped. A circle in the top left of each eye overlaps the iris and pupil to form a bright highlight, making the eye look shiny.

② Adding color

The top part of the iris is black—this is because the upper eyelid is casting a shadow over it. The area of the bright highlight is left white.

③ Turning away

In this position, we can see less of the iris and pupil and more of the white of the eye. The whole eye also appears narrower. First, sketch a circle-shaped eyeball, and within it draw a curve slightly in from the left—think of this curve as where the skin covers the eyeball. See how this changes the shape of the eyelid and eyebrow? The iris and pupil become narrower and the bright highlight is now also oval-shaped.

④ Turning farther away

Again, start with a circle but draw your curve farther to the right to make the new shape of the eyeball even narrower. Place the oval shapes for the iris, pupil, and highlight farther to the right and make them narrower too.

①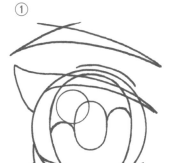

②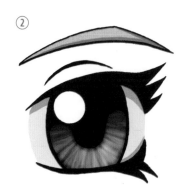

③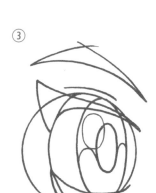

②

④

④

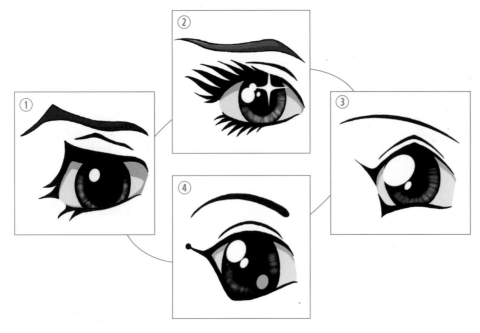

Glamorous eyes (1–4)

Manga artists have come up with a dazzling array of eye shapes and features. A lot of a character's style and personality is conveyed in the design of the eyes, so it's worth taking the time to draw them carefully. Here are a few of the kinds of eyes that could be used for glamorous female characters. None is very naturalistic, they are all heavily stylized and vary in the shapes of the lashes and brows as well as the characteristic manga sparkle and highlights.

Expressive eyes (5–7)

These are Daisy's eyes again, displaying some common manga expressions. When crying, the eyes fill with floods of tears which roll down the cheeks. An amused manga character usually laughs with eyes closed and the head tipped back so that we see the eye from the underside and arched upwards. In sleep or in thought, the closed eye arches downwards.

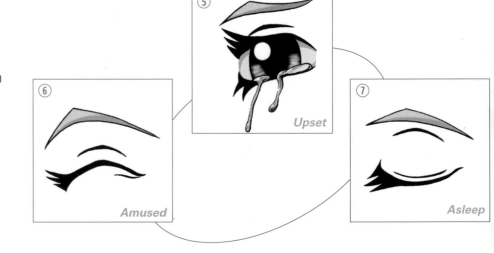

Upset

Amused

Asleep

Male and female eyes

In general, female characters have exaggeratedly large eyes and male eyes are more naturalistically proportioned. But this is not always the case. Whatever the size of the eyes, there are some general differences between the eye stylings of the sexes.

Daisy's large eye looks distinctly less feminine without the luxurious lashes. The rest of the eye remains quite unchanged, but it now seems more suitable for a young boy character.

Evil eyes

Smaller eyes can be used for female characters, especially for the baddies. Here are two similarly evil-looking eyes displaying typical gender stylizations. Though evil, the female eye is still gracefully drawn and with long lashes. The arch of the brow and the small, low-placed iris and pupil make it seem unkind. The male version has no heavy lashes, but the eyebrow can be much thicker.

It's not always easy to get both eyes of a character to look the same. Be prepared to spend some time over them, and use a sharp pencil or fine pen.

This very narrow, suspicious-looking eye, with its minimal lashes and fine brow, could equally belong to a male or female evil character.

Good Guys

Inventing characters is one of the most rewarding aspects of drawing. Here are some I've made up. You know they are good guys because they have large pupils, even when they have small irises, and their expressions are soft. You can tell they have different strengths, weaknesses, interests, and attitudes—it all shows in their faces.

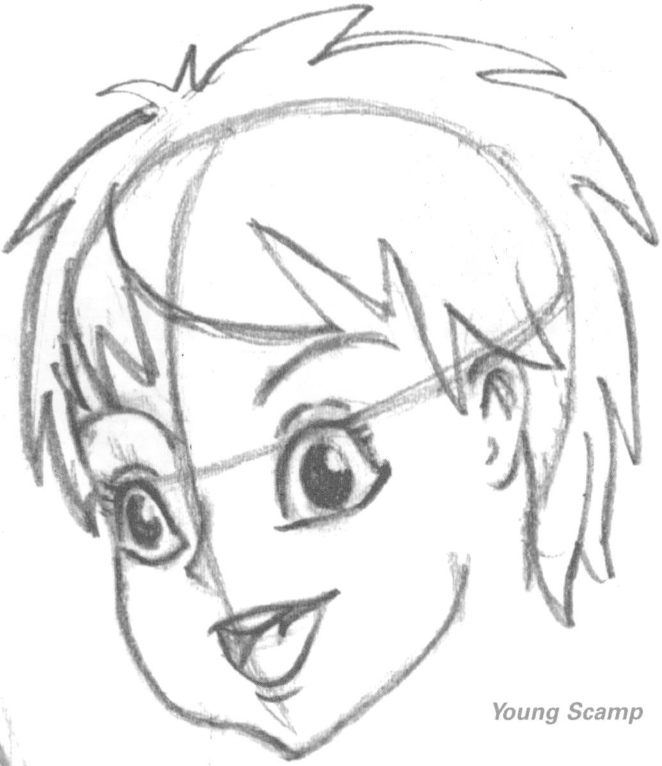

Young Scamp

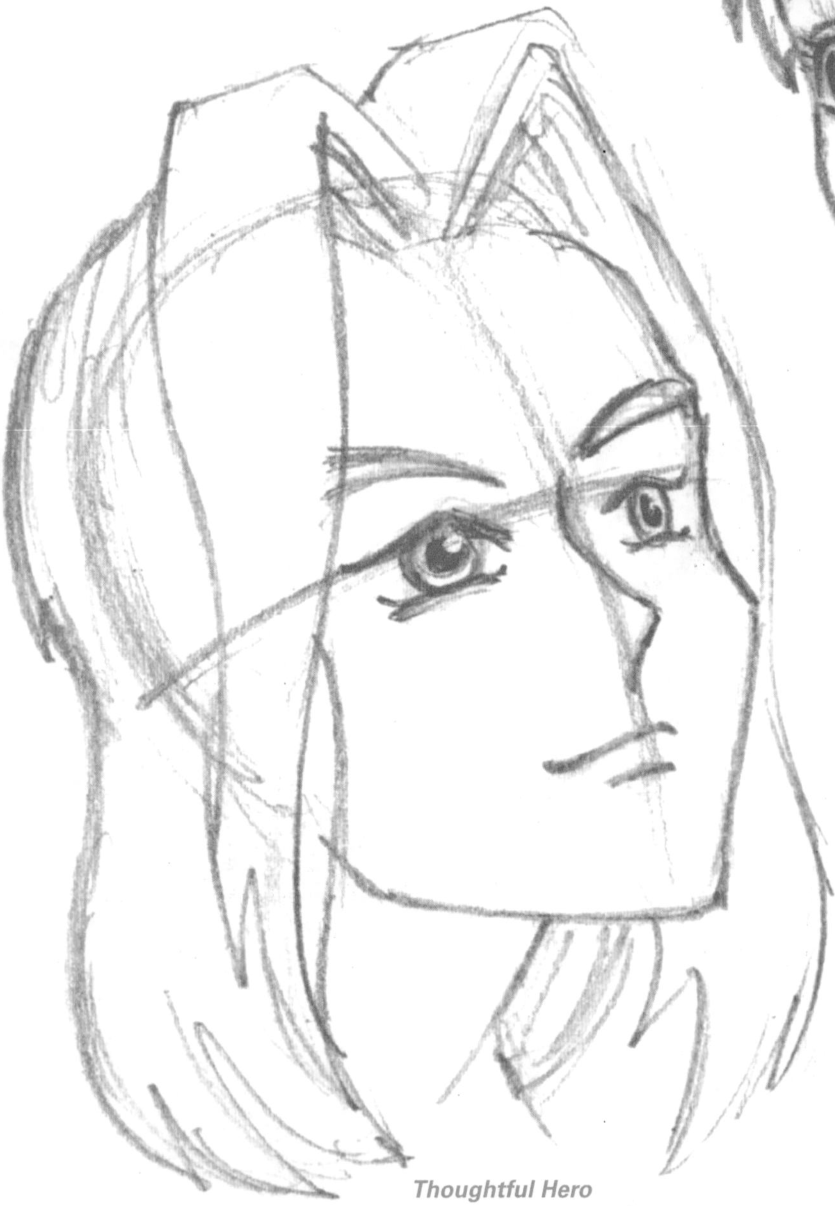

Thoughtful Hero

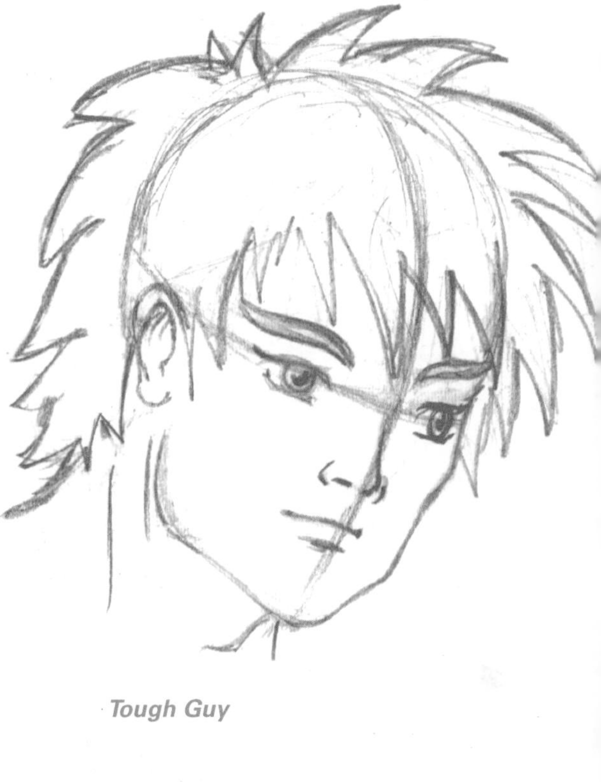

Tough Guy

Serious Type

Fantasy Hero

Streetwise Teen

Try drawing each of these characters or make up some of your own. Try changing the expressions, while retaining the friendly features of each face.

Schoolboy

Good Guys

Good Girls

When dreaming up female characters, the features are usually more subtle than their male counterparts, especially the goodies. Most manga women have similar face shapes, and very small noses and mouths. The main differences are in the eyes, hairstyles and general attitude. You may have to make many rough drawings before you can capture a certain look you are after for a good girl character.

Love-lorn

Daydreamer

City Chick

Romantic

Girl-next-door

Tomboy

Party Girl

Socialite

Your character's hairstyle is important to their overall image. Remember that hair grows out of a round skull and always flows away from the parting.

Good Boy Jai

This character, Jai, is much younger than Duke—you can tell by the shape of his head and the features on his face. You will draw him in a similar way, but the proportions will be different.

Step 1

Copy the framework for Jai's head as shown. His head isn't as long as Duke's, so make the lines forming the outline of the face and jaw much shorter. The horizontal guideline will still sit halfway down the shape, but since Jai is looking down slightly, the ends of this line will curve upward.

Step 2

Jai's eyes are large in relation to his other facial features. One eye is hidden by his hair, but the one we can see has a large oval-shaped iris.

Step 3

Add the detail to Jai's eye and draw a large eyebrow. His nose is smaller than Duke's, so make it short and rounded. Soften the jawline.

Step 4

Now work on Jai's floppy hairstyle. He has a side part—notice how this affects the way the hair falls.

Step 5

Jai has two bright highlights on his eye—a large almond-shaped one fills the top corner and a second one, shaped like a tiny oval, sits underneath this.

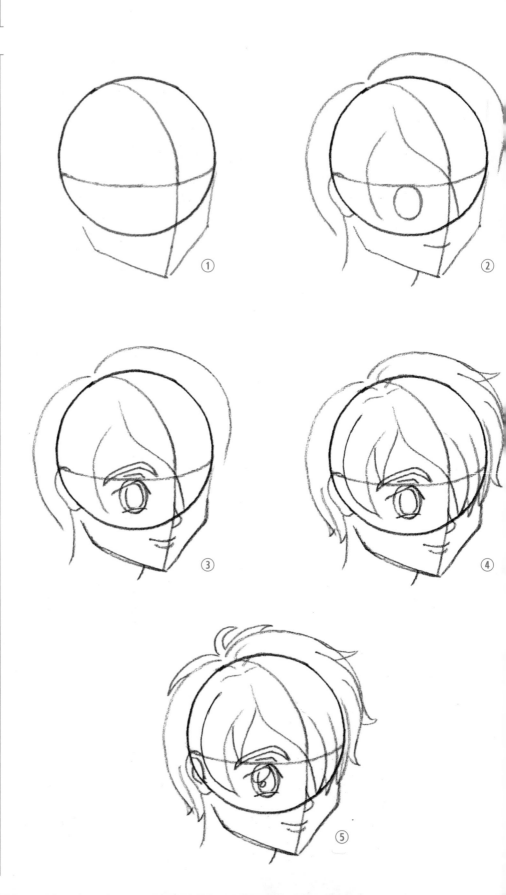

Step 6

Ink over your picture. Give the ear more definition if you think you need to. Shade in Jai's pupil, making sure you leave the bright highlights white. Leave it to dry, then erase any pencil lines that formed the original framework for the head.

If you add color to your picture, try making the smaller bright highlight a light blue instead of white. Make some areas of the hair paler to show the way the light hits the hair.

Good Girl Hale

Females of different ages have different characteristics, but the techniques you use to draw them are the same.

Step 1
Hale is much younger than Daisy. Her head is rounder, so start by drawing a circle instead of an egg shape. We'll draw her looking down and to the right, so your vertical guideline should curve out to the right. Place three horizontal guidelines as shown—they curve upward at the ends.

Step 2
Place the large irises of Hale's eyes as shown. Remember that from this angle, one will appear thinner than the other and it will sit nearer to the vertical line. Draw a small ear and two long thin eyebrows.

Step 3
Add some detail to the eyes and ear, then draw on the nose and mouth.

Step 4
Make the bottom of the hair more jagged and draw some longer pieces of hair around the sides of the face—don't cover up the ear. Place a large bow on top of the head.

Step 5
Add bangs, then work on the eyes. Each eye has three bright highlights—two are circle-shaped and sit in the top left of the eye. The third looks like a little fang and sits in the bottom right.

Step 6

Go over the light pencil lines that will form your final drawing with heavy pencil lines, erasing the lighter lines as you go. Add some lines to show the gathers on the bow. Shade in Hale's pupils as well as the top part of each iris, but make sure you leave all the bright highlights white. Now ink over your picture. Leave it to dry, then erase the rest of your pencil lines.

Add the color, or wait until you've worked through the Color section of this book and come back to your drawing later.

⑥

Young characters like Hale have plenty of space for more than one bright highlight in each of their huge eyes! The highlights can form a whole range of patterns.

Nasty Duke

Here is Duke's evil twin Dagger. By comparing these pictures of the manga twins, you can see that just a few small alterations to Duke's facial features turn him from a kind and innocent teenager into a mean and aggressive bad guy!

Make the eyes narrower and give them smaller pupils. Angle the eyebrows down toward the center and draw two deep frown lines in between them. Add some little lines at the top of the nose to show that Dagger is sneering. Now change the shape of the mouth so Dagger is curling his bottom lip. Notice how subtle changes to the color and shading adds to the effect too—a dark shadow is now cast across the eyes.

Nasty Daisy

This is Daisy's evil twin, Detta. Notice how just a few small changes to Daisy can turn her from a friendly and helpful teenager into a cold and scheming bad girl!

Drawing hints

Give Detta's eyes less height and make the pupils smaller. Angle the eyebrows down toward the center, and curl the lip at one end to make Detta scowl. Give her lots of earrings and put a ring through one eyebrow. If you decide to color in your picture, add some darker patches to her face to cast shadows across it. Make the color of her eyes more gray than Daisy's. Use a dirtier yellow for the hair.

Bad Guys & Girls

Most bad guys have tiny pupils and dramatic eyebrows. They are also usually much uglier than bad manga girls! After you've tried drawing the examples on this page, how about inventing some bad characters of your own?

Loco

Aggressive

Brat

Cunning

Sly Thug

Venomous

Manic

Schemer

Freaky

Spiteful

Bad Guy Bile

Getting the framework for Bile's head right is the key to creating this evil character.

Step 1

Start by drawing a circle with a vertical guideline curving down from the top. Carefully study the picture to copy the other vertical guidelines. Add the horizontal guideline—it should curve slightly as shown.

Step 2

Draw two small circles for the irises of Bile's eyes—notice how one sits slightly higher than the other. Copy the curves of the eyebrows. Draw the first lines of the nose, mouth, and ear and add the thick-set neck.

Step 3

When you draw Bile's eyeballs, position them so that the irises sit high up inside them. Copy the crooked shape of Bile's face and jaw. Add two little curves to form the edges of his wide nostrils.

Step 4

The eyebrows really make Bile's face look mean here—make them jagged along the top to show how hairy they are. Don't forget the lines that create bags under his eyes.

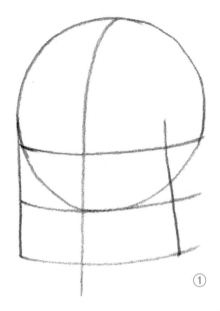

①

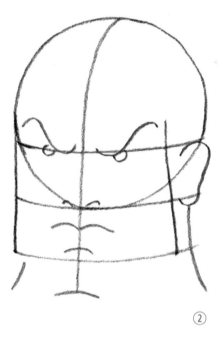

②

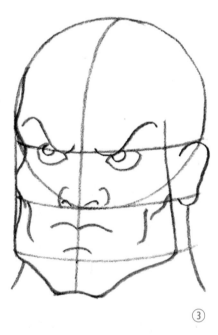

③

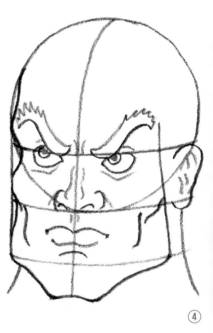

④

Step 5

Now go over your heavy pencil lines using a black ballpoint or felt-tip pen. Go over some of the lines twice to make them bolder—study the picture closely to see where I've done this. When the ink is dry, erase any remaining pencil lines, including the ones that formed the original framework for the head.

Now you can have some fun with color. I've turned Bile a sickly green and added a tinge of gray around the eyes. The orange eyebrows look like they're on fire.

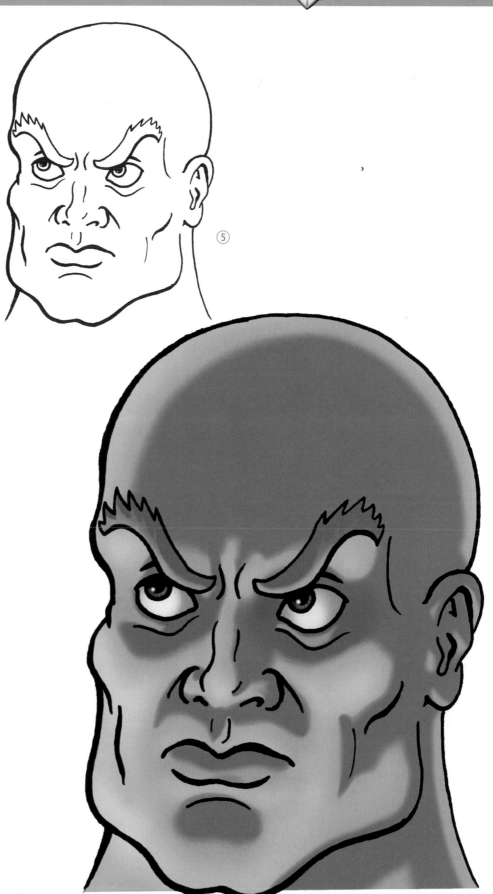

⑤

Bad Girl Ruelle

This character is a grown-up woman—and an evil one at that. We'll be drawing a ¾ view of her.

Step 1

Start with a long egg shape that is pointed at the bottom and tilts to the right. Add a vertical line that curves out to the left. Carefully copy the positions of the two horizontal lines—both curve up at the ends since Ruelle's head is tilted down slightly.

Step 2

Draw Ruelle's eyes across the top horizontal line so they sit high up on her head. Add a large curved ear. Place the mouth, neck, and hair.

Step 3

Add some more detail to the facial features. Notice how low down the top eyelids are, making the eyes look heavy. The eyebrows are sharply angled and the nose long and narrow. Draw the mouth open.

Step 4

Re-shape the face to make the cheekbone jut out more. The jaw shape is long and narrow. Add some lines to define the lank hair.

Step 5

Add a strip of hair falling across Ruelle's face and re-shape the ends to make them more straggly. Give her long eyelashes, but make her pupils small. Thicken the eyebrows and shape the lips.

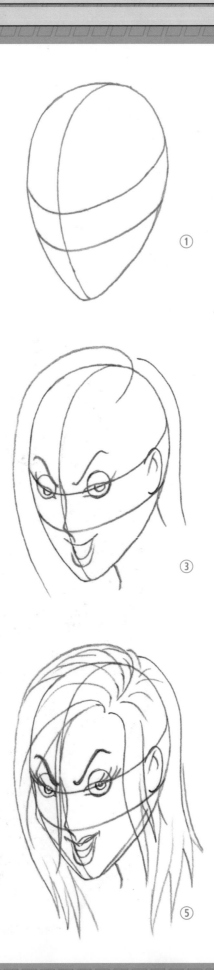

Step 6

Now go over your picture again, using heavy pencil lines to bring it to life. Shade inside Ruelle's mouth and add a couple of frown lines above her nose. Go over your final lines with a black ballpoint or felt-tip pen, and when the ink is dry, erase the rest of your pencil marks.

By using blues and grays, I've made Ruelle's coloring as cold as her character. Try using the same kinds of shades.

⑥

Designing Faces

Before we move on to drawing the body, you might like to have some more practise with heads and faces. Making copies of existing manga characters is good to get you started, but there's much more fun to be had from creating characters of your own. Here's Duke to demonstrate some things to think about when designing new character heads.

① This is Duke as we know him.

② The shape of the head is an important element of a new character, so start by deciding on head and face shapes: round, oval, angular, square. Here, I've given Duke a square jaw, which makes him seem tougher and a bit older.

③—④ The guidelines you set down to place the facial features make a big difference to a character's look. In these examples, Duke's eyes and mouth are moved up, down, in and out to produce quite different faces.

⑤ The sizes of the features also have an impact on a character. With Duke's eyes and mouth enlarged, he seems younger and more innocent.

①

②

③

④

⑤

■ Think about the age of a character before you begin.

■ Try to imagine what kind of attitude you want them to have: gentle, sadistic, heroic, cowardly and so forth.

■ See how changing expressions affects the kind of characters you are developing.

Expression

Eye shape

Already, you've seen lots of examples of eyes, head shapes, angles, hairstyles and expressions. A good way to start developing your own characters is to take elements from my sketches and diagrams and mixing them up in new ways. Then add or change any details that you think will make your characters interesting.

Here's a new character drawn from various elements of other pictures featured earlier in this book.

Face shape

Hairstyle

New character

HUMAN FIGURES

Now that you've had some experience drawing heads, you need to learn how to draw the bodies you'd attach to them to get your character moving.

The human body is a very complex machine with bones, muscles, fat, and skin all working together. You don't need to understand its entire makeup to draw a manga-style figure, but knowing something about the structure of the skeleton, and the flesh and muscle attached to it, will help make your drawings easier to construct, so that the final results are much more effective.

It might take a while to master all the various lines involved in drawing the body from different angles, but you'll start to work it out after a few exercises.

To help you understand how the shape of the body changes as it moves, study your own body in the mirror—stand at different angles and try making a variety of poses.

FIGURES
FIGURES
FIGURES
FIGURES
FIGURES
FIGURES
FIGURES
FIGURES
FIGURES
FIGURES
FIGURES
FIGURES
FIGURES
FIGURES
FIGURES
FIGURES
FIGURES

The Skeleton (male)

The skeleton can be thought of as a frame that you hang muscles, skin, and clothing on. The arms don't hang directly from the chest but are separated by shoulder bones. The legs are joined directly onto the hips. The body is able to bend because of the joints—the arms have shoulder, elbow, and wrist joints whereas the legs have hips, knees, and ankles.

① Simplified front view

This is a simplified version of the front view of Duke's skeleton to show the main body parts. The joints are drawn using dots.

② Simplified side view

When Duke is seen side on, some of his features get thinner and others disappear from view. Notice the arch of the spine from this angle.

③ Simplified ¾ view

As Duke starts to turn toward the side, the shape of his rib cage and hips will look different again.

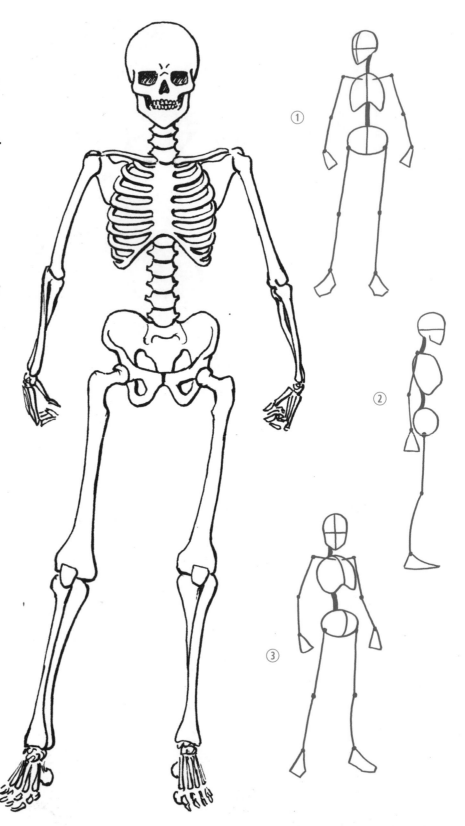

Muscles (male)

Duke is a typical manga teenager—larger than life. A real boy of his age would probably carry far less muscle than this.

① **Body outline—front view**
Duke's outline mostly follows the shape of the skeleton—it curves out more where the body is particularly muscular, and tapers in at the joints.

② **Muscles—front view**

③ **Muscles—side view**

④ **Muscles—rear view**

These pictures of his body show how the flesh and muscles wrap around Duke's bones. Study these pictures carefully. Understanding the muscle structure under the skin will make drawing it easier. You may like to refer to these pictures when you are drawing your own action characters.

To draw a character with a larger build, draw the body outline farther away from the bones and use stronger curves. For a skinny body, keep your lines closer to the bone.

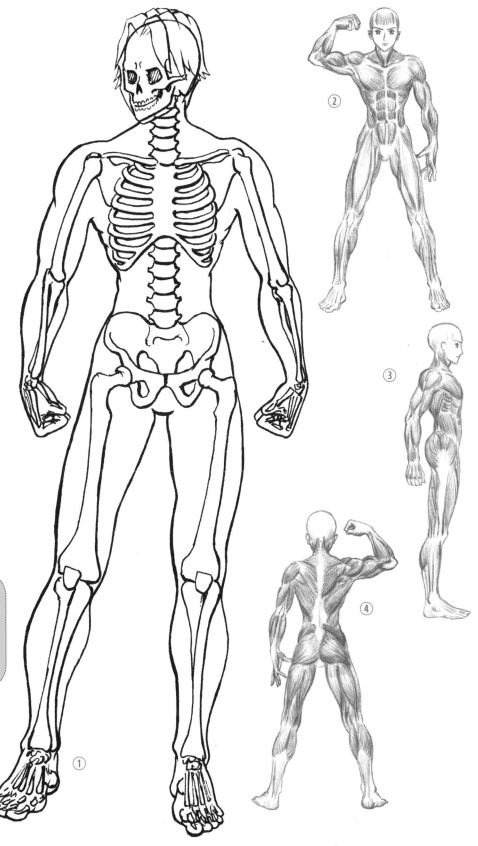

Proportions (male)

Manga artists work out the relative sizes of their characters using head lengths. This is Duke at four different ages. As he gets older, the shape of his body doesn't change as dramatically as that of a manga woman, but there are still important transformations.

① **Toddler Duke**

This is Duke at about three years old. The younger a character is, the larger his head tends to be in relation to the rest of the body. You can see from the guidelines that Duke's whole height is four times the height of his head. Manga children are much chubbier than manga adults.

② **Preteens Duke**

At nine years old, Duke is about six heads in height. His chest is becoming broader and he is generally more muscular.

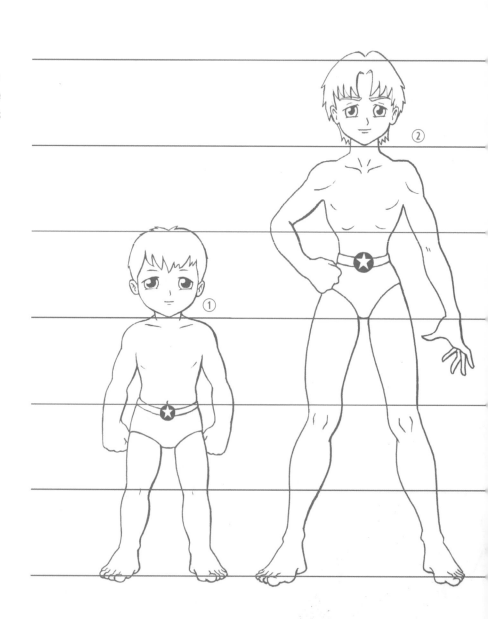

③ **Teenage Duke**

Duke is now well into his teens, so he is nearly fully grown. His muscles are now well developed. At seven heads in height, Duke is quite tall for his age—as heroes often are. Some manga males are only about this height when they are fully grown adults.

④ **Adult Duke**

This is Duke at his fully grown adult height of eight heads. Male manga characters can be up to 10 heads tall, but this tends to be the incredibly strong or evil ones. As well as having developed even bigger muscles, Duke has more flesh around the waist, making his chest less defined. His thigh muscles are also larger in relation to the rest of the legs.

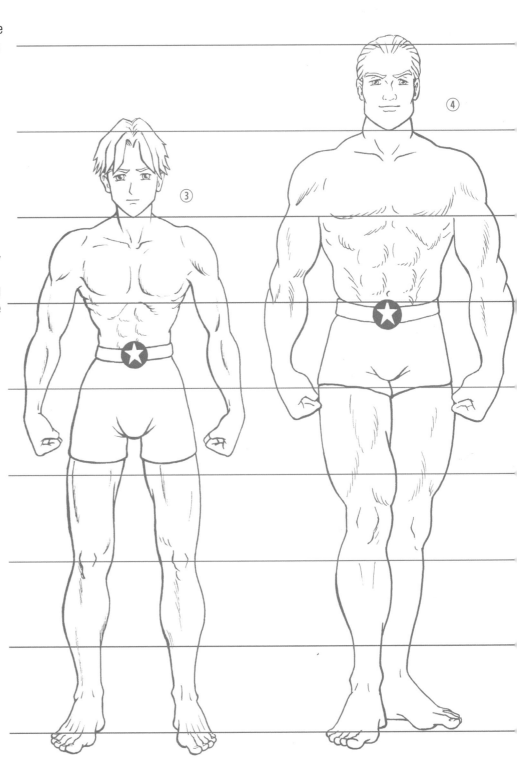

Front View (male)

This is Duke's body as viewed from the front. This is the easiest angle to draw, so it is a good one to start with.

Step 1

Start by drawing a vertical line to help you make your picture symmetrical. Draw the framework for the face as you learned to do on page 16. Copy the shape of the chest here—it's a large oval that curves in at the bottom to represent the shape of the rib cage. Now draw an oval lying on its side to make the hips. The gaps in between these body parts are for the neck and stomach. Add the limbs (arms and legs)—notice how much longer the legs are than the arms. Use dots to mark all the joints. The hands and feet can be drawn as simple triangles to begin with.

Step 2

Add some rough guidelines to mark where the flesh and muscles will go—don't worry about the joints yet. Copy how these lines curve farther away from the bones around the more muscly parts of the body like the shoulders and calves.

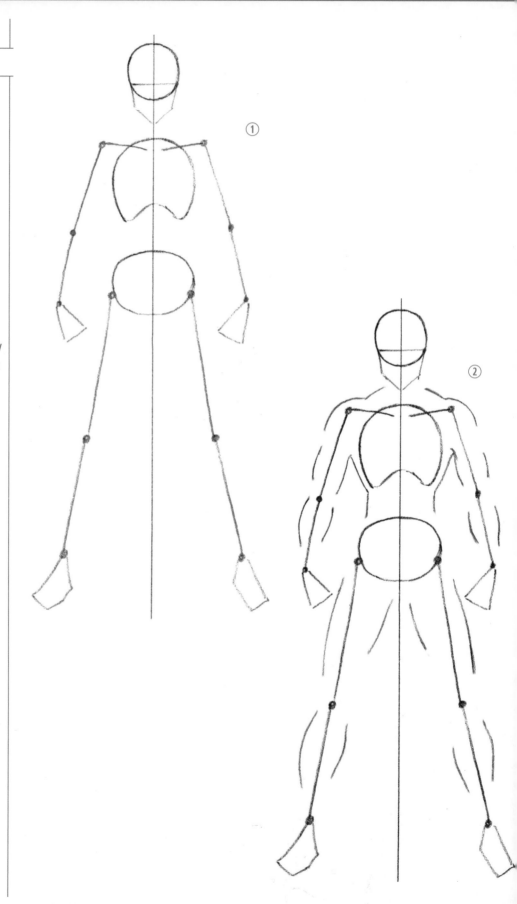

Step 3

Start joining together the parts of the outline you drew in the last step. Carefully copy where the lines curve inward like at the elbows, wrists, and ankles.

Step 4

Now it's time to give the muscles on the upper body more definition by drawing some curved lines on the arms and chest. Copy the pattern of the shapes that form the stomach muscles. Try holding your hands like Duke's and looking at them in the mirror to help you work out how to draw them. We'll look at drawing hands in more detail later in the book. When you finish the outline at the bottom of the legs, copy how it juts out at the ankle bones. Copy the curves of the toes and the ball and heel that you can make out on the inside of each foot. When you've sorted out the main parts of the body, outline the hair and facial features, remembering what you learned in the Head section of this book (refer back to pages 16–23 if you need to refresh your memory). »

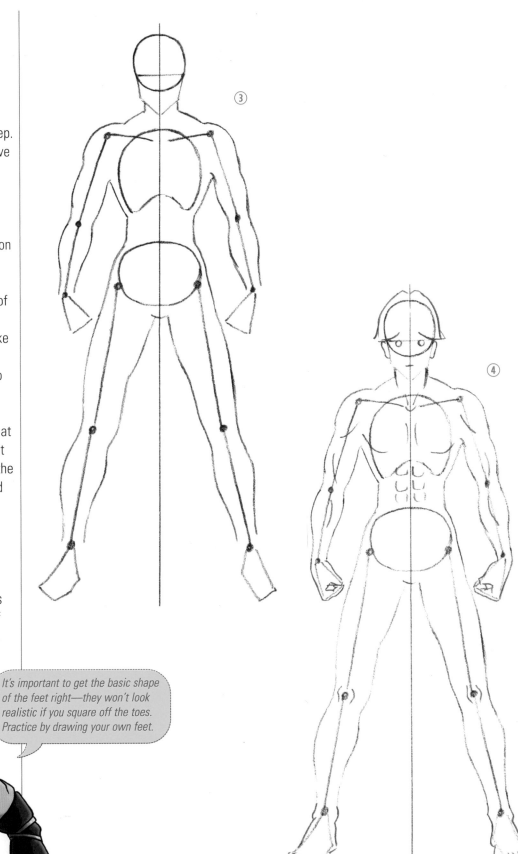

It's important to get the basic shape of the feet right—they won't look realistic if you square off the toes. Practice by drawing your own feet.

<<
Step 5
Go over your final pencil lines with a black felt-tip pen or, if you don't have one, a ballpoint pen. Mark the lines of Duke's swimming trunks and give his fingers and toes more definition as shown. Work on the face and hair too. Add some extra little lines and curves to Duke's body to highlight where his muscles and bones protrude.

Step 6
When the ink is dry, erase all the guidelines you drew for Duke's skeleton. That's your first manga body finished!

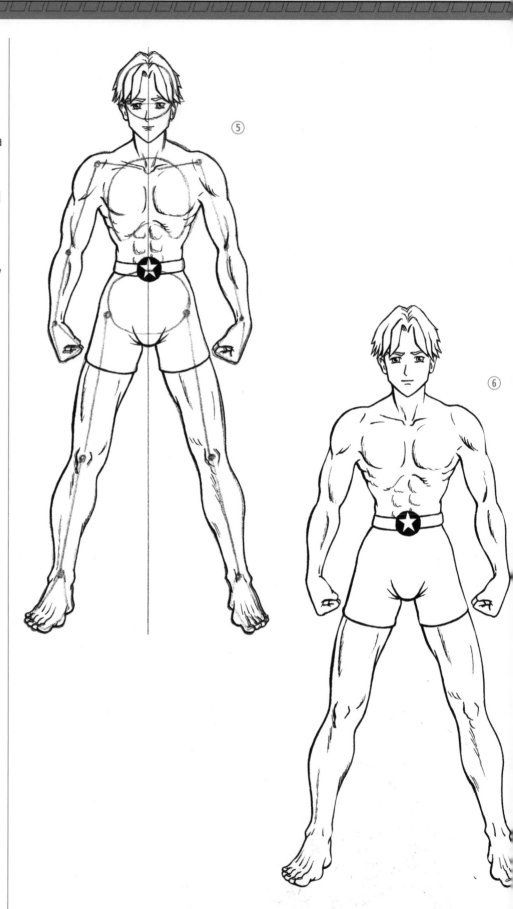

Step 7

Now you're ready to color in the picture if you want to. Notice how I've shaded some parts darker than others—turn to the Color section of the book for some tips on this.

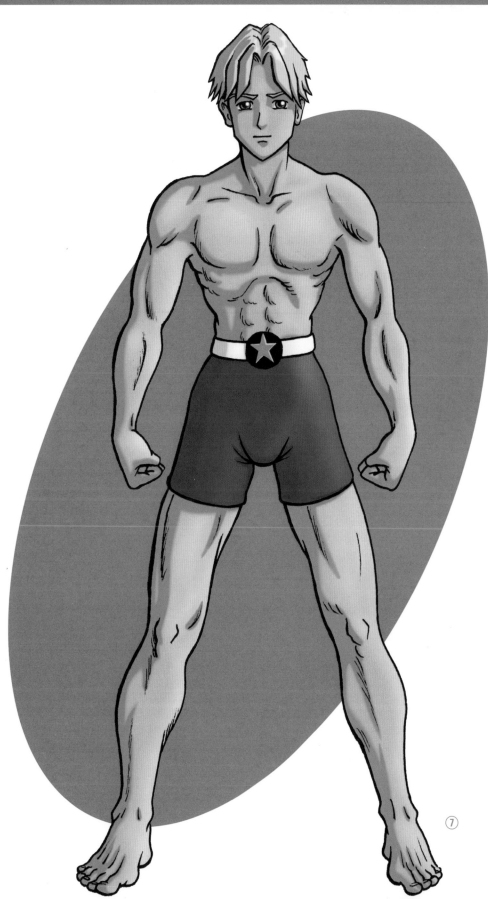

⑦

Profile (male)

Duke has turned to the side and changed his pose slightly. When he stands like this, we can see only one arm and one leg.

Step 1

First draw the head, chest and hips. You need to shape the head as you did on page 62 except that Duke is now facing in the opposite direction. The chest is a tilted oval shape with a piece missing near the bottom. The hips are almost circular. Add the curved lines forming the neck and lower part of the spine. Carefully copy the way the limbs are attached to the body. When you draw the leg, curve out the calf bone.

Step 2

Now for some flesh and muscle. Draw some rough lines around the main bones of the body as shown. It's very important that you get these right before you start thinking about completing your outline.

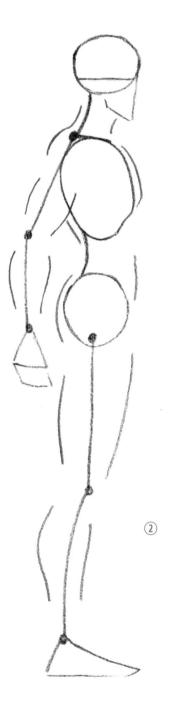

Step 3

Once you're happy with where you've placed the main parts of your body outline, fill in the gaps. Study the picture to see how the outline curves in and out around the joints. Notice how the stomach is made up of short curves to define the muscle.

Step 4

Now add some lines to the upper body to make the muscles stand out. You may find it helpful to refer to the muscle diagrams on page 59. Shape the hands and feet, outlining the fingers and toes. Add a little line around the knee and ankle bone to define these. Next start working on the outline of the hair and place the facial features.
»

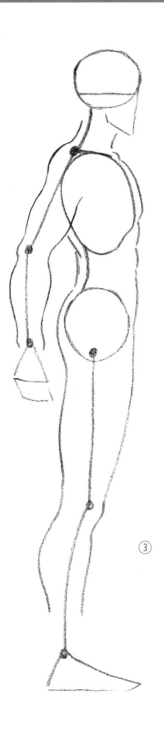

③

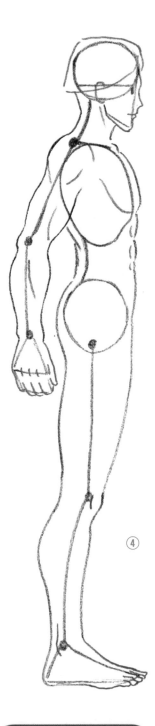

④

<< Step 5

Draw on Duke's swimming trunks—you won't be able to make out the shape of the star on the waistband from this angle. Now go over your pencil lines with a black felt-tip or ballpoint pen, adding more detail to the hair, face, hands, and feet as you go. Draw some extra little lines around the chest bone to define the rib cage. Study the picture to see where else you could add some lines to emphasize the muscle or bone, like on the neck and thigh. Small details like these can make all the difference to your final picture, making it much more lifelike.

Step 6

Once the ink is dry, erase all the pencil lines of your skeleton framework to leave a clean drawing.

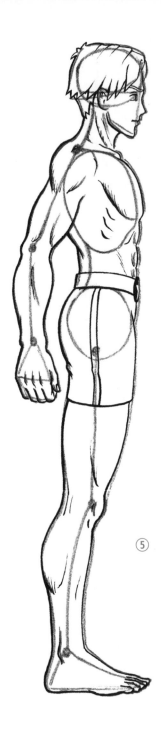

⑤

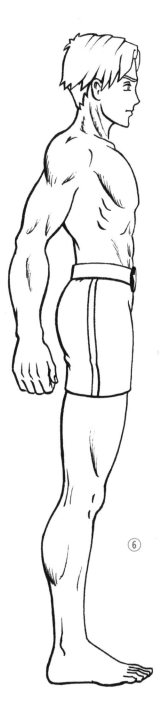

⑥

Step 7

Now color in your picture if you want to—you could try experimenting with different color schemes to change Duke's hair color and skin tone as well as the design of his swimming trunks.

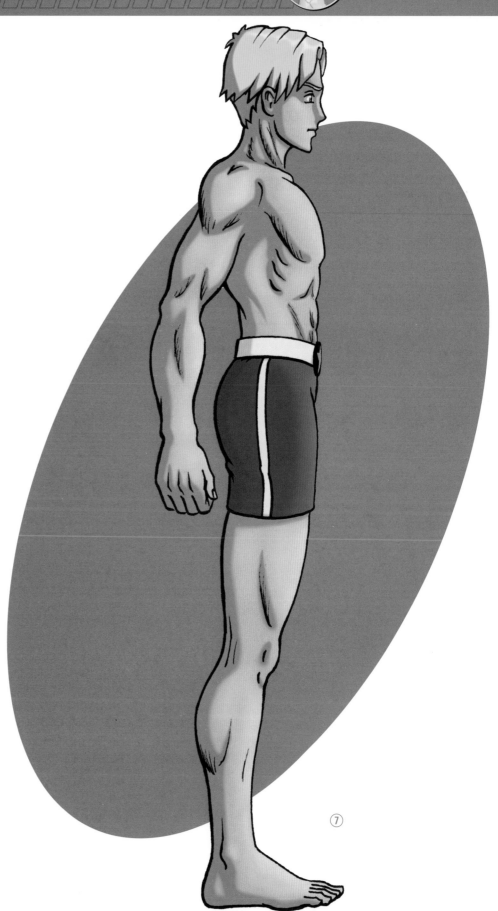

⑦

¾ View (male)

This viewpoint is slightly more complicated to draw, but it creates a much more interesting picture, so it's worth spending some time trying to get it right.

Step 1

Remembering to use light pencil lines, draw the skeleton framework as shown. Notice how each of the main body parts has a curved vertical line on it—the lines all curve out to the right. The lines for the neck and lower part of the spine also curve out to the right. Position the limbs as shown.

Step 2

Add the main lines that mark the flesh and muscle around your skeleton framework.

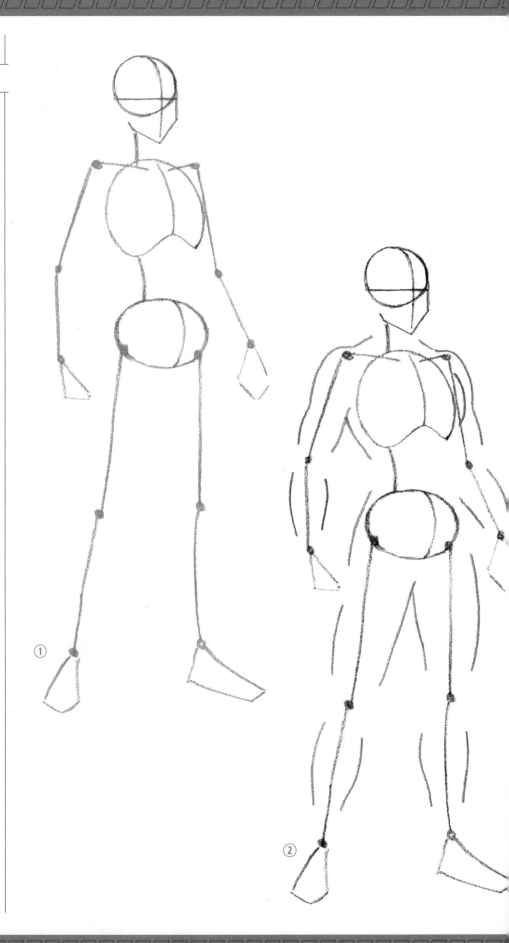

Step 3

Fill in all the gaps around Duke's body outline as shown. When you are drawing a figure at this angle, notice that the line of the neck to the right of your picture is farther from the spine than the other one. The same is true for the waist.

Step 4

Add some more lines to the upper body to define the bone structure and muscle—the muscle diagrams on page 59 will help you to understand what's going on here. Add the hands and feet to your outline, then start to shape the hair and facial features.

»

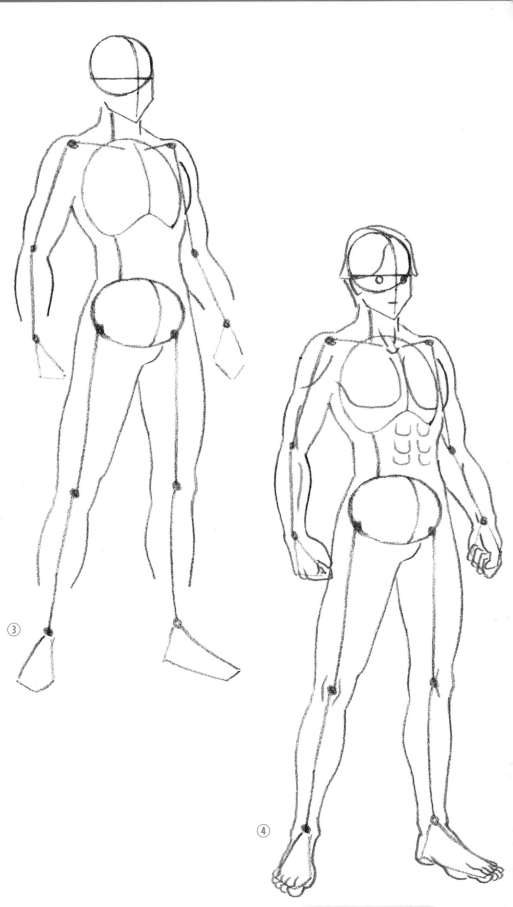

<<
Step 5
Add Duke's swimming trunks, then go over all the main lines of your drawing in pen, finishing off the final details. Don't forget all the extra little lines on Duke's neck, chest, arms, and legs, as well as on his stomach. Spend some more time on his face, especially the eyes.

Step 6
Once the ink is dry, you can erase the rest of your guidelines.

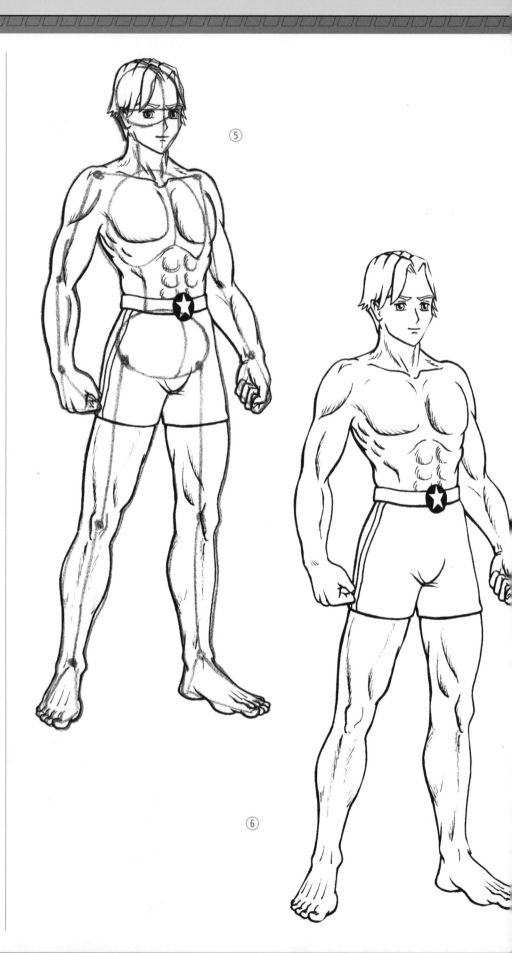

Step 7

This is quite a sophisticated picture, so if your finished drawing looks anything like this one, you're doing really well. If it hasn't quite worked out, don't worry—that's perfectly normal! Just keep practicing.

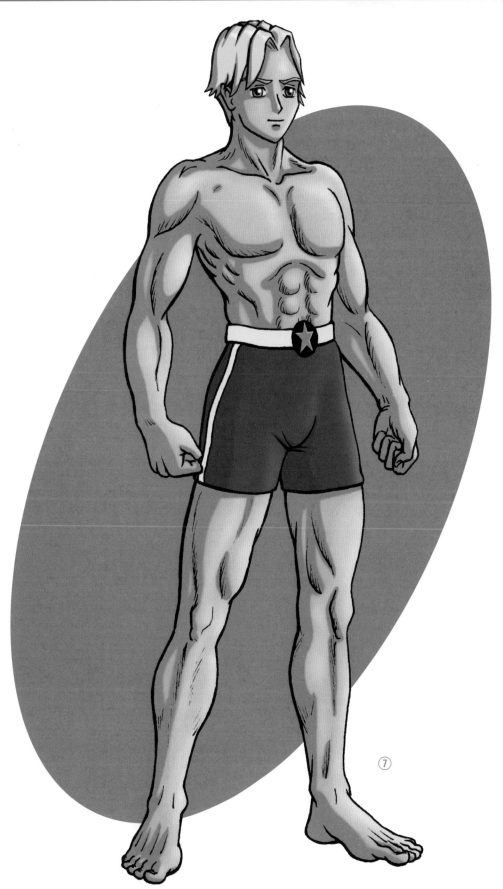

⑦

The Skeleton (female)

Think of the skeleton as a frame upon which you can hang muscles, skin, and clothing. Although it's quite complicated, you don't need to know about all the bones—you just need to think about the basic structure. The body is able to bend because of the joints. The arms have shoulder, elbow, and wrist joints, while the legs have hips, knees, and ankles.

① Front view

This is a simplified version of Daisy's skeleton. The head, chest, and hips can all be drawn as simple oval shapes, separated by short vertical lines for the parts of the spine at the neck and lower back. Notice that the arms do not hang directly from the chest but are separated by shoulder bones, while the legs are joined onto the hips. The joints are all drawn as small dots.

② Side view

Earlier in this book we saw how when Daisy turns her head to the side, some of the features get thinner or disappear from view. The same is true for the whole body. Notice how from this angle, you can see that her back is slightly arched. The arms are slightly bent and the leg bones curve.

③ ¾ view

Here, the three vertical guidelines (one each on the head, chest and hips) have moved off-center and curve out to the right.

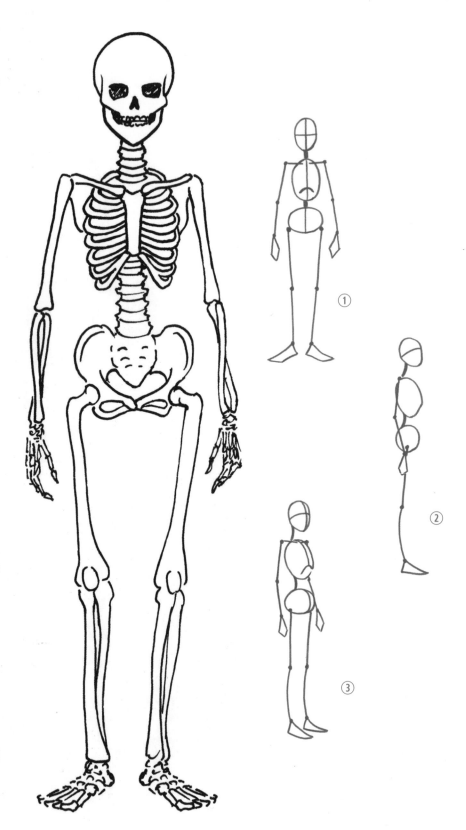

Muscles (female)

Here's Daisy's skeleton again with an outline drawn around it to show how the flesh and muscles wrap around the bones. Like most manga women, Daisy has a muscular, athletic look. Her outline mostly follows the shape of the skeleton, except that in some places, like where there are powerful muscles over the shoulder joints and on the thighs, the outline curves out more. The outline tapers in at the joints. Some parts of the body have no muscle, so you can notice the bones under the skin. These parts are highlighted with red dots.

① **Side view**

Notice how the outline curves at the top of the leg at the front for the thigh muscle. Lower down, it curves in the opposite direction for the calf muscle.

② **¾ view**

The lines showing the curves of the muscles on one leg will follow the shape of the lines on the other leg. One leg also overlaps the other.

③ **Thinner characters**

To make your character thinner, draw the body outline closer to the skeleton structure and make your pencil line more angular, to reduce the bulges.

④ **Larger characters**

To give your character a larger build, make the outline curve more. The skeleton remains the same for these different body types.

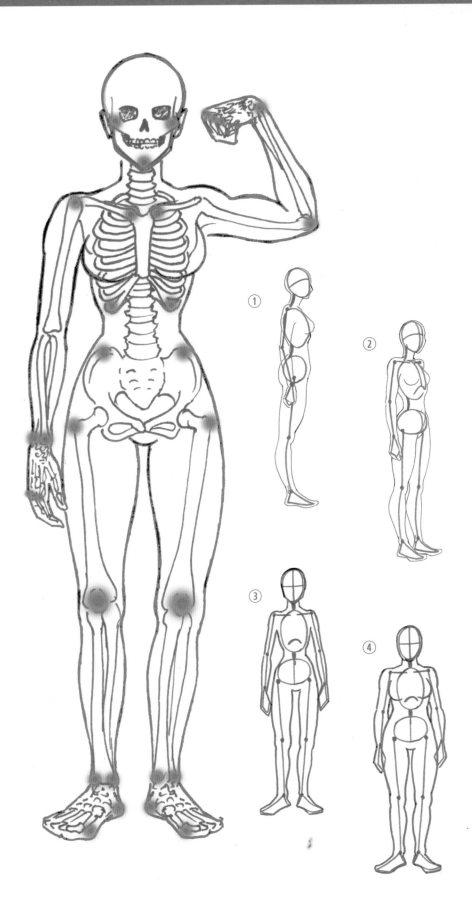

Proportions (female)

Earlier in this book, we looked at how the proportions of the head change as a person gets older. The same is true of the body. Manga artists work out the relative sizes of their characters using head lengths. These pictures show Daisy at four different ages.

① **Toddler Daisy**

The younger a character is, the larger her head will tend to be in relation to the rest of her body. At about three years old, Daisy's whole height is four times the height of her head. Manga children of this age are much chubbier than manga adults.

② **Preteens**

At around nine years old, Daisy is about six heads in height. Her body is more shapely than when she was younger, but she is still quite skinny.

③ The teenager

Daisy is now 17, so she is nearly fully grown. She's seven heads tall—some manga adults are also around this height. Daisy is tall for her age to make her look more glamorous. Compare Daisy here with the pictures of her when she was younger and see how much more developed her muscles are now.

④ Adulthood

This is Daisy at her fully grown adult height of eight heads. Not only is she taller, but her body is broader at the hips and her limbs are more curvy. Real human beings are rarely eight heads tall, but this is very common in manga stories. Sometimes characters can be as tall as 10 heads, but they tend to be male characters, and only the extra-strong or evil ones. Manga females of eight or more heads in height are usually fashion models or action heroines.

It is uncommon for female characters to be heavily muscled, even if they are dynamic action types. Their bodies are more often tall and graceful.

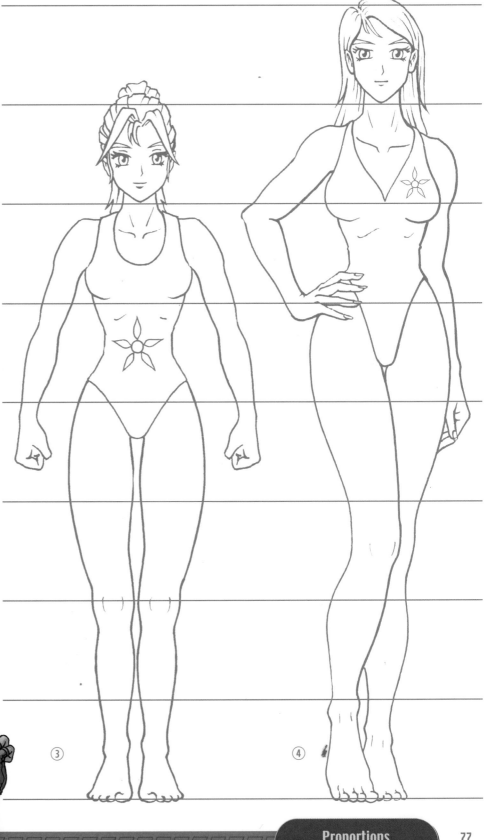

Front View (female)

Daisy has volunteered to stand very still while we draw her body.

Step 1

Start with a vertical line to help you make your picture symmetrical. Draw Daisy's egg-shaped head at the top. The chest shape is like a large oval with a chunk taken out to show the shape of the rib cage. An oval lying on its side makes the hips. Space out the three shapes to leave space for the neck and stomach.

Add the limbs (arms and legs). Start by drawing the two collarbones coming out of the chest. Study the picture to see how long the limbs should be—marking the joints will help you get the proportions right. The legs are much longer than the arms. Notice how the wrist joint of the hand on the left of your picture is level with the joints at the tops of the legs.

Step 2

Draw some curves around the major bones to mark where the flesh and muscles will go—don't worry about going around the joints yet. Remember that the tops of the legs (the thighs) will be broader than the sections below the knees (the calves). The upper arms should be slightly broader than the forearms. Draw in the neck and shoulders too.

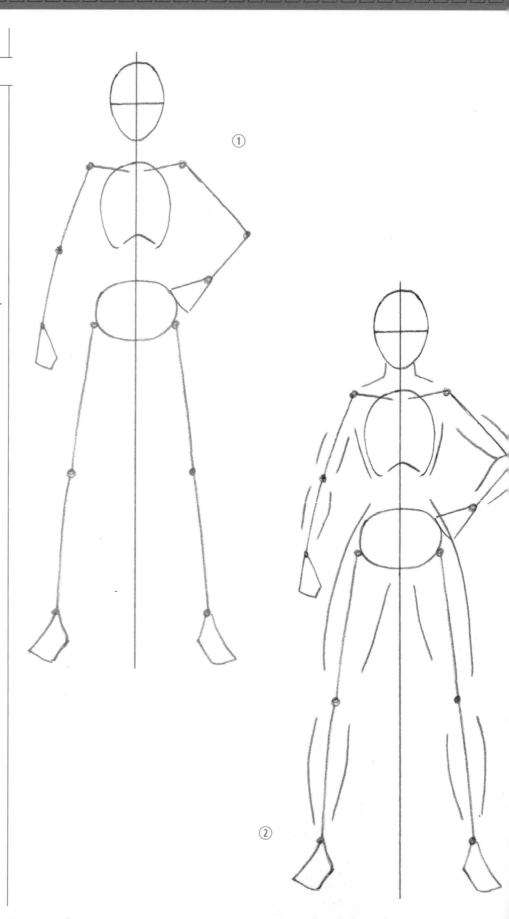

①

②

Step 3

Fill in the missing parts of your outline and see the body take shape before your eyes. Curve out your lines to make the shoulders look strong. The outline curves in at the elbows and wrists, but there should be a little kink on the outside of each wrist to show the bone. Draw some curves for the chest as shown and add the lines of the waist. Now for the legs—from this viewpoint, the knee and ankle joints bulge out at the sides slightly.

Take a stab at giving the hands some shape—notice that the thumbs have a muscly part, so make the outline more curved here. Add the feet, but don't worry too much about them since we'll look at hands and feet in more detail later. Finally, start outlining the features on the head, applying the techniques we looked at in the previous section.

Step 4

Mark the lines of Daisy's swimsuit and give her fingers and toes more definition. Now add a few details to the face and hair—look back at page 24 of the Head section of this book if you need some more help with this.

>>

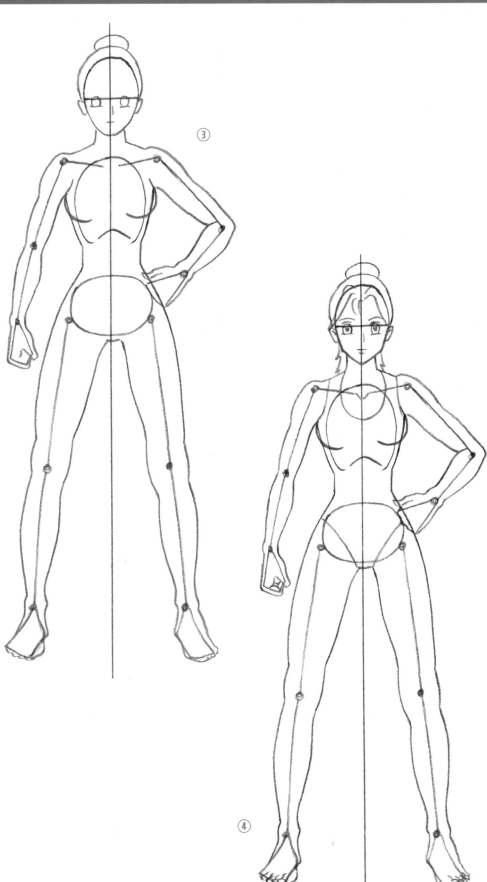

Step 5

Go over your final pencil lines with a black felt-tip pen or ballpoint pen. Now draw some little lines to define Daisy's neck muscles, collarbones, and rib cage. Add some detail to the knee joints, then work on Daisy's face and hair.

Step 6

When the ink is dry, erase all the guidelines you drew for Daisy's skeleton. That's your first manga body finished!

⑤

⑥

Step 7

Color in Daisy if you want to—or wait until you've worked through the Color section of this book.

⑦

Profile (female)

Daisy has turned to the side and changed her pose slightly—you can see one arm but both legs.

Step 1

Draw the basic shapes of the head, chest, and hips, carefully copying where they sit in relation to one another. The head is quite circular from this angle and sits slightly ahead of the chest and hips. The oval of the chest tilts backward at the top. From this angle, the hips form a circle shape. Add the neck and lower part of the spine. Notice how both parts curve, particularly the lower part—this arch of the back is very important to the style of manga artwork. Add the limbs— start by marking the joint at the top of the arm to help you position the collarbones and arm bones correctly. When you draw the legs, notice how the calf bones curve to give the legs a more glamorous profile. Just draw rough outlines of the hand and feet for now.

Step 2

Draw some rough lines around the main bones of the body for the flesh and muscle. It's very important that you get these right before you complete your outline.

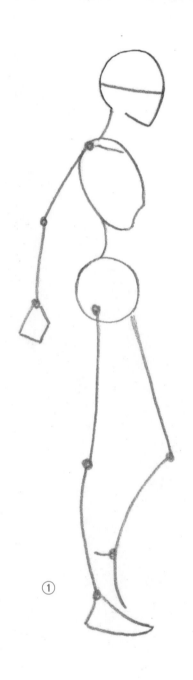

①

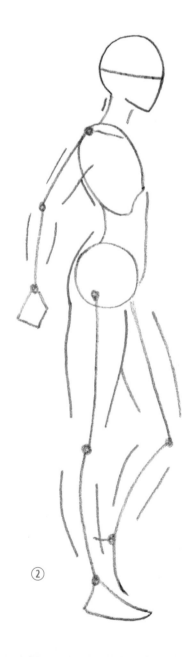

②

Step 3

Fill in the gaps of your outline. Study the picture to see how it curves in and out around the joints. Add the hand and the feet. When you outline the hair, notice how the ponytail falls down at the back so you can see the bottom of it between Daisy's arm and the arch of her back. Now place her facial features.

Step 4

Draw in the lines of Daisy's swimsuit at the top and bottom. Now add more detail to Daisy's hair. Remember to think about what way it is flowing. Add more detail to the eye. Now mark her toes and draw a little line around the outside of her ankle to give it definition. Small details like this make your final picture much more lifelike.
»

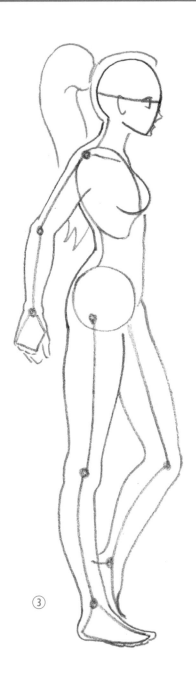

③

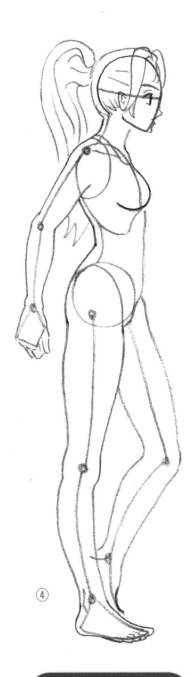

④

<<
Step 5

Draw over the main lines of your picture in heavy pencil, adding more detail to the hair, face, hands, and feet as you go along. Don't forget the flower on Daisy's swimsuit—you'll only be able to see half of it from this angle. Go over your heavy pencil lines with a black ballpoint or felt-tip pen.

Step 6

Once the ink is dry, erase all the pencil lines of your skeleton framework.

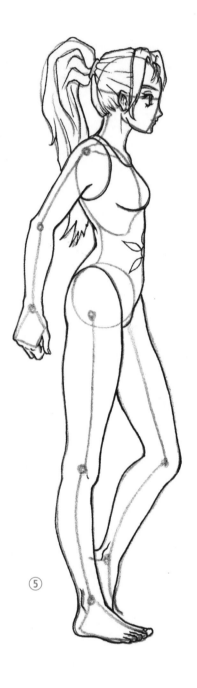

⑤

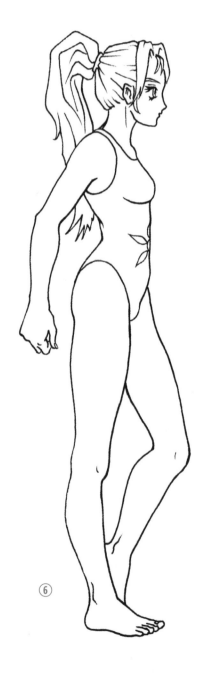

⑥

Step 7

Now you can color in your picture if you want to—try experimenting with different color schemes to change Daisy's hair color, skin tone, and swimsuit design.

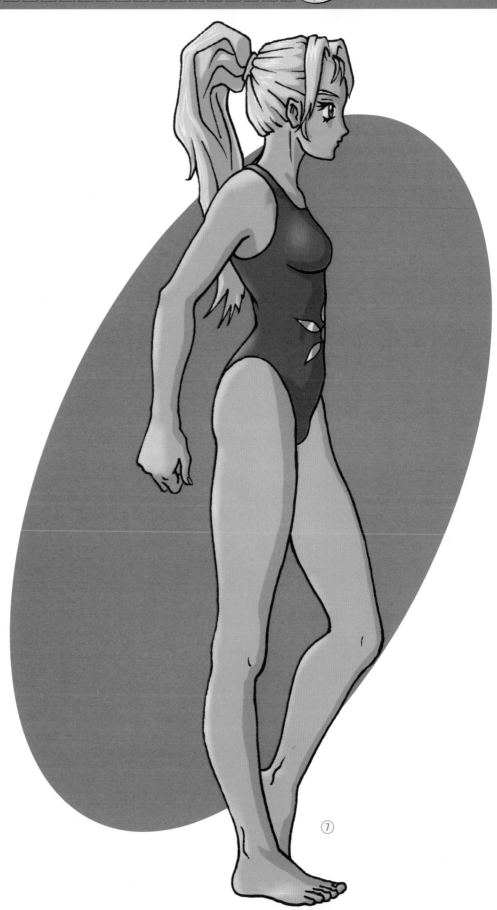

¾ View (female)

In addition to standing at a different angle, Daisy has changed her pose again, so she now appears as if she is walking.

Step 1

Using light pencil lines, draw the head, chest, and hip shapes as shown. Draw a curved vertical line on each of these body parts—notice how all the lines curve out to the right. Add the lines for the neck and lower part of the spine—these also curve. Add the bones and joints of the limbs. Notice that the upper part of one of the arms is slightly hidden by the chest. The lines for the legs should cross over each other as shown. Copy the shape of the back foot to show how Daisy's heel is raised.

Step 2

Add the main lines that mark the flesh and muscle around your skeleton framework. When you are drawing Daisy standing at this angle, one of the neck guidelines is farther away from the guideline for the spine than the other one. The same will be true for the waist in the next picture.

Step 3

Fill in all the gaps around Daisy's body outline, including the hands and feet. Now add the lines for her chest, hair, eyes, and mouth.

Step 4

Draw in the lines of Daisy's swimsuit. Give the fingers and toes some definition, then work on the hair and face. Look back at pages 24–31 if you need reminding about how to draw these.

>>

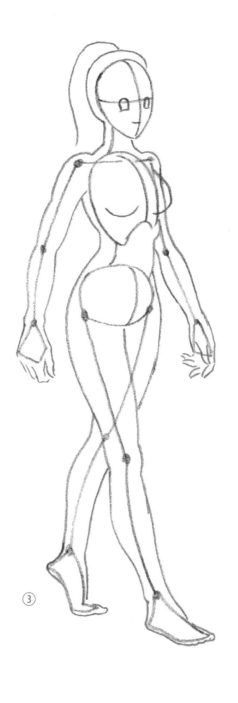

③

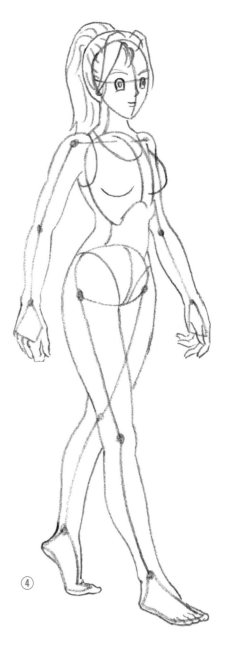

④

<<
Step 5

Go over Daisy in heavy pencil. Draw the flower on her swimsuit—you can see almost all of it from this angle. Don't forget all the little lines on Daisy's neck, rib cage, elbows, knee, and ankle. Add in her fingernails and big toenails. Spend some more time on Daisy's face, especially her eyes. Use a black ballpoint or felt-tip pen to go over all the final lines of your drawing.

Step 6

Once the ink is dry, erase any remaining pencil lines.

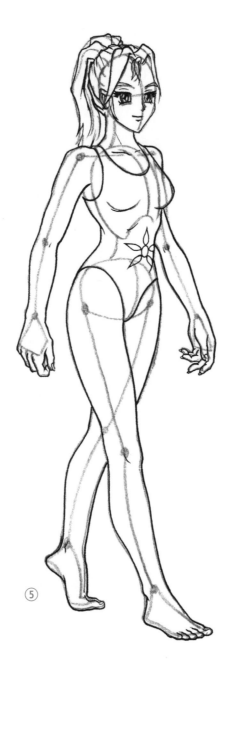

⑤

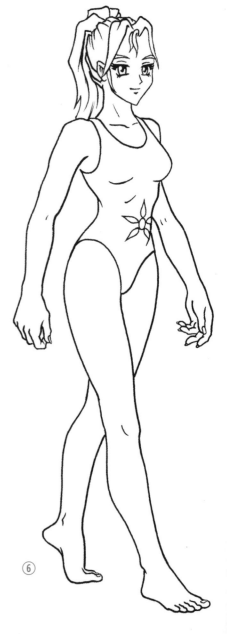

⑥

Step 7

This is quite a sophisticated picture, so if your finished drawing looks anything like this, you're doing really well. If you haven't gotten it perfect, don't worry—that's normal! Try to work out where you've gone wrong and then have another go at it.

⑦

Clothing

Every item of clothing will fall, fold, hang, and wrinkle slightly differently because of its shape and material.

① **Everyday clothing**

The clothing here is quite baggy. This emphasizes the effects of the body's movement upon it. Where the limbs are bent at the knees and elbows, the cloth gathers into tight folds. Where the limbs stretch, the cloth is pulled tight but still forms wrinkles. Notice how raising an arm causes the fabric under the armpit to form folds that radiate away from the joint. In places where the cloth is not pulled or gathered, it hangs more freely.

② **Tunics and capes**

Manga characters are often dressed quite differently from real people. They might have flowing garments like tunics and capes. When the character is standing still, all the folds will hang vertically due to the pull of gravity. In this sketch, even though I haven't drawn the body, you can tell there is movement or wind affecting the cape, causing the folds to flow in different directions.

③–⑤ **Materials and shape**

It is essential to think about the weight of the cloth. A thicker fabric, like in picture 3, makes bigger folds. Folds also occur where the fabric is loose-fitting, like in picture 4. Manga characters often wear tight-fitting clothes which have simple wrinkles, like in picture 5. These are easy to draw—as long as you have drawn the body underneath them well.

Manga Style

The clothes you choose to give your manga characters can say a lot about their personality and status as well as when and where they live. Here Daisy has been let loose in a manga clothes store and she is modeling some typical manga outfits. There is not much detail in these drawings and no color or texture, but you can still tell from the folds and creases that they are made from different materials and that the style of the clothing also affects the way it hangs on her body.

Hands

Hands are not easy to draw, but mastering how to draw them will give your pictures an expert quality. Just like the rest of the body, they can be broken down into basic shapes.

Step 1

To draw the back of the hand, you need to draw a rough outline of the overall shape before you add the individual bones—the shape is a bit like a fan.

Step 2

Draw a large circle at the bottom to form the wrist bone, then draw the finger bones and joints radiating out from this. The bones are the straight lines and the circles are the joints. The thumb sticks out to the left of your original shape.

Step 3

Draw around the bones to add the flesh and muscle. Make the outline more curved around the fleshy parts of the thumb.

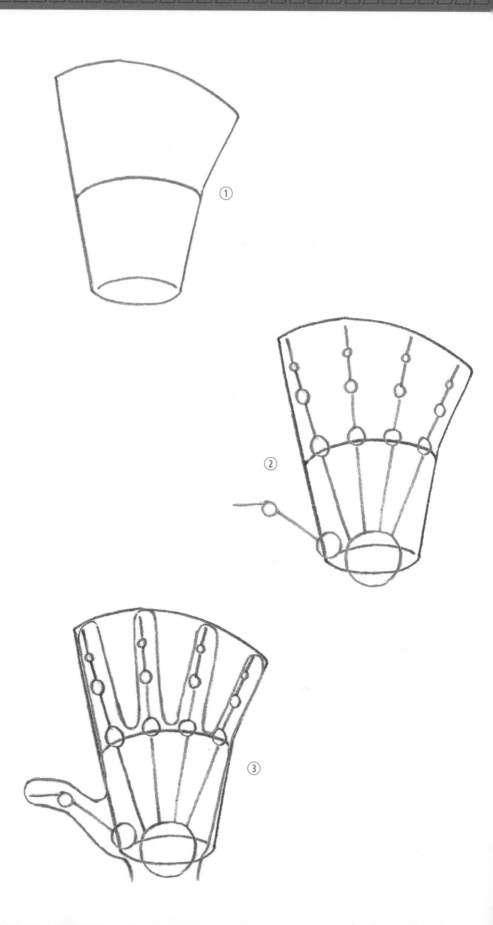

Step 4

Draw on the fingernails and some little lines to define the knuckles.

Step 5

Use a black ballpoint or felt-tip pen to go over the final lines of your drawing again. When the ink is dry, erase all the pencil lines of your original framework.

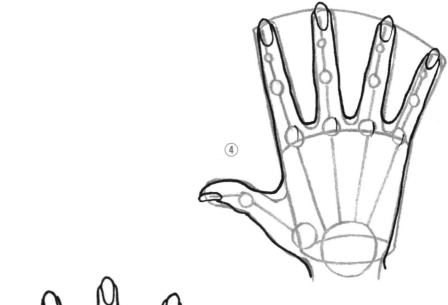

④

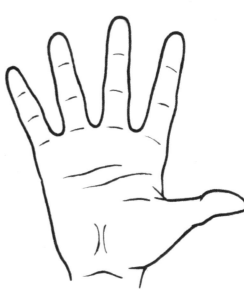

⑤

To draw the palm side of the hand, reverse the drawing you did in steps 1, 2, and 3, then copy all the crease lines you can see here.

Artists often use their hands as models. Practice drawing your spare hand. Try rotating it so you can draw it from different angles. Look at it in the mirror too.

MANGA

Hands in Action

There's not much a person can do with their hands if they keep them flat all the time, so you will need to learn how to draw hands from all kinds of different angles, in all sorts of positions.

① **Poses**

Here are a few examples of Daisy's hands in action. I've added some guidelines to help you work out how they are constructed.

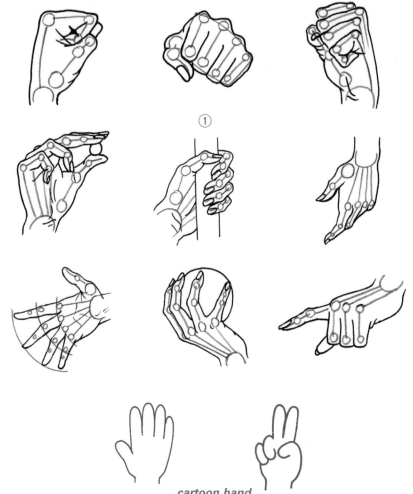

② **Simplifying hands**

Cartoonists have many different ways of simplifying hands. Try out each of these styles. However you draw them, hands must always look like they belong to the body they are attached to.

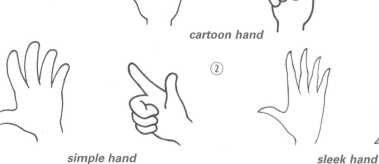

cartoon hand

②

simple hand

sleek hand

③ **Different ages**

It's obvious that these hands belong to characters that are very different in age. The baby's hands are chubby, so the bones and joints aren't very defined. The older hands have less flesh, so they look much more bony and wrinkled.

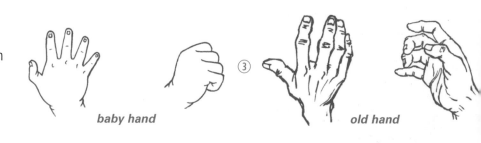

baby hand

③

old hand

Feet

Feet are made up of just as many bones as hands. Although your manga characters will often be wearing shoes, they will sometimes be barefoot—if they practice martial arts, for instance.

① **Daisy's feet**
Here are Daisy's right foot and ankle drawn from different angles. Try copying them. I've used circles and lines to mark some of the main parts that form their structure. The two main bulges on the foot itself are the ball and heel. Notice that the two bones that jut out on either side of the ankle are not directly opposite each other—one is higher up. And just like the bones of the hand, the toe bones run in lines along the feet, radiating from the ankle.

② **Feet inside shoes**
Even when you are drawing characters with their shoes on, it will help you to imagine the shape of the foot inside the shoe.

③ **Basic shapes**
Try to think of feet as triangles to begin with. If you get this basic shape right, the other details should fall into place.

④ **Simple feet**
Even if you decide to simplify the feet, it's still important to get their basic shape right. The toes should form a pointed shape, as in the first picture. If you draw them like they are in the second picture, they will look too square.

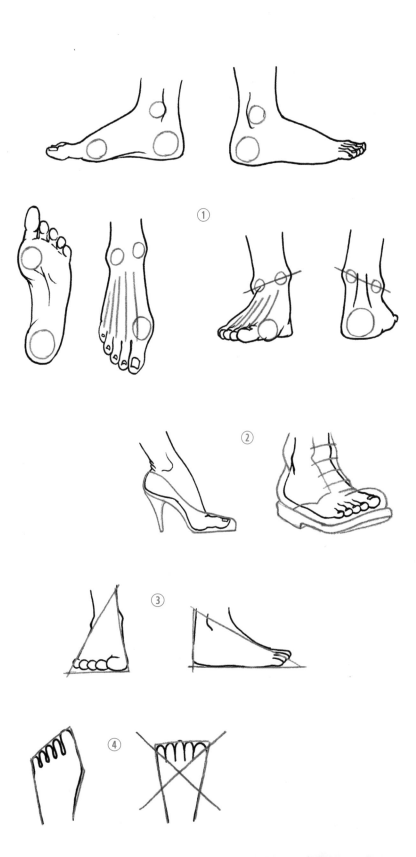

Action proportions

Now that you have had a little experience of drawing Duke's body, you might like to think about some other ways that the same skeleton can be fleshed out for differences in character and drawing style

① Muscles natural

Duke, as you have drawn him, is a typically well-muscled manga teenage action character. A real person of his age would probably look more like this drawing; much less defined musculature and much less 'manga'.

② Defined bulk

Now that you have seen how the muscles of the body fit together, you can further exaggerate his form and add definition to his muscles for a super-fit character.

③ Muscles distorted

Another thing you could try, is to selectively exaggerate certain muscles and further define those muscle shapes. Thus you can create new types of characters and develop your own drawing style.

④ Female muscles distorted

Here's a drawing to highlight the differences between manga male and female characters. You can't play around will female proportions so much. Too much muscular definition and they start to look a bit weird!

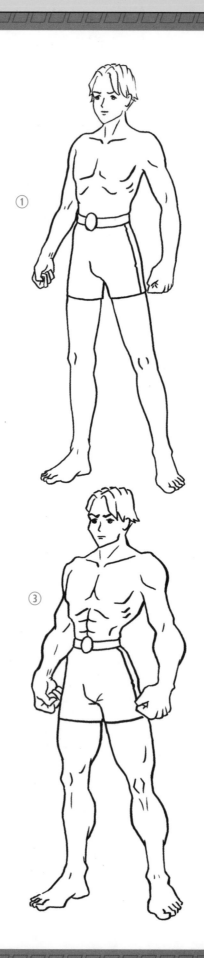

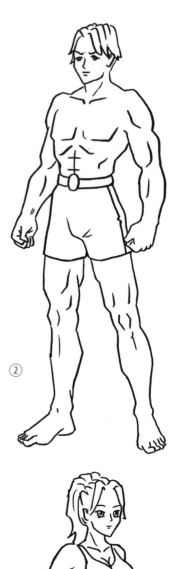

⑤ Adult natural

With knowledge of musculature and proportion, there is no end of possibilities for how you can manipulate your character's body shapes. Compare Duke's adult body form with the more extreme distortions of adult manga bodies here.

⑥ Adult bulk

Even if the adult Duke is already very well muscled, the size of the muscles and skeleton within can be pushed to greater extremes. Making the head relatively smaller increases the effect of a massive figure. This kind of body will normally be used for bad characters.

⑦ Adult lean

You could go the other way and make characters which are extra lean and tall. This body shape could be for good as well as bad guys. Depending on how you draw the details and the way they move, they could equally be graceful or awkward-looking with such elongated limbs.

⑧ Adult extreme

Here's a kind of blend between the two extremes of bulk and height: more elegant than the bulky version, but much stronger than the lean one. This kind of body form is used for superhero and supervillain characters.

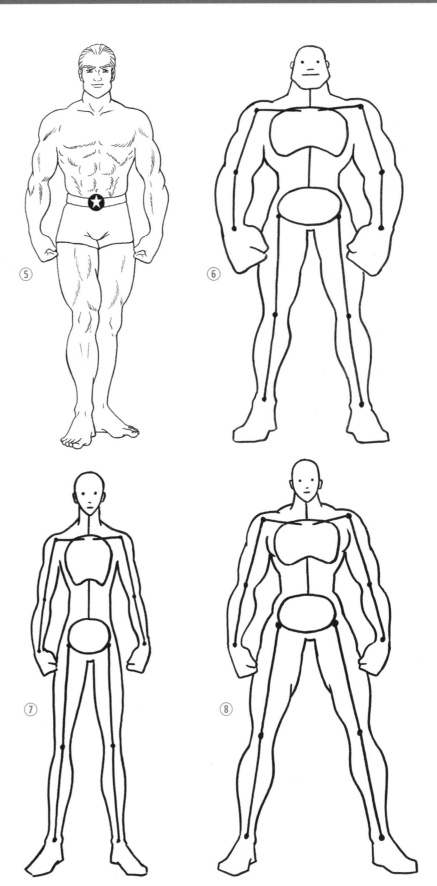

Child characters

These figures, if a little exaggerated in parts, are fairly naturally proportioned and are typical of the proportions of many manga children and early teenage characters. Compared with western comics, it's far more common for manga to feature characters of these ages.

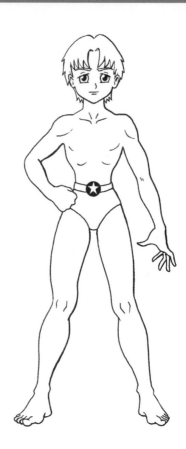

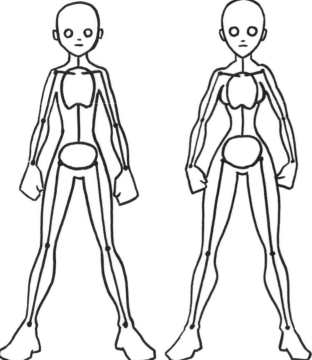

If they want action heroes, manga artists adapt their child characters' proportions to make them more dynamic than in real life. Here the male and female body types are streamlined and their musculature quite well defined. They may even be imbued with some very adult qualities, such as curvy figures for the girls.

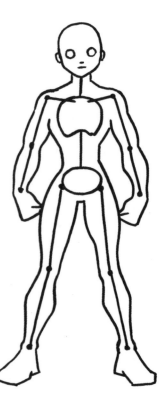

Boy characters are often drawn with very bulky muscles, very unusual in the real world, but perfectly acceptable in the world of manga heroes.

Very young characters

Even tiny kids can be turned into manga action characters with a few tweaks of proportion. The differences are subtle, but important. A narrowed torso gives the impression of increased maneuverability, and sturdy wrists and ankles suggest more strength than the average toddler.

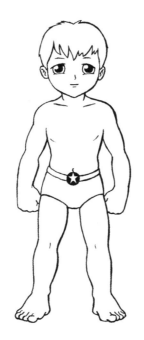

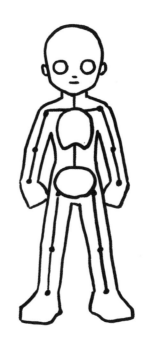

Feminine characters

With female characters, it is uncommon for them to be too heavily muscled, even if they are to be dynamic action types. It is more usual that their bodies are drawn very tall and graceful. They may have well-developed breasts, but they will not be very broad at the hips. Their muscles should look strong and well defined, but not bulky. Manga women are always very feminine.

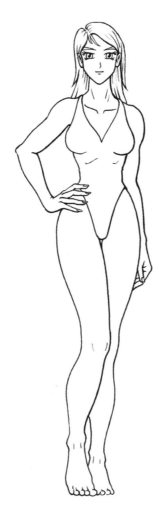

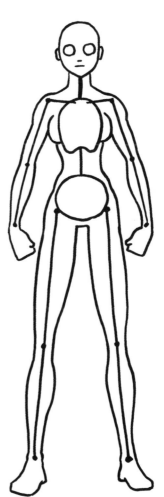

New Characters

By this stage, you've had a go at all sorts of manga drawing disciplines. You should know all you need to invent your own manga characters and draw them in all sorts of poses, from all angles, in whatever clothing you want to invent for them. A good way to progress at this stage, is to draw lots and lots of new characters, trying to make each one as different as possible from the last. If you flick back through the book, you'll find dozens of my sketches which will give you a wide range of faces, hairstyles, clothing, poses and body types to refer to. You could mix and match elements throughout the book to come up with new combinations. Then you could progress to borrowing bits of manga characters from comics and games. Or why not try giving your new characters hairstyles copied from your friends, clothes copied from catalogues and poses and expressions from newspaper photographs? Inspiration can come from anywhere. Keep your eyes open, keep trying new things in your drawings and enjoy the act of creation. The more you do it, the easier it will become and the more you will enjoy your manga art.

Here's a couple of new characters I have put together from some of the previous pages of this book. There are hundreds of possible combinations. When you add details, poses and characteristics of your own, the possibilities are endless!

Pose

Hairstyle

Face

New character

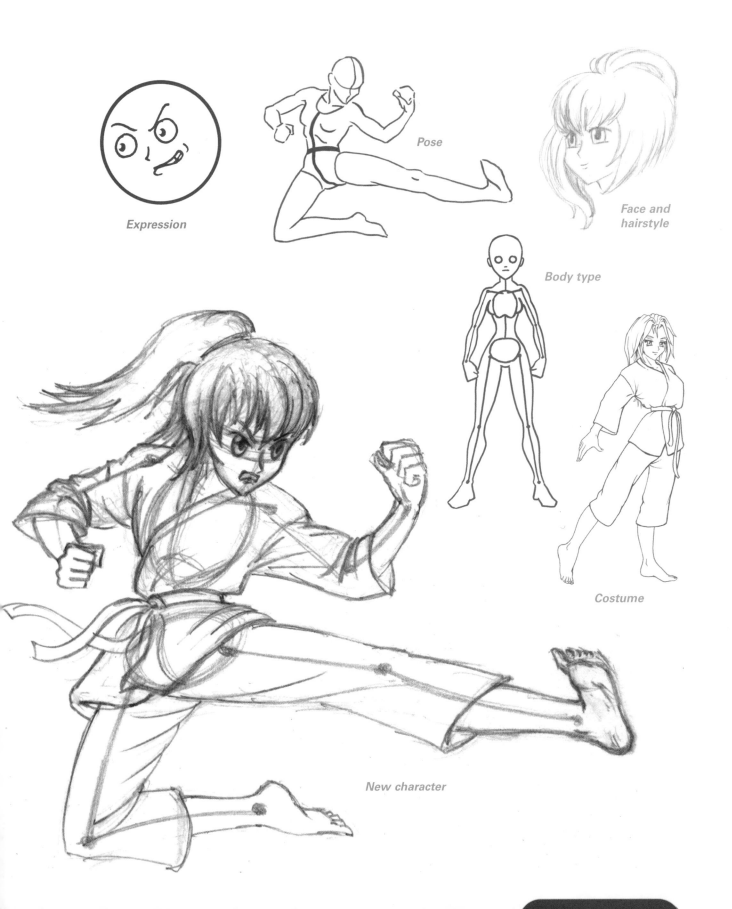

Expression

Pose

Face and hairstyle

Body type

Costume

New character

HUMANOIDS

Hybrid characters that are a mixture of humans and animals are very popular in the most recent comics coming from Japan. All kinds of half-human, half-animal monsters are to be found battling alongside or against favorite manga action heroes and heroines.

We've adopted a similar approach in this next section of the book. You'll also find here a great many robotic characters. Many of these mechas can display all sorts of surprisingly human-like qualities.

Monsters and mechas based on humans are known as humanoids. To create them, you need to know how to construct the heads and bodies of humans, so as a starting point I'll take you through the basic stages of drawing manga males and females.

Once you've mastered drawing the humanoids in this section, you'll have all the skills you need to concoct a tribe of your own fierce and powerful manga beings.

HUMANOIDS

HUMANOIDS
HUMANOIDS
HUMANOIDS
HUMANOIDS
HUMANOIDS
HUMANOIDS
HUMANOIDS
HUMANOIDS
HUMANOIDS
HUMANOIDS
HUMANOIDS
HUMANOIDS
HUMANOIDS
HUMANOIDS
HUMANOIDS
HUMANOIDS
HUMANOIDS
HUMANOIDS

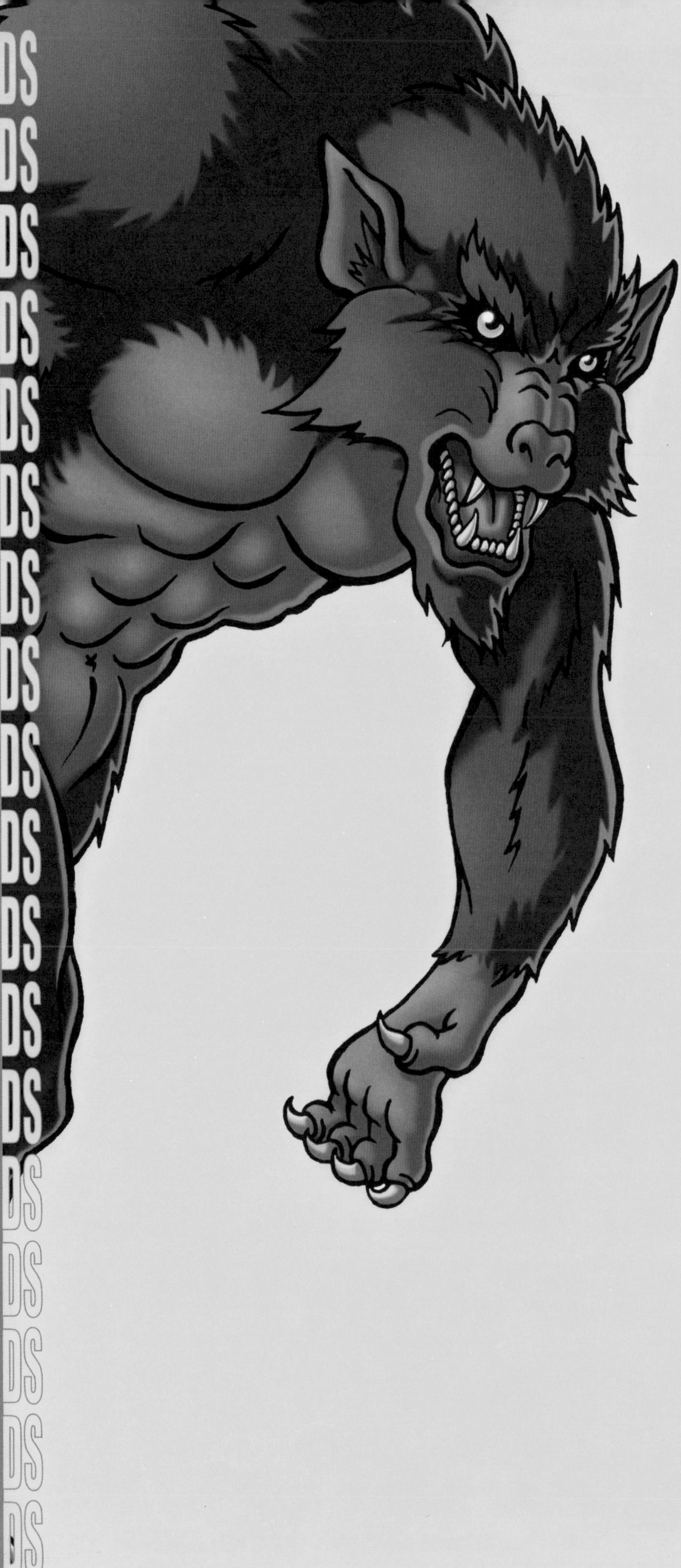

MANGA

Male Mutations

Once you've practiced drawing a human head, you can alter the features to transform it into animal mutants. Compare each of these pictures with the front view of Duke to see how they differ.

① **Ape boy**

Short tufty hair, thick eyebrows, protruding cheekbones, dark eyes, and crease lines that show the wrinkled skin all work together to give an ape-like appearance.

② **Lion boy**

The hair here has been styled to resemble a lion's mane. A rough edge has been added to the jawline to imply fur. Fur has also been added to the ears, which are high up on the head. The eyes point down toward a wide nose and mouth.

③ **Lizard boy**

The rounded head shape here is accentuated by a lack of hair. The bony spikes on top of the head, the protruding eyeballs, the noseless nostrils, and the thin, wide mouth complete the reptilian look.

④ **Bird boy**

These large round eyes resemble an owl's. The hair is shaped to look like feathers, and the nose takes the shape of a beak. Notice that eye lashes have been added—these are rare on male human characters.

①

②

③

④

Female Mutations

Taking Daisy's head as your starting point, the same approach can produce more feminine animal mutants.

① **Bear girl**

Rounded ears that sit high up on the head, a clear hair line around the face and a nose that takes the shape of a snout all give Daisy a bear-like look. Large round eyes and short tufty hair complete the effect.

② **Fish girl**

To create an aquatic look, sweep the hair up into a point, add scales to the ears and draw large round eyes that sit far apart. Notice the distinctive shape of the mouth too.

③ **Monkey girl**

Compare this picture with the ape boy. The eyes are slightly bigger, as manga girls' eyes tend to be, and the hair longer but still tufty.

④ **Sheep girl**

A matted hairstyle and long curly horns easily identify the animal here. The look is enhanced by sharply angled eyes and eyebrows.

⑤–⑥ **Robot girl**

Most manga robots are human-based too. Here are a couple of different styles based on Daisy's face. See what other variations you can come up with—the great thing about robots is that there's no right or wrong about the way they look!

Cyborg Girl

Cyborgs are usually the result of a horrific accident or battle where a human character has been injured and has had to have surgery to replace real body parts with mechanical elements. This usually turns them into powerful bionic beings. This cyborg girl has retained a very human shape, apart from the flame-throwing weapon that replaces her left arm.

Step 1
Draw the basic shapes for the head, chest, and hips as if you were sketching a human character. Add the sections of the spine and the limb bones—the bottom section of the mechanical arm is much longer than an ordinary forearm would be.

Step 2
Draw the curves of the flesh and muscle around your skeleton framework. The figure has strong, rounded muscles that are much more defined than those of most non-bionic manga females.

Step 3
Draw some lines to form the basic shape of the flame thrower. Add the outline for the hands and feet, then start to work on the facial features and hair.

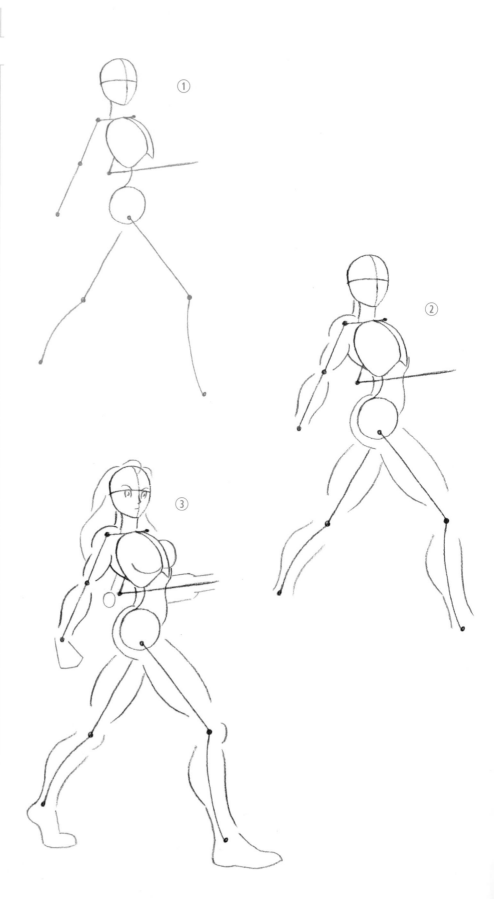

Step 4

Work on all the metalwork that surrounds the cyborg's feminine body as shown. Add the protective armor to the head and finish the lines forming the shape of the mechanical arm.

Step 5

Fill in more of the detail on the metal suit like the ribbed sections that allow the knees to bend. Add the long curved blade to the end of the good arm and shape the fist. A few little curves at the end of the barrel of the flame thrower will create the impression of smoke.

Step 6

Go over all the final lines of your drawing with a soft pencil, including all the detail, so you can clearly make out your final picture.

>>

Step 7

Spend some time carefully going over all your heavy pencil lines with a black felt-tip pen. There's a lot of detail, so it's best to use a very fine point. When the ink is dry, erase all the remaining pencil marks.

Step 8

Next go over some of the lines again using a pen with a slightly wider point to vary the thickness of your outline. This cyborg has an extremely slick look, so your line work should be smooth and graceful. Now the challenge is to use solid black to suggest reflections in her shiny body parts. As with any metallic object with various surfaces, the light will catch it in many different ways, and so create all sorts of visual interest.

Step 9

On pages 184–195, you'll learn how to create these coloring effects digitally. If you don't have a computer, don't worry. You can achieve a very good result using felt-tip pens. Any mistakes you make while coloring can be corrected afterward with the help of some white drawing ink and a fine brush.

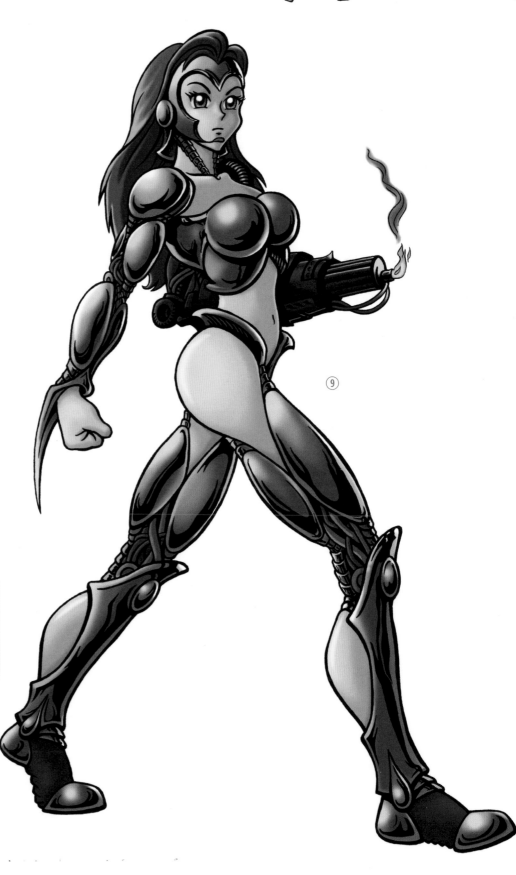

⑨

The next time you pass a highly polished car or motorcycle in the street, study the shadows and reflections on the chrome and other metallic surfaces. This will help you create these same effects on robotic characters you draw in the future.

Creating Magnus

This is a ¾ view of Magnus the robot with lines added to help you get the perspective right. We'll look at perspective in more detail in the Action section of the book.

Step 1

Draw three oval shapes for the body parts as shown. Add a curved vertical guideline to each body part, then draw a horizontal guideline across the head—the ends curve downward. Copy the angles of the three sloping perspective lines.

Step 2

Add the arm and leg bones—notice that the perspective lines run through the joints.

Step 3

Make the shape of the upper arms and legs by drawing different-size circles connected by parallel lines. Outline the large boots too.

Step 4

Now outline the metalwork of the forearms, hands, and lower legs.
>>

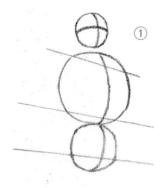

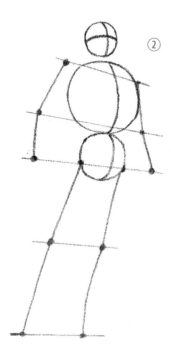

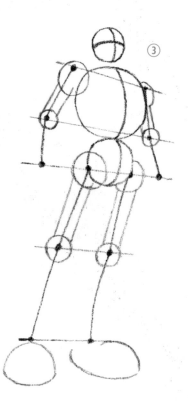

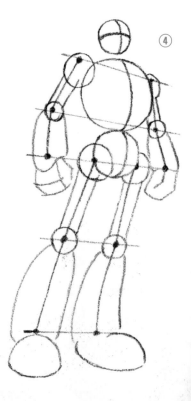

Step 5

Draw on the outline shape of the metal suit surrounding the chest and hips. Work on the main features of the head and add a bit more detail to the lower legs and feet.

Step 6

The rows of horizontal lines down the front of the body create a sub-frame made up of metal disks. Add the letter M to the chest and work on the detail of the giant hands—the thick metal fingers have large circular joints.

Step 7

Pick out all your good lines to form the shape of your final drawing and go over these in heavy pencil. Now go over all your final lines again using a black felt-tip pen. Finally, study the picture carefully to see if you've missed any little details.

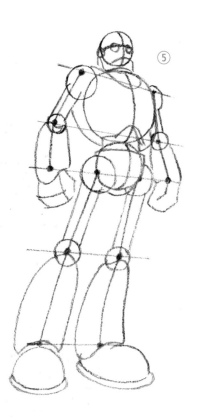

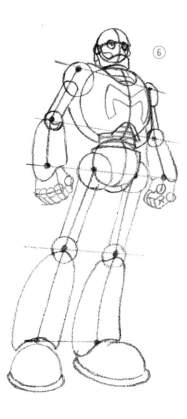

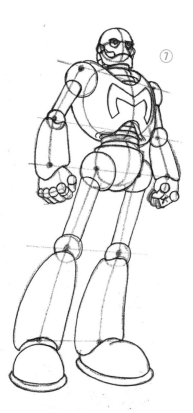

Step 8

When the pen ink dries, erase all the pencil lines that formed your original framework to leave a clean drawing of Magnus. There are full instructions for inking and coloring Magnus on pages 182–183.

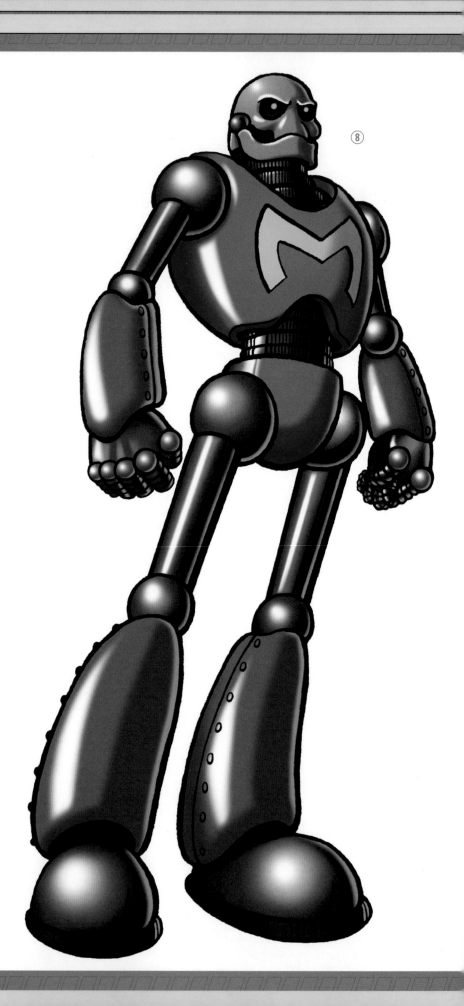

⑧

ant Robot

fore you start drawing, take a ook at the finished character on e next page so you know what ou're aiming for.

Step 1

Start with the basic masses that orm the head, chest, and hips. Like Magnus the chest is much larger han the head and hips. Notice how he vertical guideline is in a different position on the hips as the igure is twisting.

Step 2

Although this robot doesn't really have bones and joints, drawing them vill help you establish the relative engths and positions of the robotic imbs and work out where they bend. I've added some perspective ines to the lower body to help you draw the legs—the leg to the right of your picture is farther away, so it appears shorter.

Step 3

Turn the chest into a cube and draw a rectangular box around the hips. Use a ruler if it helps. Copy the blocky shape of the upper legs, making the nearest leg thicker. Draw semi circles for knee joints.

Step 4

Add more blocks to form the rough shape of the lower legs and the robot's arms.

>>

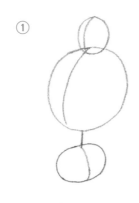

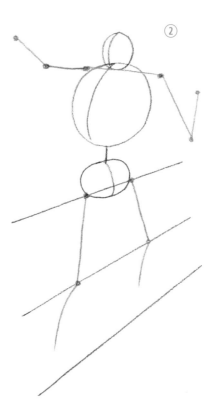

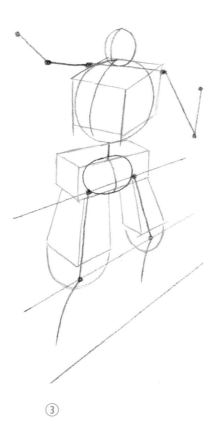

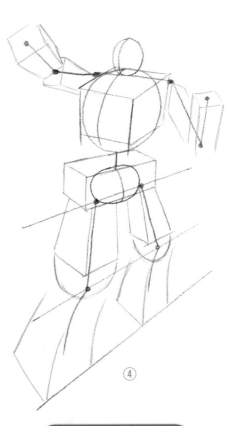

«

Step 5

Start to refine your robot's shape. Make the chest more angular, turn the waist into a narrow, curvy tube, and add a power pack to the robot's back. Carefully copy the rest of the metalwork and make the basic shapes of the hands—to draw the giant outstretched hand, start with the framework for the finger bones, then map in the palm and the sockets for the fingers.

Step 6

Add the segmented parts of the fingers. I've also refined the shape of the hand to the right of the picture. Copy all the panels on the chest and draw the tread on the soles of the metal feet. I've added a helicopter to the picture to give the robot a sense of scale—we can now see that this robot is about the same size as a skyscraper.

Step 7

Go over all your good lines in heavy pencil, then in black felt-tip pen. Add some more detail to the helicopter, including the rows of curved lines that show the spinning blades.

⑤

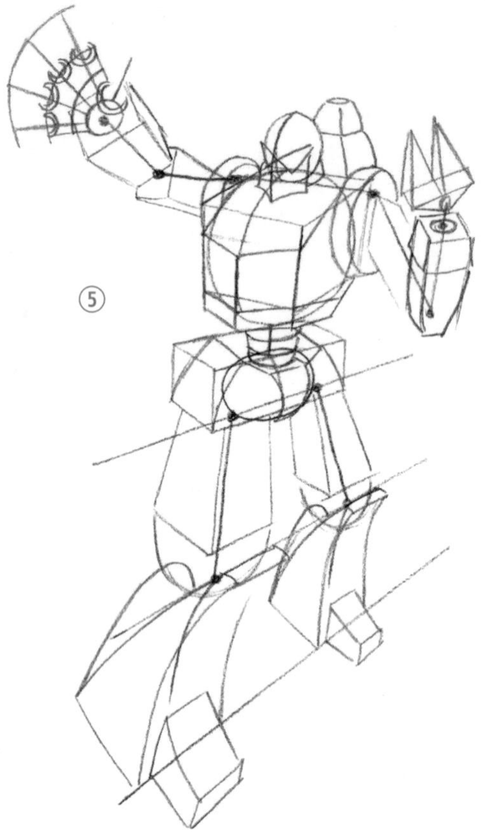

⑥

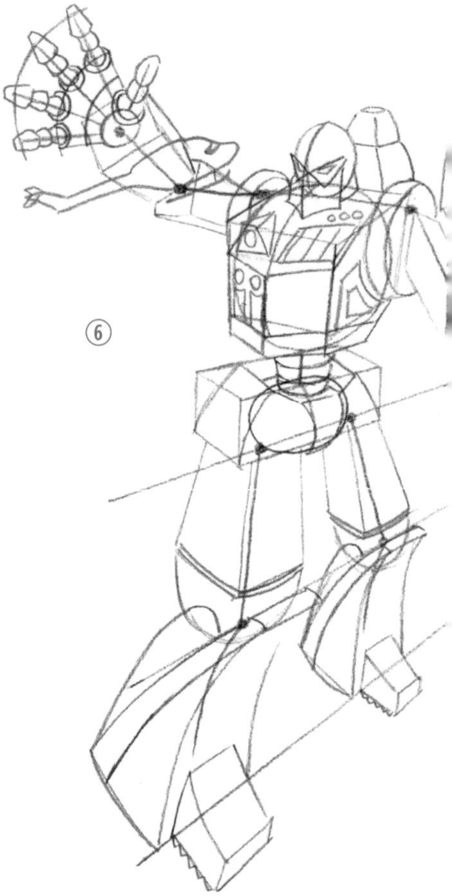

⑦

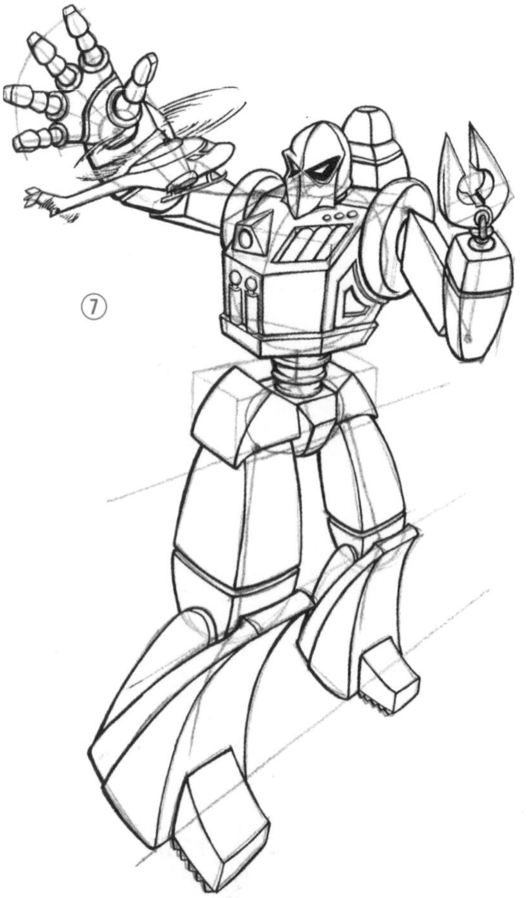

Step 8

When the ink is dry, erase all your pencil marks. Now you can enjoy adding color. I've added some strips of white to make the metal look like it's reflecting the light. The helicopter is bright green so it stands out against the colors of the robot's body.

⑧

Centaur

One of the simplest ways of combining human and animal body forms is a straight forward half-and-half split. The top or bottom half of a human is attached to the opposite half of an animal. One creature that takes this form is the centaur, which has featured in stories for thousands of years. It has the torso of a man attached to the body of a horse.

Step 1

Since this figure involves drawing two different species, it's best to concentrate on one creature at a time, so start by drawing the human half as shown. The chest takes the shape of an oval with a chunk cut out to show the edge of the rib cage—the oval is tilted to show that the chest is being thrust forward.

Step 2

Now for the horse—draw a large oval where the man's hips would normally sit to form the horse's rib cage. The man's spine is now also the horse's neck bones. Add the horse's backbone and leg bones—copy the shape of these carefully to capture the centaur's active pose.

Step 3

Start drawing the outline shape of the flesh and muscle around the bone structure as shown. Notice the deep curve of the horse's underbelly and the strong muscles around the upper arms of the human half and the hind legs of the horse.

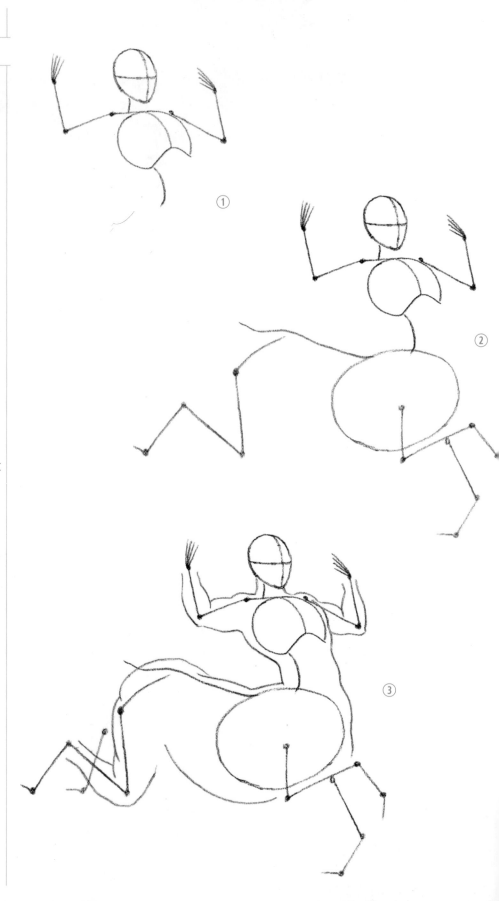

Step 4

Work on the legs and hooves. Notice how the outline curves out around the knobby joints.

Step 5

Place the facial features and work on the shape of the hands. When you draw the sword, make sure it looks as if it has been thrust back, ready for battle. The ponytail on the head should be flying up at the back, just like the horse's tail. Use long, confident pencil strokes to create the curves of these.

>>

④

Human and animal forms can be combined in many different ways, as you will see in the variety of creatures that are brought to life in this section.

⑤

Step 6

Add some more detail to the facial features. I've made the centaur's jawline more angular and drawn lots of little lines on the upper body to define the muscle. A few more curves on the body of the horse will add more definition to the muscle and bone here too. Notice the lines on the hair—these help to show the direction in which it is flowing.

Step 7

Pick out the good lines of your sketch and go over them with a soft pencil to produce your final picture. Next go over all your final lines again using a black felt-tip pen. Shade in the eyes, leaving a tiny circle of white on each one.

Step 8

Erase all the pencil lines that formed your centaur's skeleton framework, then add the color. I've chosen to give my centaur a zebra's body. I've made his hair black to match his tail.

⑧

Werewolf

The characteristics of a wolf and man are blended together here so that every feature and body part has the flavor of both species.

Step 1
Copy the skeleton framework as shown—the angle of the head and oversized chest is crucial to the beast's overall stance. The short legs make the body appear even heavier.

Step 2
When you add the outline of the flesh, use a high arch to create the hunchback. This will make the head appear to hang even lower.

Step 3
Now work on the head. The ears should be pointed and the eyes small. The beast has a long snout and square jawline. Add two rough triangle shapes to the sides of the face for the fur here.

Step 4
Draw the mouth open to display the teeth. Work on the lines forming the hair, including the bushy eyebrows and chin.

Step 5
Add the hands and feet, including the sharp, curved claws. Copy all the curves that define the chest and stomach muscles. Now use some zig-zag lines along the beast's back and on other parts of the body to show the rough texture of the fur— don't overdo this, since you want the body to retain a human feel too.

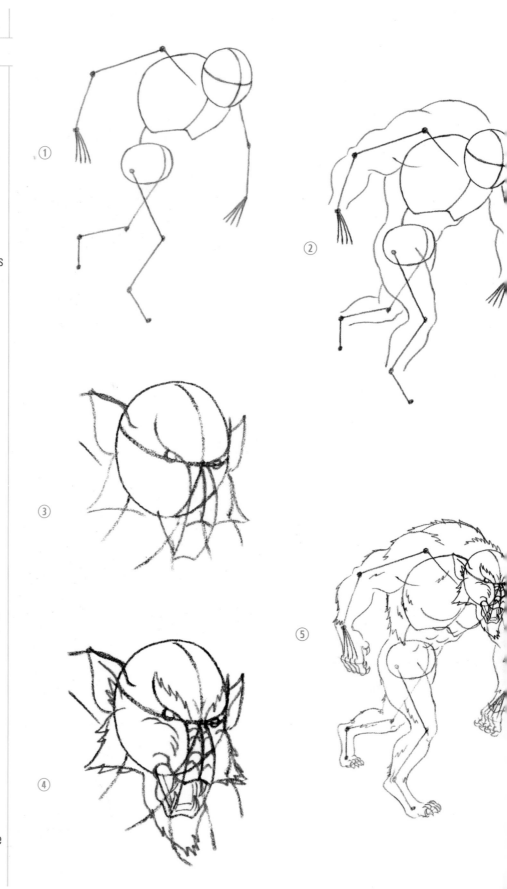

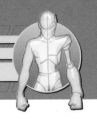
Step 6

Go over all the final lines of your drawing in heavy pencil or go straight to ink if you feel confident enough. When the ink is dry, erase all the pencil marks. Shade around the eyes to make the character look more sinister, then apply the color. Notice how the shadows work to make the beast more imposing. The yellow of the piercing eyes adds to the creature's less than friendly appearance.

⑥

Designing a Robot

Just as manga artists use the features of animals and humans to create mutant creatures, all sorts of everyday objects can provide inspiration for drawing robots.

Here are some of the objects I found lying around my home. They are all quite ordinary things, but any of their features or geometric qualities could be incorporated into the design of a new robot character.

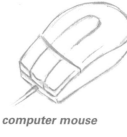

computer mouse

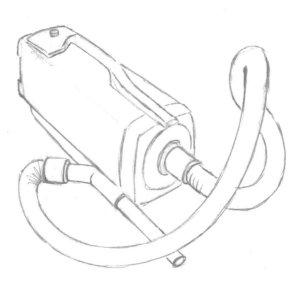

vacuum cleaner

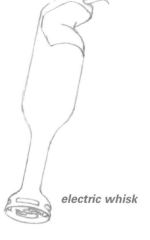

electric whisk

box cutter

soap dispenser

pliers

binoculars

perfume bottle

hairdryer

kettle

watering can

Junk Robot

Here are all the household objects assembled into a very rough robotic form. I've used some objects more directly than others and also changed their relative sizes—notice, for instance, the giant binoculars that form the power pack on the back. This design still needs a lot of work—the last thing a manga super mecha wants is to look as if he's made from giant kettles and vacuum cleaner parts. Before you turn this page and find out how I develop him further, try the following exercise.

Exercise

Find some objects that interest you around your home or pictures of objects in books. They might be airplane parts, engines, tools, electronic items, or anything else that could be made to look robotic. Build up a few pages of small sketches of these items, then try using all or part of each object to assemble a robot of your own. Developing new characters is a lot of fun, but it can also be a lengthy and involved process.

Developing a Robot

To bring our collection of junk to life requires a few more stages of development.

Step 1

I've chosen a chunky human form for my robot.

Step 2

Because the physique I've decided on is very bulky, my robot could easily look cumbersome, so I've gone for a dynamic pose.

Step 3

A mechanical version of my running human is now easy to draw.

Step 4

Next I built up my robot part by part, basing the design on my sketch of a junk robot from the previous page. This time, however, I only used the household objects as an inspiration and instead invented new parts to suit my machine. Deciding on the final shape of these parts can involve a lot of redrawing, but going over your final lines in heavy pencil and erasing all the mistakes will make your final design much clearer.

Step 5

To farther disguise my source material and to give more of a manga feel, I've added some extra details like the slatted metal visor and chest panel. When you're happy with your robot, go over it in black pen. Once the ink is dry, erase all remaining pencil marks.

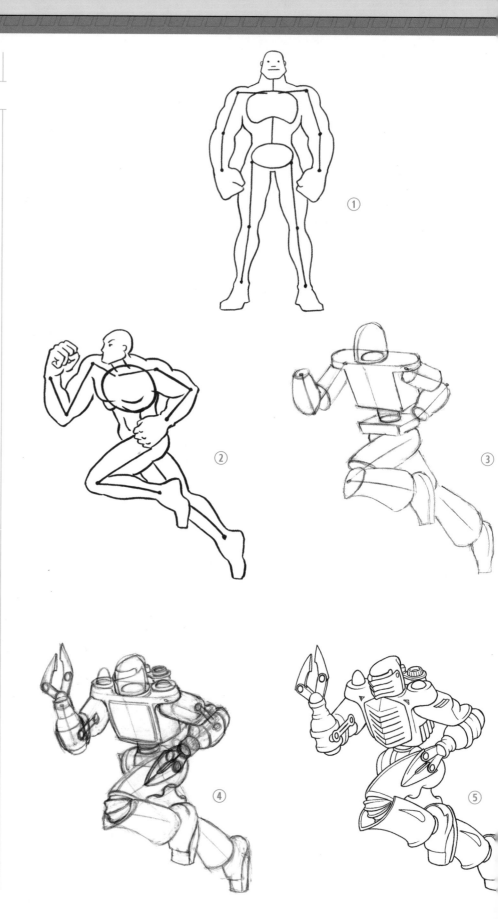

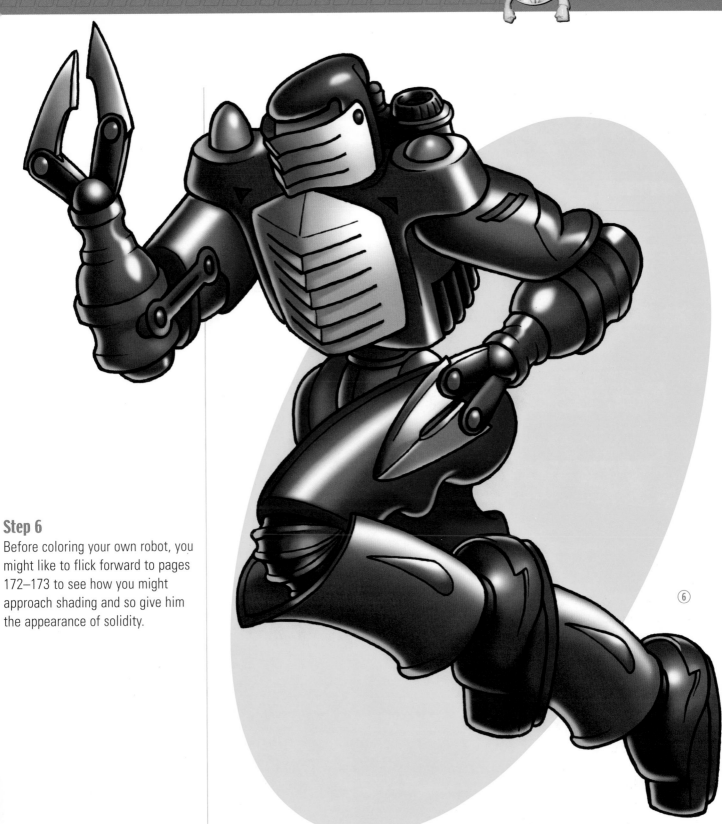

Step 6

Before coloring your own robot, you might like to flick forward to pages 172–173 to see how you might approach shading and so give him the appearance of solidity.

⑥

CREATURES

For manga artwork aimed at younger children, cutesy cartoon-style characters are very common and can be an essential element of the plot line and action.

Even in stories aimed at a more mature audience, cute animals often feature as stooges to the main characters, or provide some light relief from the violence of a fight scene.

Whatever kind of creature or character you want to draw, the drawing principles are the same. You start with a set of simple geometric shapes that form the main body masses, then work on smaller details as your drawing skills progress and your confidence grows.

You'll see too how by making a few simple alterations to some cute creatures, they can be changed into evil little characters —so even if cuddly cats and fluffy bunnies aren't your type of thing, it will be useful for you to become proficient at drawing them. You never know what they might develop into.

CREATURES
CREATURES
CREATURES
CREATURES
CREATURES
CREATURES
CREATURES
CREATURES
CREATURES
CREATURES
CREATURES
CREATURES
CREATURES
CREATURES
CREATURES
CREATURES
CREATURES

Cute Cat—Front View

You could probably do a good job of drawing this cute cat just by copying the final picture. But if you learn to construct it one step at a time, this will help you when you are drawing more complicated characters and viewpoints.

Step 1

Take a hard pencil and use light lines to draw an oval for the head. To help you make your picture symmetrical, put a vertical and a horizontal line through the center of it—it's good to get used to drawing lines like this freehand rather than using a ruler. For the eyes, draw two ovals with pointed ends. The ears and long fur around the face can be drawn as rough triangle shapes.

Step 2

Adding a few more simple lines will complete the facial features.

Step 3

Extend the vertical guideline to help you draw the body. Two overlapping circles make its basic shape.

Step 4

The smaller circle will help you draw the slender chest and front legs. The bigger circle will help you position the back legs. The tail sits upright.

Step 5

Add some jagged lines to create the texture of the fur—longer strokes will make a fluffier cat and shorter strokes will make the coat smoother. Add the paws.

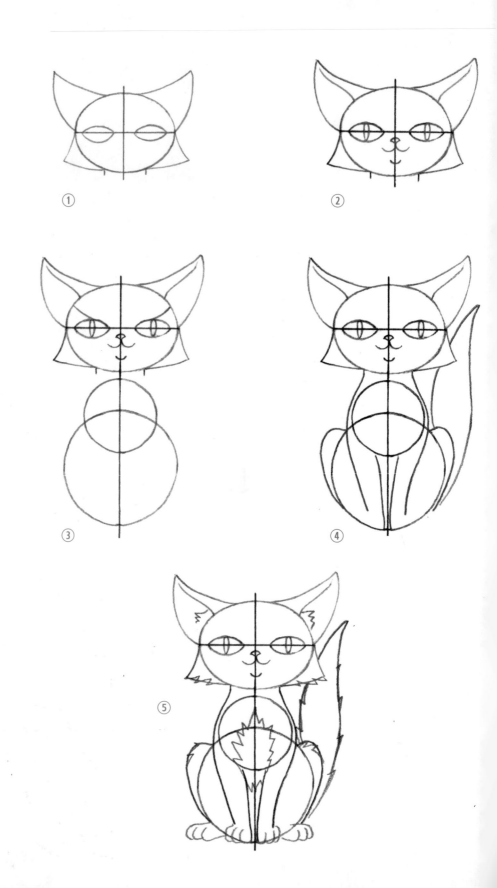

Step 6

Use a soft pencil to make the good lines of your drawing heavier. Erase your rough lines as you go along. Shade in the pupils, but leave a circle of white in the top left of each eye to form the bright highlights that characterize manga artwork. Go over your final lines again with a black felt-tip pen. When the ink is dry, erase any remaining pencil marks.

Step 7

This is what your finished drawing should look like. I've colored mine on a computer—you can find out how to do this later in the book. You might want to color your cat with pencils, paints, or felt-tips instead. Or you can move on to the next exercise and leave the color until later.

Cute Cat—Side View

Here our cute cat has turned his body to the side. His head, however, is turned only halfway between the front and side, so it is at a ¾ angle.

Step 1

Draw an oval shape for the head, but make it more squashed than the one you drew for the front view. The change of viewpoint also means that the vertical and horizontal guidelines now curve to follow the rounded shape of the head as shown.

Step 2

Use your guidelines to help you place the facial features as shown. Notice that the eye to the right of your picture is drawn smaller because it is turned farther away. The ear on that side is smaller too.

Step 3

Draw two overlapping circles to help you form the shape of the body. Study the picture to copy the size and positioning of the circles.

Step 4

Add the cat's body outline using your circles to guide you. Make the upright tail long and curved.

Step 5

Add some jagged lines to show the texture of the fur. Shape the paws and add a circle to each eye for the bright highlights—the circle on the eye to the right of your picture will be smaller than the one to the left.

Step 6

Use a soft pencil to go over the lines that you want to form your final drawing—erase your rough lines as you go. Shade the pupils of the eyes black, leaving the bright highlights white. Next go over your drawing again using a black felt-tip pen. When the ink dries, erase any remaining pencil lines, including the framework for the head and the circles that formed the body shape.

Step 7

The great thing about manga creatures is that they can be whatever color you choose— color your cat as you did before or try using a different color scheme.

⑥

⑦

Cute Proportions

In manga, as with all styles of drawing, characters are measured in head heights. This refers to the size of the character's body in relation to its own head. Changing the body's proportions can have a big effect.

The cute cat featured in the previous two exercises is about two-and-a-half heads tall, which is fairly standard for characters of this type. Three heads and two heads tall are also quite common. Remember that the smaller the body is in

relation to the head, the younger and cuter the character will look. Study the pictures below to see how I've used different-size circles to change the body shape. Try drawing the cat you drew before but make him shorter or taller.

3 heads tall   *2½ heads tall*   *2 heads tall*

Cat Varieties

Artists can draw many variations of one animal. Here are a few of the different ways that a cat can be interpreted, depending on the style of manga drawing.

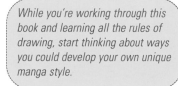

While you're working through this book and learning all the rules of drawing, start thinking about ways you could develop your own unique manga style.

Transformations

If you have a good understanding of how to draw a cute cat, it's easy to work out how you can change its personality—or even turn it into a different animal altogether. The principles are exactly the same— just a few of the details differ.

① This is a ¾ view of our cat, but here I've made him a little more rounded so he looks even cuter.

② Notice how easy it is to turn our cute cat into a fierce enemy. Slanting the eyes and eyebrows and adding some sharp teeth and claws produces dramatic results. An artist can do many other things to convey character and emotion through the features on the face—the cat can be made to look dopey, confused, or excited, for instance—but in most manga scenarios naturalistic animal characters do not normally have a great range of expressions. They simply appear either good or evil.

③ Starting from the same body and head shapes, the cat can be turned into a mouse by changing the shape of the ears and eyes and adding two long front teeth. A long thin tail completes the transformation, but you could also add a chunk of cheese for effect!

④ The same cat can be used to create a
   pig, squirrel, rabbit, or dog. Try
   drawing each of them. Turn each one
   into an evil character too. Look in
   other books to find pictures of animals
   and so help enrich your store of ideas
   when it comes to portraying cute
   manga creatures or their evil cousins.

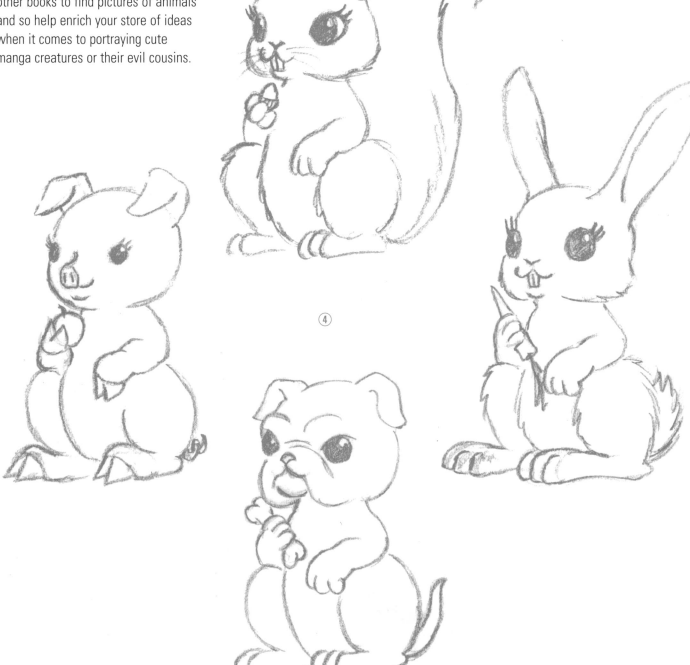

④

Lioness—¾ View

Here is one of the cute cat's relatives—the lioness. Imagine the head as a large ball, with a smaller ball making up the muzzle.

Step 1
Draw two overlapping circles as shown. Draw a curved vertical line on each one to mark the center of the lioness's head. Now roughly sketch in the shape of the eyes, nose, and mouth.

Step 2
Draw on the ears. A few more lines will shape the jawline and neck.

Step 3
Carefully copy the lines I've added to make the lioness more lifelike—notice the creases in the skin above the nose that add to her snarl and the jagged shapes that form the fur.

Step 4
Now for the whiskers, teeth, and tongue. Take some time to get these right since they are crucial to the beast's threatening appearance.

Step 5
Go over all your good lines with a soft pencil so you can clearly see the shape of your final drawing—erase the rough lines as you go. Go over the lines again with a black felt-tip pen. I've used the black pen to shade the nose and mouth area for effect. We'll look at this technique in more detail later.

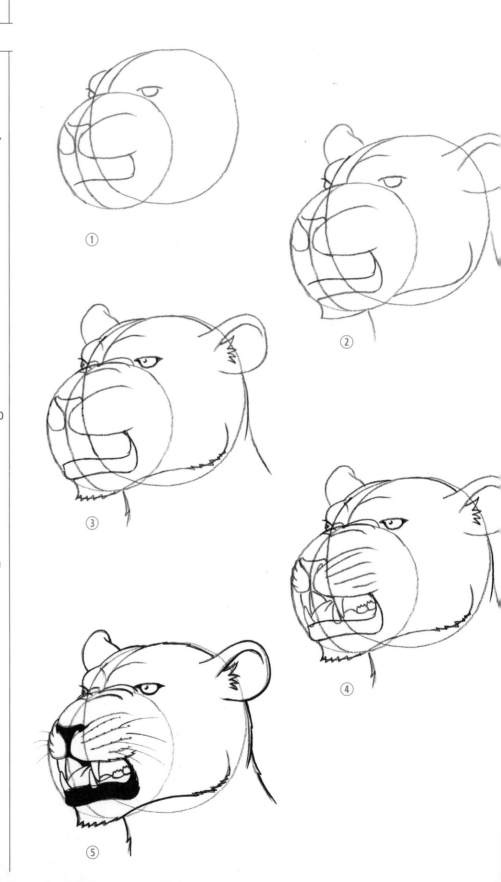

Step 6

Now you can erase the rest of your pencil guidelines, then add some color. Copy the way I've colored the lioness here—notice the different shadows on her face.

⑥

Lion Body—Side View

Let's get more ambitious and draw complete animal bodies. We'll start with a fully grown male lion.

Step 1

Start with the head and body shapes, then add the spine and the bones of one front and one hind leg.

Step 2

Add the outline of the flesh around the bones—carefully copy the curves as shown in the picture so you capture the build of the lion's body—notice the lion's puffed-out chest. When you've drawn the line of the belly, add the second hind leg.

Step 3

Work on the rough shape of the muzzle. Add the second foreleg—you can only just see it from this angle. Draw the paws firmly placed on the ground.

Step 4

Add some curves to outline the shape of the face, mane, and tail.

Step 5

Work on the detail of the face and add lots of little curves and curls to the mane to show that the texture is different from the smooth hair on the body. Add a tuft of fur under the chin and on the tip of the tail.

Step 6

Go over your final lines, erasing any earlier mistakes. Ink over the lines in black pen. Add rows of dots for the whiskers and solid black on the nose and mouth.

Step 7

When the ink is dry, erase all your pencil guidelines. If you're not satisfied with the finished result, go back over the steps to see where you went wrong—it may have been the build of the body, the texture of the mane, or the distinctive shape of the eye. When you've figured out which part you really needed to do more work on, try again. Once you've got a drawing you're happy with, add the color.

⑦

Lion Styles

Although there isn't a great deal of variation in the way larger animal characters are drawn, that doesn't mean they never differ. Here are some ways you could bring a bit of personal style to a creature like a lion while keeping a manga feel—but of course you're free to draw animals in whatever way you want.

① This sculptural style would be appropriate for drawing either a spirit or lion-god. The noble beast is created using lots of sharp lines to give an angular look.

② This is a type of cute cartoon drawing style that can be applied to larger animals to make them look more friendly for younger children. You'll notice that although there's a very spiky quality to the lines, the lion still looks gentle because of its big, round, glossy eyes.

③ You can soften the ferocity of a wild animal without making it too cutesy—reduce the size of the teeth, round off the sharp edges of the fur, and keep the eyes round.

④ Here smooth strokes have been drawn using a Chinese brush pen, but the eyes and teeth of this beast show that he is far from friendly—small slanted eyes with tiny pupils and some large sharp fangs do the trick. I've also added eyebrows, even though a lion wouldn't really have them. When they're angled down toward the nose, they help to make the lion appear even more fierce.

⑤ These drawings show how the lion is interpreted in traditional Japanese paintings, statues, and puppets. Neither figure looks much like a real lion. The styles have been developed over centuries as one artist copied another but added a little of their own style along the way. These kinds of lions are still used in manga today, especially in fantasy stories or samurai adventures.

⑤

④

Proportion Distortion

You might be surprised to learn that when manga animals aren't supposed to be cute, they are usually drawn with a degree of naturalism, like the lion on the previous pages. Even though the proportions of manga human characters are often highly exaggerated, those of animals seldom are. But some manga artists, influenced by Western comic styles and Hollywood animation, are beginning to give their animals more dynamic characterizations.

① Here's a lion drawn to naturalistic proportions, showing its simplified skeleton and the shape of the head underneath its mane. The lion, as you can see, is long and quite low to the ground. This is because it has to stalk its prey and does not want to be seen above the long grass of the plains.

② Compare this treatment of the same animal. I have enlarged parts of the body and reduced others to emphasize the most powerful parts. The chest is deeper and the legs more solid, and these changes are made more apparent by slimming down the hindquarters. The head and feet are also enlarged to make room for huge teeth and claws.

In the real world, a lion with these proportions would be at a disadvantage in catching its prey, but in the world of manga, such considerations are unimportant. What matters is that the lion looks impressive and threatening.

③ Now that I've revised the proportions in a rough diagram, I can make a finished drawing of the lion in a suitably ferocious pose. The stance of this new lion is not very different from that of the lion on the preceding pages, but the changes result in a very different-looking drawing with more dynamic proportions, a ¾ angle of view, the head turned, the facial expression, and a display of teeth.

④ With the addition of color, the transformation is complete. In line with the changes to the lion's natural form, I've exaggerated the color.

④

Fox—¾ View

One animal that often crops up in Japanese folklore and comics is the fox. Its head is much more angular than that of a lioness.

Step 1

Start with a rough oval shape for the main part of the head, then add a long narrow muzzle. Copy the curves of the vertical and horizontal guidelines. These lines will help you place all the features symmetrically.

Step 2

The ears immediately make your picture identifiable as a fox. The eyes start as two small circles. Outline the nose and mouth too.

Step 3

Keep building up the features of the face. Add the loose fur to the sides of the face. Some simple scribbles form the fur inside the ears.

Step 4

Go over all your good lines in heavy pencil. Add the whiskers and teeth, then go over all your final lines in black ink. A few extra marks will show the texture of the fur around the eyes and at the top of the muzzle. Shade the pupils black, leaving a white circle inside each one. Use solid black on the nose and mouth too.

Step 5

Erase all your pencil marks then add the color. Notice how using white on the eyes adds to the fierceness of the fox's glare.

Variations

Once you've mastered drawing a fox, making a few changes to it can develop its character—or turn it into a different beast altogether.

① I've used the same basic framework for this fox, but I've made it look much more evil by slanting the eyes and making the pupils smaller and the teeth longer. I've also used sharper lines for the fur.

② A friendlier fox can be created by making the eyes larger and rounder. I've also made the fur more tufty and used curved lines to make the muzzle less angular. I haven't drawn any teeth, so it appears that they are covered by the tongue.

③ Here's my initial fox sketch, placed next to one of a wolf. You can see that they are really quite similar. To draw the wolf, break it down into the simple steps you followed for the fox, but look at this sketch at each stage to work out what's different—notice that the ears sit farther apart and the eyes are narrower. The muzzle is wider and the snout more pointed. When you've finished, find a photograph of a domestic dog and try drawing it using the same steps. Exaggerate the features to make it look good or evil.

The more you draw animals, the more you'll realize how important it is to look at photographs of real animals to help you capture their features.

Animal Movement

Animals don't tend to stay still for long, especially in manga, so you need to learn to draw them in all sorts of poses—from sitting, standing, and lying down to stalking, running, and jumping. These pictures show some typical animal poses. I've left the skeleton framework on each body to help you see how the joints can and can't bend.

① These two poses are typical of a lion's behavior. Notice how different the legs look when a lion is sitting down compared with when it's stretching. Although the lion isn't in motion in either picture, the head shows that it's alert, and one of the poses shows that it's ready to pounce.

② There is definitely a sense of movement in each of these drawings. The feet of the cheetah are off the ground and the head is held forward. Each picture suggests imbalance—an impression that if the animals weren't moving forward, they would fall over.

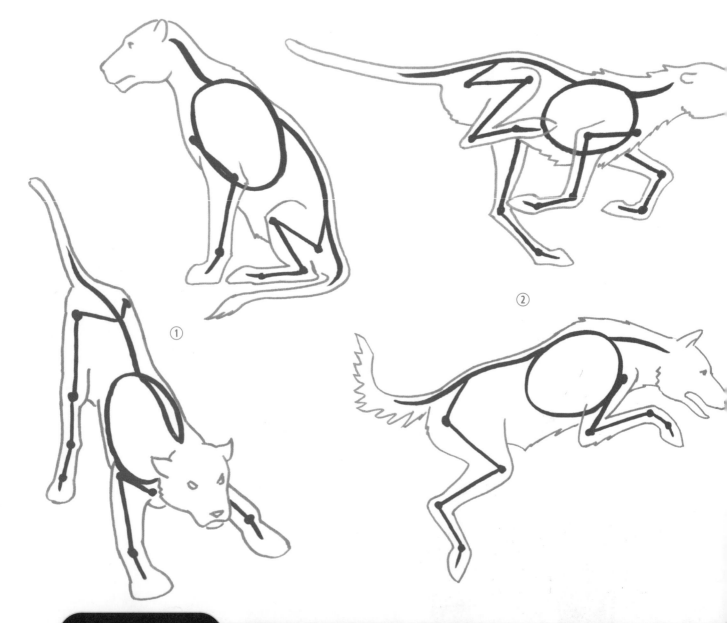

③ Even though these poses aren't balanced, the horse doesn't appear to be moving forward because it has two feet placed firmly on the ground. We still get a sense of the effort it's putting into each stance and the tension in the limbs as the horse lifts itself against the force of gravity.

③

The ways animals move are as varied as the species and breeds themselves. When you're watching a movie or TV program featuring animals, watch closely and pick up as much information as you can. You could make some quick sketches of some of the poses and movements you see.

Wolf—Side View

These stages for drawing the body of a wolf from the side also show you how to bring movement into the pose.

Step 1

First draw the main body shapes—the muzzle should be more pointed than that of the lion and the chest takes the form of a large oval lying on its side. All but one of the legs are raised so the bones form zig-zag shapes. The tail is flying up at the back as the animal speeds along.

Step 2

Add the body outline—where you need to create more flesh or muscle, like around the wolf's powerful hind legs, curve the line farther away from the bone.

Step 3

Work on the features of the head—the ear should lie flat, the nose is high in the air, and the mouth is open. Outline the feet and complete the curve of the tail.

Step 4

Lots of little jagged lines around the body outline will help show the texture of the fur. Define the paws and work on the mouth too—the tongue hangs out slightly to show that the wolf is panting.

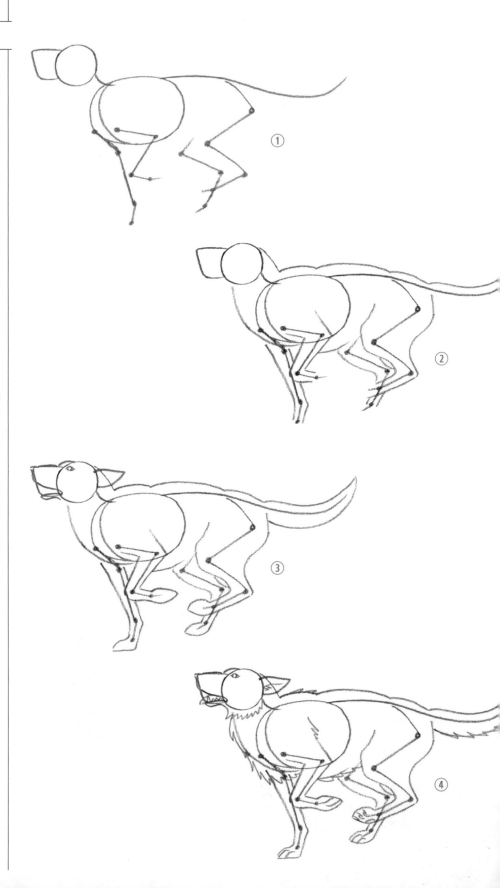

Step 5

Go over your final lines in heavy pencil. Next go over the lines again with a black felt-tip pen, adding some claws to the paws as shown.

Step 6

Erase all the pencil lines that formed the framework for your running wolf, then color him in.

⑤

⑥

Monster Dog

Turn back a few pages and you'll see how I changed a rather ordinary-looking lion into a more ferocious version. You can do this to any creature, and the wolf on the previous page is no exception. This time I'm going to distort the nonthreatening animal even more to create a vicious and demonic monster dog.

① - ② Here's a wolflike dog in a jumping pose. By making very slight changes to the skeleton—adding just a little more length to the spine and heightening the neck joint—he can be made to look quite different. The limbs are leaner and closer to the bone, though the outline bulges around the joints to suggest the thickness of the bone endings. The thicker, longer neck works well, as does the slimming down of the stomach area.

This example shows the importance of the skeleton in your drawings: if the skeleton works, then whatever alterations you make to the skin should work too.

③ Before making a finished drawing, I worked out some more details of how I'd like the head to change. I'll strip away all the elements that could look cute: the large, soft ears are reduced to leathery spikes, and the friendly eyes become mere slits and are moved to a higher position on the head. The teeth are an obvious thing to change too. Allowing the fangs to protrude over the lips is a good trick, and a snarling expression always looks effective.

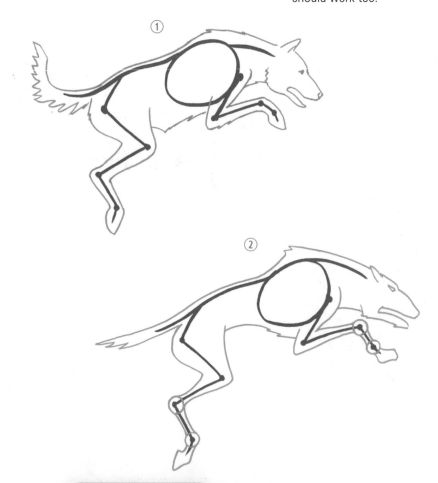

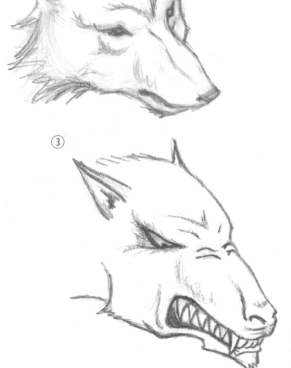

④ I think you'll agree that there's nothing friendly about this beast. Along with the changes to the proportions, I have also drawn the outline of the monster dog with a simplified, angular style. I want to convey a feral creature, ungroomed, half-starved, and hungry for blood. A few lines to suggest ribs and neck sinews are a useful addition.

⑤ This dog is definitely a creature of the night, so I have chosen colors that will blend in with the shadows. In contrast to his body color, the bright mouth and flashing teeth and claws stand out as perilous weapons.

More Skeletons

So far, we have been concentrating on mammals, but there are many more members of the animal kingdom that you might want to draw. Luckily, nearly all animals that live on land have the same parts to their skeletons, even though the proportions may be very different. The human body is also constructed with exactly the same framework as all of these diverse creatures.

① Frog and crocodile

The skeletons of a frog and crocodile have the same parts as a mammal's skeleton—each is made up of a head, rib cage, and spine, plus limbs and joints. It's not just the relative size of these body parts that distinguishes these creatures from mammals. Their posture is also very different—the limbs are more tightly folded, making the animals more squat.

② Eagle and crane

These birds feature heavily in Japanese folklore and have also found their way into many manga stories. With its wings spread, we can see how tiny the eagle's arm bones are in relation to the overall size of the wings. The drawing of the crane shows the way the arm bones bend when its wings are folded against the side of its body.

③ Dinosaur and crow

This dinosaur can stand fairly upright since its strong back legs can bear its weight. Over millions of years, birds have evolved from dinosaurs and still retain some of the same characteristics. The crow also stands on two legs. Its forelimbs are wings, but the overall bone structure is the same. Notice how the proportions of its skeleton differ from the crane's.

④ Wasp and spider

There are exceptions to most rules, as these last two pictures show. Wasps and spiders are invertebrates, so they have no spine. Like all insects, wasps have three main body segments and six legs—the legs are always attached to the middle body segment and the wings have no bones. Spiders have just two main body parts and an extra pair of legs.

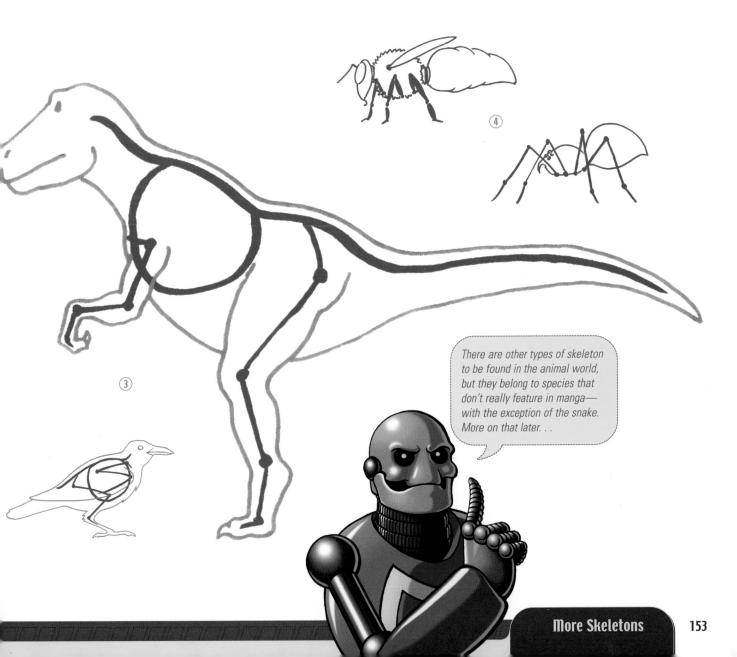

There are other types of skeleton to be found in the animal world, but they belong to species that don't really feature in manga— with the exception of the snake. More on that later. . .

Dinosaur—¾ View

This exercise shows how to draw a dinosaur in action from a 3/4 viewpoint. Drawing the body from this angle is a bit trickier but following the steps will help you.

Step 1

A large roughly drawn circle forms the ribcage. Position and shape the skull, then add a curved line to this to mark the center of the head. Add the parts of the spine and all the bones of the limbs. Once you've completed the skeleton framework, use it to help you outline the flesh of the body.

Step 2

Finish off the forelimbs—the claws are curled under so that they are hidden. When you work on the head, copy the curves above the eyes. The mouth should be wide open, ready for you to add the teeth.

Step 3

Now fill the mouth with jagged teeth. Draw the center crease line of the tongue and draw on the nostrils. Some tiny curves along the dinosaur's back will show the bumps of the spine. Adding crease lines to the body will show the folds of the thick skin. Put some sharp claws on the toes.

Step 4

Go over your good lines with a soft pencil. Then go over these lines again with a black pen.

Step 5

Once the pen ink is dry, erase any pencil lines. Now you can add the color—instead of making the dinosaur look naturalistic, I decided to use bold blues and greens. You can choose whatever color scheme you want.

(5)

Creating Hybrids

Several different animals can be combined to create an entirely new species, like the manga dragon we'll draw over the next few pages. Take a look at the finished picture of this dragon on page 159, then study the pictures on this page so you can get an idea of where its different parts derived from.

Lion, snake, and crocodile

The manga dragon has a face similar to that of a traditional Japanese-style lion. Its body and head shape are like a snake's, and its limbs sit like those of a crocodile. But it has features of other animals too—it has the antlers of a deer, the whiskers of a catfish, and the mane of a horse. Its feet are a mixture of human hands and an eagle's claws.

Japanese Dragon

This is a very sophisticated creature, so take your time over each step.

Step 1

Copy the head shape as shown, then add a long curvy tube for the body—overlap the curves of this snake-like shape as if the body is transparent. Later you can erase the lines that make up the sections of the body you wouldn't really be able to see since they lie underneath other sections.

Step 2

Add the bones of the four limbs and copy the frameworks I've drawn for the hands. They are shaped to give the impression that the beast is ready to lash out at any moment.

Step 3

Draw the outline for the flesh around the bones—the lines you drew across the finger bones in the last stage should help you see where the knobby joints are so you can curve your outline around these.

Step 4

Let's leave the body for now and concentrate on the head. First, block in the main shapes—the eyes, nose, jaw, ears, and antlers.

Step 5

Use jagged lines for the fur and teeth. Two curves on the antlers will mark where the skin finishes. Don't forget the tiny pupils and the long curved whiskers.

>>

<<

Step 6

Add a row of spiky fur along the dragon's spine. Remember that the dragon is twisting and turning, so some parts of its back aren't visible. Draw some long curved guidelines along the body to help you position the ribbed belly in the next stage. Add the sharp claws.

Step 7

As you draw all the lines on the ribbed belly, remember that the belly is rounded, so these lines will curve slightly. Study the picture carefully to work out which way they curve as the body bends in and out—getting this right will add solidity and three-dimensionality to your picture. Add the tip of the tail and attach some fur to the dragon's elbows.

Step 8

Now you should be ready to pick out all the final lines of your drawing and make them heavier by going over them with a soft pencil, then with a black felt-tip pen. If you can easily make out all your good lines, just use a pen. Study the picture carefully to see if there are any lines you missed. Add some extra black to the eyes.

Step 9

When the ink is dry, erase all your pencil lines. Now you can decide on a color scheme. Notice the colors I've used for the fur to make it resemble flames. The inside of the mouth is black to help highlight the ferocious teeth. Don't forget to leave a circle of white on each eye.

⑨

Complex Hybrids

As you get more experienced at drawing animals, you can start to put more of your own ideas into your work. Try creating your own hybrid creatures by mixing the features of different animals. Here are a couple of examples to give you some ideas but if you flip through this book, you'll find lots of skeletons and poses that you could also base your new creations on.

① To come up with this new species, I studied the features and poses of a crane, horse and crocodile, then mixed some of these elements together. Making up mutant animals like this can be great fun. Each new creature can be the starting point for a new manga adventure.

② I created this cute little animal by looking at some pictures I drew in my sketch book a while ago—my new creation has the head shape of a bulldog. A bird's beak takes the place of a nose. The body and pose are similar to a bear's, but the legs are short to help make the character look cute.

Here are some more animal pictures for you to work from to make up some new manga hybrids of your own. Try changing the proportions of the features you are using. Draw the limbs of one animal in a pose you would usually associate with another creature. Practice drawing different-sized creatures—some fierce, some cute, some subtle, some weird. Use different viewpoints too.

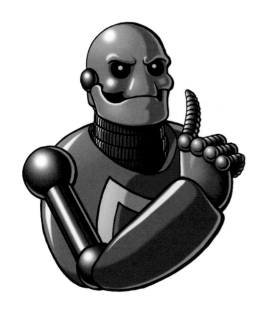

Creating an Alien

There's no parcticular route to creating new characters. Each character evolves in its own way through many stages of drawing—especially if your principals come from other planets. When you aren't sure what you want to draw, there's nothing more daunting than a blank sheet of paper.

① **Doodling**

A good way to get started is to give yourself a problem to solve. Take a pencil and some scrap paper and lightly draw a squiggle.

② **Imagining**

Looking at your squiggle from different angles, try to make out a face or body hidden among the lines. Draw directly onto your squiggle to develop what you see. This squiggle made me think of a bird-like form.

③ **Shaping ideas**

After repeating this process several times, I start to get inspiration for the kind of alien I want to create, and see insect and crablike qualities that might work well for an alien creature.

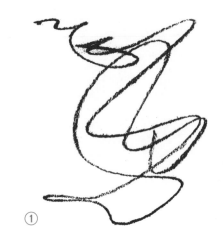

For more inspiration, try dipping tip of a large brush into some ink and dripping splotches on to som scrap paper to see what kinds of creatures emerge.

Seeking Inspiration

Having arrived at the kind of look I want to achieve, I turn to my sketch books for further inspiration. All the examples shown were done during a trip to a natural history museum, and provide good reference for my alien project. Incorporating features based on the natural world can help to make your creatures look believable.

Sketching an Alien

Working from my rough doodles and sketch books, I start to develop some alien life forms. Gradually a character starts to evolve, and each picture takes me one step closer to creating a character I'm happy with. I want my alien to be fearsome yet graceful and appealing.

If you visit a natural history museum, take a sketch book with you to draw any animal features that appeal to you. Look at pictures in wildlife books or on the Internet too.

Developing the Alien

① Color sketch

Roughly adding some color to my favorite design helps me to visualize how a finished version might look. It's almost there, but I feel it could still be made to look more scary and other-worldly.

② The pose

For a start, it needs a more dynamic pose. Drawing the skeleton framework of a human allows me to see if a pose will work.

③ Design changes

During the process of sketching my alien in its new pose, I continue to develop its body features.

④ The final sketch

Producing a final sketch, I further refine the details and proportions. I could continue to change elements, but at some point you have to settle on a final design. I'm now ready to ink and color my final picture, but in the next few pages I've broken it down into steps for you to copy it.

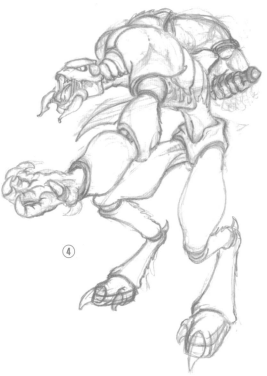

Alien

Here are the steps to making a precise drawing of the final alien character I came up with on the previous pages.

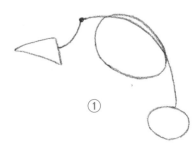

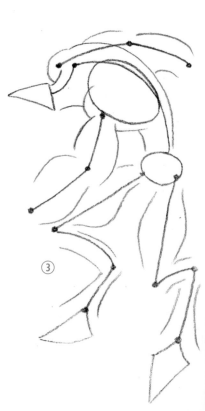

Step 1

Although this alien's overall body shape is quite human in form, there are some vital differences in the make up of its skeleton. The outline for the head is triangular, and I've put an extra joint in the neck to make this longer and more mobile. Notice the dramatic arch of the spine too. The chest oval is much larger than the oval for the hips.

Step 2

Place the arm bones and joints as shown. For clarity, one arm is drawn as if it isn't connected to the body. Notice how the legs differ from a human's. The section between the knee and ankle is short and the ankles sit high up, more like those of many animals.

Step 3

Add the main parts of the body outline as shown—the body is made up of lots of separate segments.

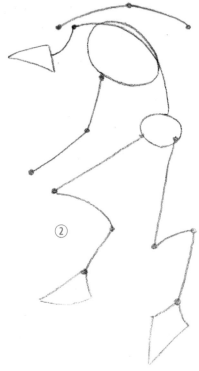

Step 4

Fill in the gaps of your alien's body outline—if you turn the page, you'll see a picture of the finished beast, which will help you work out what body parts all the different lines belong to. Work on the shape of the head too. The hands resemble a human's, while the feet are more like an animal's hooves.

Step 5

Build up the definition of the creatures gradually—here I've drawn in the flesh of the fingers and worked on the shape around the hips and limb joints.

Step 6

Now for some of the more lethal parts, like the giant fangs and claws. Add the sharp blade of the weapon too. Work on all the segments running down the neck of the spine and the plates that form a shell to protect the creature's back.

➜

Step 7

Work on the rest of the detail, like the features of the snarling mouth and the jagged spines on the legs. Add some little lines to show the protruding ribs and draw the curves that show the muscles on the tiny stomach. Notice the extra lines that show the fleshy parts of the hand.

Step 8

Use a soft pencil to go over all the good lines of your drawing so you can easily make these out.

Step 9

Ink over all your heavy pencil lines using a black felt-tip pen. When the ink is dry, erase all the remaining pencil marks, especially the lines forming the skeleton framework.

Step 10

Now add color to your picture—this is what it will look like if you color it digitally. After coloring, you could have some fun thinking about what kind of creature this beast might be attacking—once you've come up with a design for the enemy creature, put the two beasts together in one picture.

⑩

COLOR

In this section, we're going to look at inking your drawings, coloring, and applying tone. You'll also learn something about how different colors work together.

Colored pencils are the easiest to use, so you may want to start with them and then move on to felt-tip pens and watercolor paints. Once you start working with paints, you'll want to use thicker paper since this won't buckle when it gets wet.

Experienced artists have their own preference for using certain materials depending on their style and on what they enjoy working with most.

Although adding color can produce fantastic results, it can also ruin a good drawing if the color isn't applied well. Spend some time experimenting with different materials to see how you get on with them, and so you learn about the different effects that can be created with them.

Art materials can be very expensive, but you can get by quite well with just a few. All the examples in this book were done with the kinds of materials you might already have in your own home—so look around before you start spending money!

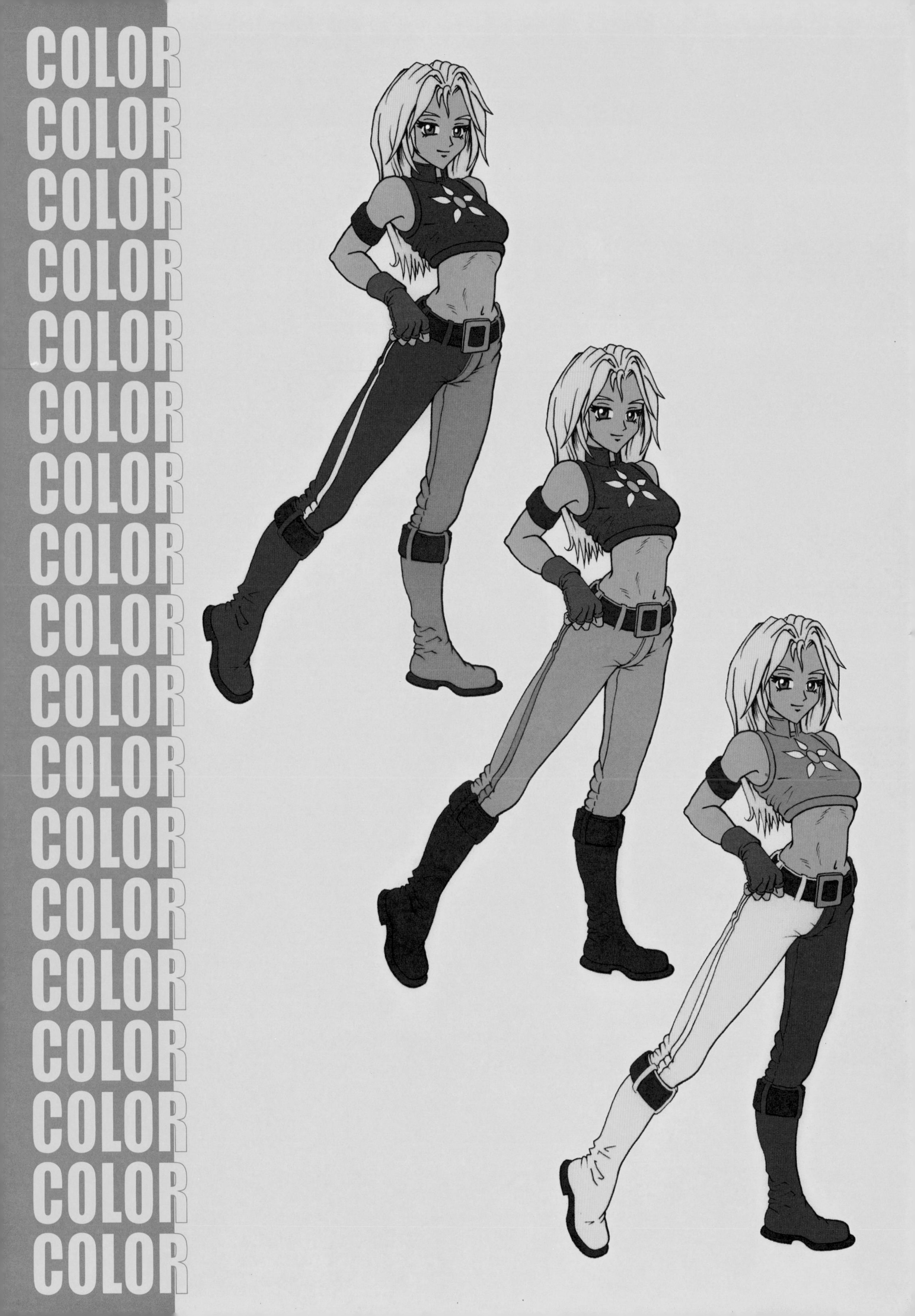
COLOR
COLOR
COLOR
COLOR
COLOR
COLOR
COLOR
COLOR
COLOR
COLOR
COLOR
COLOR
COLOR
COLOR
COLOR
COLOR
COLOR
COLOR

①

②

Light & Shade (basics)

To use color effectively, you need to understand how light and shade affect an object.

① Daytime shadows

The shapes shown here form the basis of most objects. Light is hitting them from an upper-right direction. The surfaces facing toward the light will therefore appear brighter than the parts that face away. The parts facing away will not be completely black, however, because light also bounces off walls, floors and other objects to faintly illuminate these areas.

② Night-time shadows

At night, when objects are lit directly from artificial light sources, there may be no light reflecting off other things to help illuminate the parts of an object that face away from the light source, so these areas can merge into the darkness.

③ Simple shading

First decide on the direction the light is coming from, then lightly shade the surfaces of your picture that aren't facing the light directly. In my picture, the light is coming from top right again. I've used a very soft pencil, holding it at an angle but without pushing down too heavily.

④ Creating shadows

Some parts of a complicated object like this robot will block out the light from other parts—an arm might cast a shadow on a leg, for instance. Keeping the light direction in mind, imagine where various body parts might cast shadows on other parts and shade those areas darker.

⑤ Hidden areas

Some parts of the robot are tucked away, like the little crevasses under close-fitting joints. Shade these parts more heavily.

⑥ Angles

Polish your picture by working across each body part and imagining the subtle ways that light falls on it. Shade the parts to different degrees, depending on the angle of each part in relation to the direction of light.

⑦ Adding backgrounds

Here is my finished picture against two different backgrounds. A gray background makes the lighter areas stand out more and helps show the effects of reflected light around the left and lower edges of the body parts. I've also put the same drawing on a black background and removed the reflected light. Now you can see that it blends in with the background completely. This effect is often used in manga to create atmosphere.

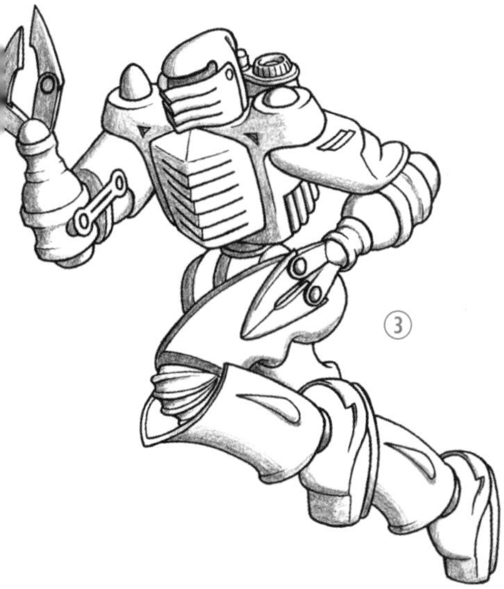

③

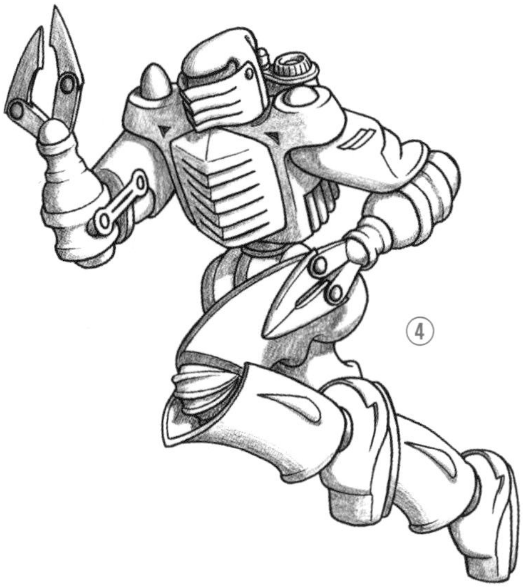

④

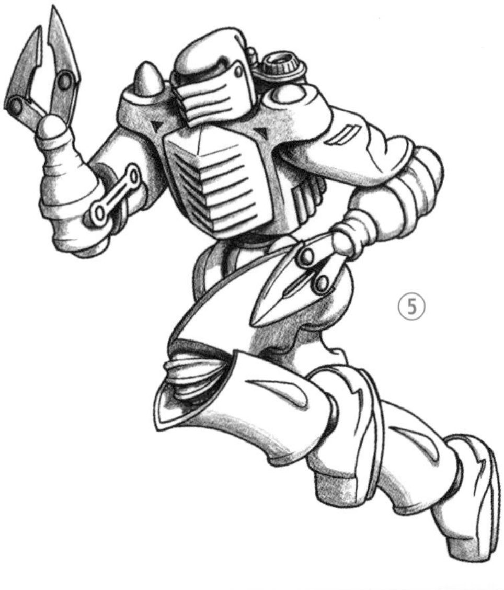

⑤

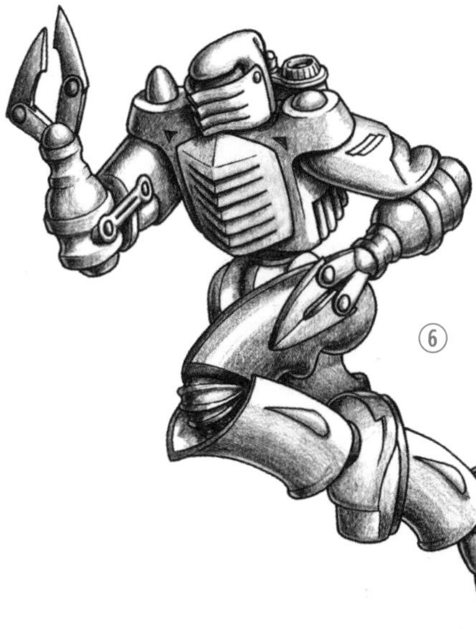

⑥

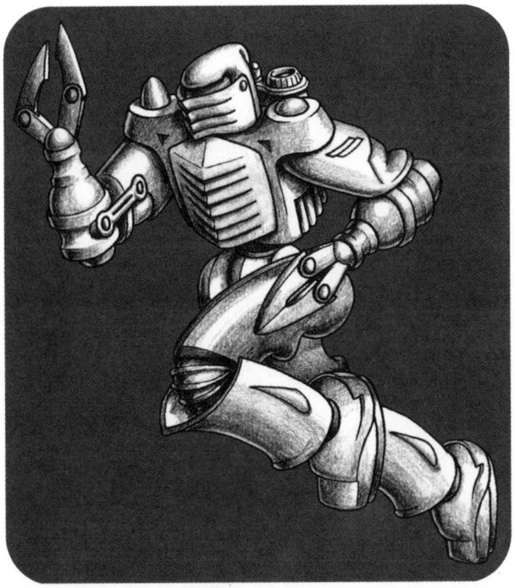

⑦

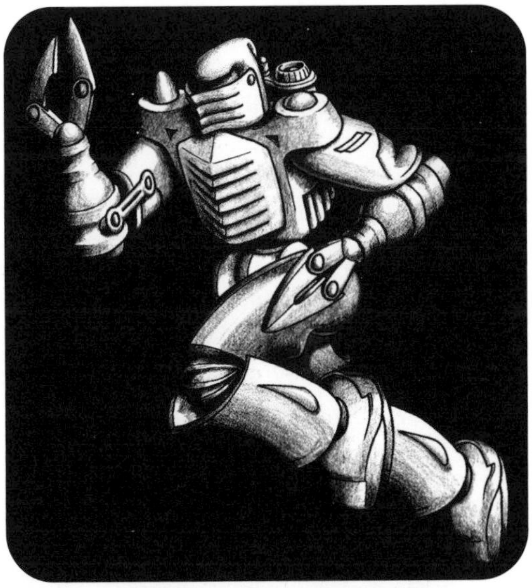

Light & Shade (faces)

Pencils are great for drawing lines, but they are also good for shading. Making some parts of your drawing darker will create the illusion of solidity and depth. Think of shading as coloring in black and white, but don't get too carried away with your pencil—leave plenty of white paper showing. The lighter some parts are, the darker and more dramatic the shadowy areas will look.

① **Line drawing**
This is Atta. Her face is drawn in simple pencil line. The only shading is on her irises and pupils. It looks fine, but it could be made much more interesting by using shading to show how the light is falling on her. When light falls on an object from different angles, it brings out different aspects.

② **Front lighting**
Imagine that light is falling on Atta directly from the front. The center of the face, where the light hits full-on, will naturally be better lit than the top of the head and the sides of the face, where the light hits at sharper angles—these areas should receive the heaviest shading with your pencil. Using a soft pencil, start by shading very lightly and gradually build up the darker areas layer by layer. Notice how the highlights in the eyes have changed position— they should always face the direction from which the light is coming.

③ **Lighting from above**
Now the light source is above Atta so the top of her head has the least shading. Notice how the shading is darker below the brows and under

the chin since shadows would be cast on these parts of the face.

④ **Lighting from the side**
The light source is to the right of the face. The areas of heaviest shading are on the side away from the light.

⑤ **Lighting from below**
You can use lighting to make a picture much more dramatic. When the face is lit from below, it takes on creepy qualities.

⑥ **Adding backgrounds**
When you put the shaded drawings of Atta against a dark background, this makes the effects of shading her differently much more easy to see.

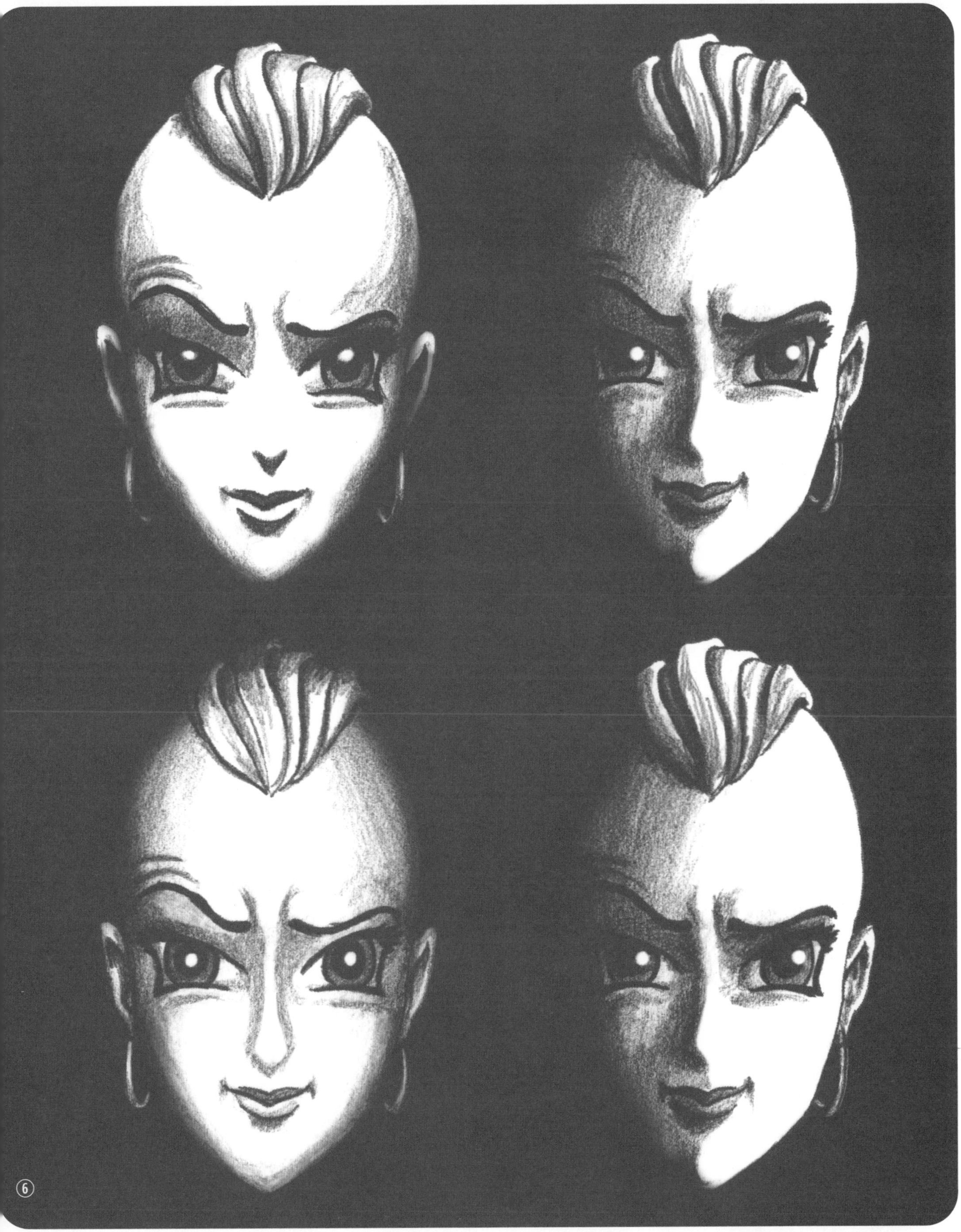
6

Inking & Coloring

Over the next couple of pages, we'll look at some shading and colouring techniques and materials. All of the following examples are based on the same drawings and all are lit from the same upper-left direction, so that you can compare the results.

Pencil

Using only a pencil, this is the simplest form of shading, but the results can be rich, refined and quite satisfying. In these examples, there is no ink and no dark outlines. You don't often see pencil-shaded pictures in comic books, but you can learn a lot by practicing with this method.

Simple pen line

Here, I've copied the same designs and outlined them using a fine-tipped black pen; the kind that you can buy quite cheaply from any art shop or stationer's. With all my rough pencil marks erased, the drawing is clean, but it will need more work to capture the manga flavour.

Finished pen line

Traditionally, manga artists use a metal pen, which they dip into black ink. This can produce lines of varying thickness, depending on how hard you press the pen against the paper, but it can be tricky and messy to use. Similar effects can be produced more easily with felt-tipped pens by retracing the lines of the initial ink drawing, varying the width of the lines to accentuate curves. A useful trick is to make the lines bolder in areas that face away from the light source.

After completing the full ink line drawings, I photocopied them several times to finish them in different ways. Working on photocopies allows you to experiment without the fear of ruining a carefully inked drawing.

Tonal wash

For this version I used black watercolor paint mixed with a lot of water to make it thin and easy to apply. You can use watered-down ink instead, if you like. This technique is known as *wash*. To paint like this, make sure that the pen you use for the outline has waterproof ink, otherwise it will blur when you put the wet paint on. It's a good idea to work on fairly heavy paper, because wet paint will make thin paper buckle. And, of course, you'll need a brush. It is worth investing in one of decent quality, with soft hairs and a fine point. Good brushes are not cheap, but if you clean them carefully after every use, they will last a long time.

Colored pencils

The easiest way to add color to your pictures is to use colored pencils. They will not give you really professional results, but they can look good if you use them carefully. Colored pencils are especially good for quickly sketching new color schemes in rough. A handy feature of colored pencils is that you can blend colors together to create new shades. For these pictures, I did not have exactly the colors of pencil that I wanted, so I blended other colors together, working one color over the top of another.

Felt-tips

Another medium you may have used before is felt-tipped pens. They produce very vibrant colors very quickly and they come in a vast range of colors. For this picture, I have used felt-tipped pens of artists' quality. These are very expensive indeed, so unless you are extremely committed to manga artwork, you would be advised to experiment with the cheaper variety. White drawing ink can be used on top for bright highlights and to correct mistakes. There's more about felt tips on pages 182–183.

Digital coloring

The sleekest and most vibrant coloring effects are achieved with a computer. More and more manga artwork is colored by computer, but long before these were invented manga artists were producing very stylish artwork. You will need the appropriate software and it takes a bit of time to learn, but the principles are quite simple in essence. We'll look at digital coloring in more detail later in this section.

Color Theory

There are a few basic rules to follow when you're using color and they will make all the difference to the overall look of your finished artwork. Here's Daisy to demonstrate.

① **Primary colors**

Red, blue, and yellow are the basic colors that all other colors are mixtures of. These are called *primary* colors, and I've used them for Daisy's clothes here. If you can only afford three colored pencils, pens, or paints, these would be good ones to buy.

②–④ **Secondary colors**

The next range of colors are green, orange, and purple. These are called *secondary* colors. Each one is a combination of two primary colors. Here the colors of Daisy's pant legs are the ones that would be mixed to make the color of her shirt.

⑤ **The full spectrum**

The three primary and three secondary colors represent the full spectrum of pure bright color, like you would see in a rainbow. If you use them all in one drawing, you can see that the result can be quite overpowering, so don't use too many different colors in one picture.

⑥–⑦ **Tints and shades**

White and black can also be added to a color to change its qualities. Colors that have had white added to them are called *tints* and look pale and pastel, like in picture 6. Colors that have had black added to them are called shades and look darker, like in

picture 7. Using tints and shades will make your pictures look much more sophisticated.

⑧ **Complementary colors**

Some colors go better together than others. Good combinations can be made by using *complementary* colors. Each primary color has a secondary color as its complement which is a combination of the other two primaries. So red is complemented by green (a mixture of blue and yellow), blue is complemented by orange (a mixture of red and yellow) and yellow is complemented by purple (a mixture of red and blue). Here Daisy is dressed in various tints and shades of yellow and purple. She has even dyed her hair to add to the effect.

⑨ **Harmonious color schemes**

You don't need to use many colors at all to create a harmonious color scheme. The only color used for Daisy's clothes here is red, which has been turned into different tints and shades by adding white or black.

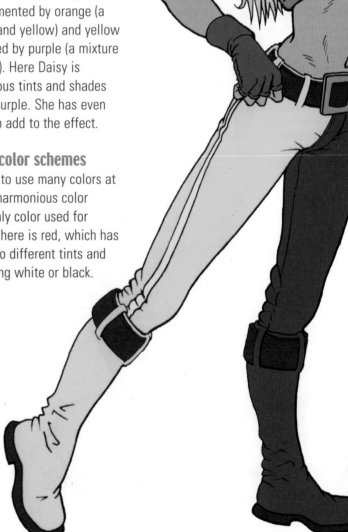

①

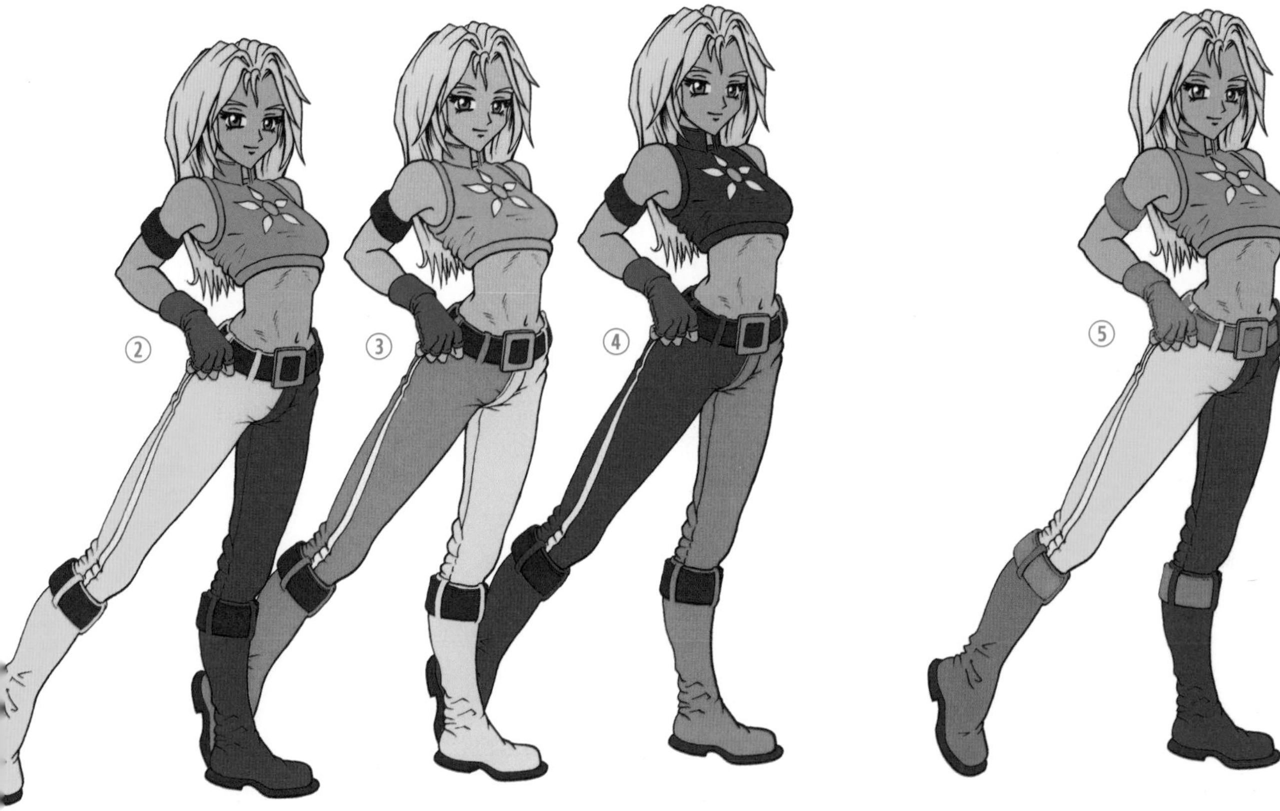

②
③
④
⑤

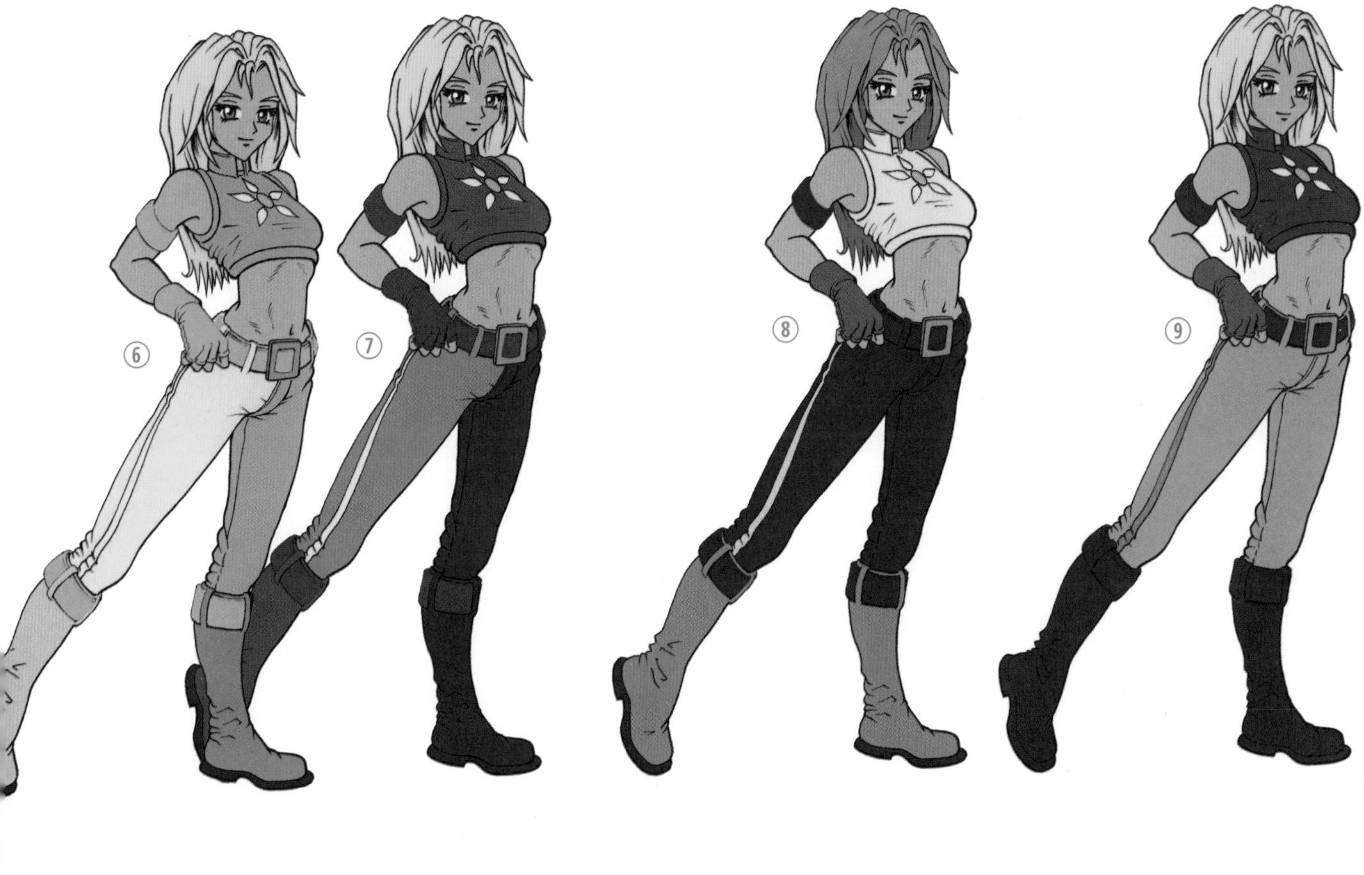

⑥
⑦
⑧
⑨

Inking & Coloring Magnus

Manga artwork is usually characterized by slick outlines and smooth shading and coloring. Using the drawing of Magnus that we created step-by-step on pages 110–112, I'll show you some simple tricks to bring him up to manga standard.

① Black outline

This is the basic drawing of Magnus outlined with a thin black pen. It's not bad, but it could be made to look a lot stronger without much more work.

② Adding ink

Thickening the whole outline makes Magnus look much bolder and more solid. I've varied the width of the lines too—they're thicker along the right-hand side of each body part and on the underneath edges, which helps to suggest that these parts are facing away from the light source. For this, you could use real artist's pens with flexible points for dipping into ink, but these are difficult to use and the same effects can be achieved with a thicker felt-tip pen. I've also added some lines to the fingers to show the metal grooves and filled a few areas with solid black, like the corners of the mouth and the underside parts of the robot's metal jacket.

③ Line shading

The same pens can be used to add some metallic effects to the body work. I've shaded the robot's cylindrical body using lots of little vertical lines. I've also added some small circles to the arms and legs to make the rivets that fasten the pieces of metal together.

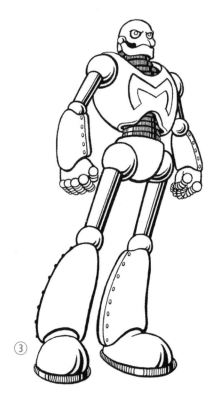

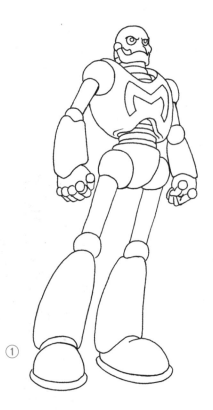

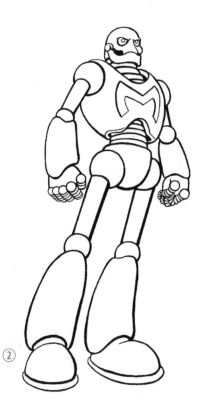

Here I'm using artist's quality marker pens to color Magnus, but you can get similar effects with ordinary felt-tip pens.

① Robot color swatches

Magnus is really only five colors: gray, blue, green, yellow, and gold. To show how light falls on him (from top left), we also need to use darker shades of each of these colors, so you'll need felt-tip pens in the different shades you can see here.

② Adding the color

First use your darker shades—the colors you need are shown next to the picture. Apply them to the areas facing away from the light and to areas that are in the shadow of other parts of the body.

③ Larger areas

Now you can color the bigger areas using lighter colors—when you do this, leave some strips of white. This will have the effect of making the surfaces look shiny.

④ Smaller parts

Continue to add color using the swatches next to the picture to guide you—notice how I've used different grays to enhance the shine patterns on the metalwork.

⑤ Final color

Once you've finished with your felt-tip pens, you can clean up your picture with the help of a bottle of white ink and a fine brush. Use these to blot out color around the edges of your picture where the color has bled over the lines. They are also good for adding highlights and sparkle to the metalwork. I've used them to help me add a glow of reflected light to the right-hand side of the picture—I drew thin strips of white on the head, chest, and arm, let this ink dry, then colored these strips light blue.

①

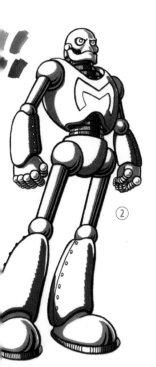

②

③

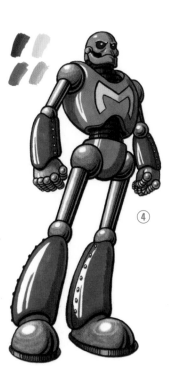

④

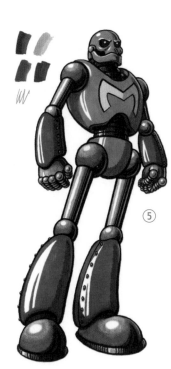

⑤

Computer Coloring

The computer is the favorite method of coloring manga artwork, especially among younger artists working in the style. The process can take a while to master completely, but the principles are quite straightforward. Various software packages are available for the purpose. To follow the exercise I'm going to show you next, you'll need Adobe Photoshop, one of the most common packages.

Scanning and preparation

Before you can start coloring, you have to convert your drawing into a digital file for the computer. To get the best result, set the scanner to a high resolution—say, 500 dpi—and choose the grayscale option. This will give you sharper lines to work with later. When the image is open in Photoshop, reduce the resolution to 300 dpi. This is about the maximum you'll need to print with; higher resolutions will slow down your computer.

Now convert the image (in Image>Mode>) to RGB (Red/Green/Blue) to allow you to start using color. At this point it's a good idea to look at your work close up and clean up any obvious blemishes. Don't be too fussy about this—as long as you sort out the major imperfections the small ones won't catch the eye. Use the Eraser tool for this.

Making sure your background color is white, choose Select All (Apple or Ctrl + A) and then New Layer Via Cut (Apple or Ctrl + Shift + J). Set the Blending Mode of this layer to Multiply, name it Line Art, and then lock it with the Lock icon. You shouldn't need to touch your original artwork again.

Hint: I use an Apple Macintosh computer, for which the command key is labeled with an Apple symbol. If you use a P.C. the same function is achieved with the control key labeled 'ctrl'.

Eraser

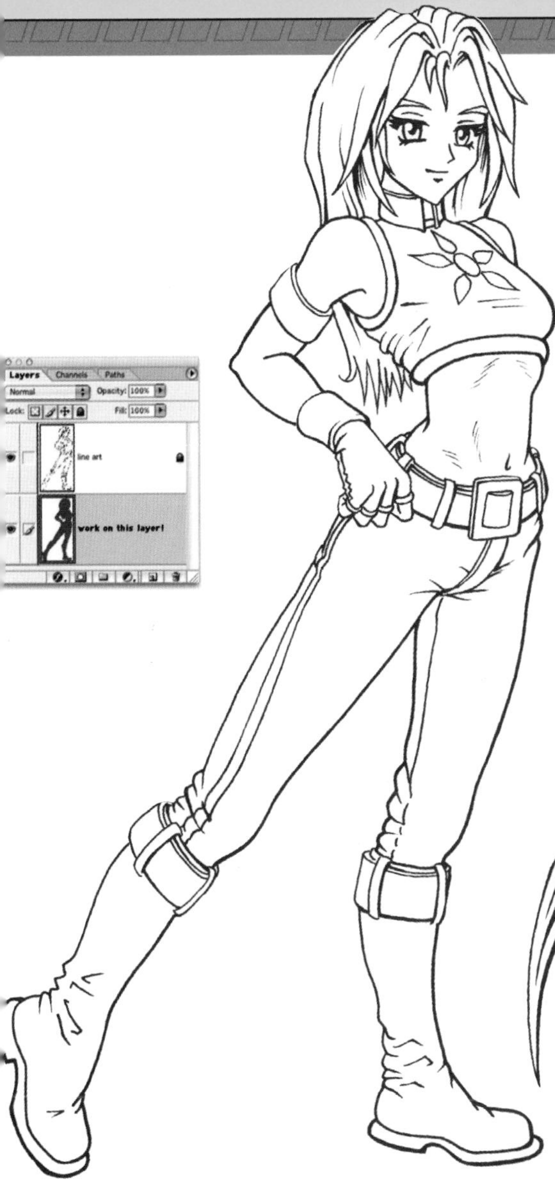
Layers
Channels
Paths
Normal
Opacity: 100%
Lock:
Fill: 100%
line art
work on this layer!

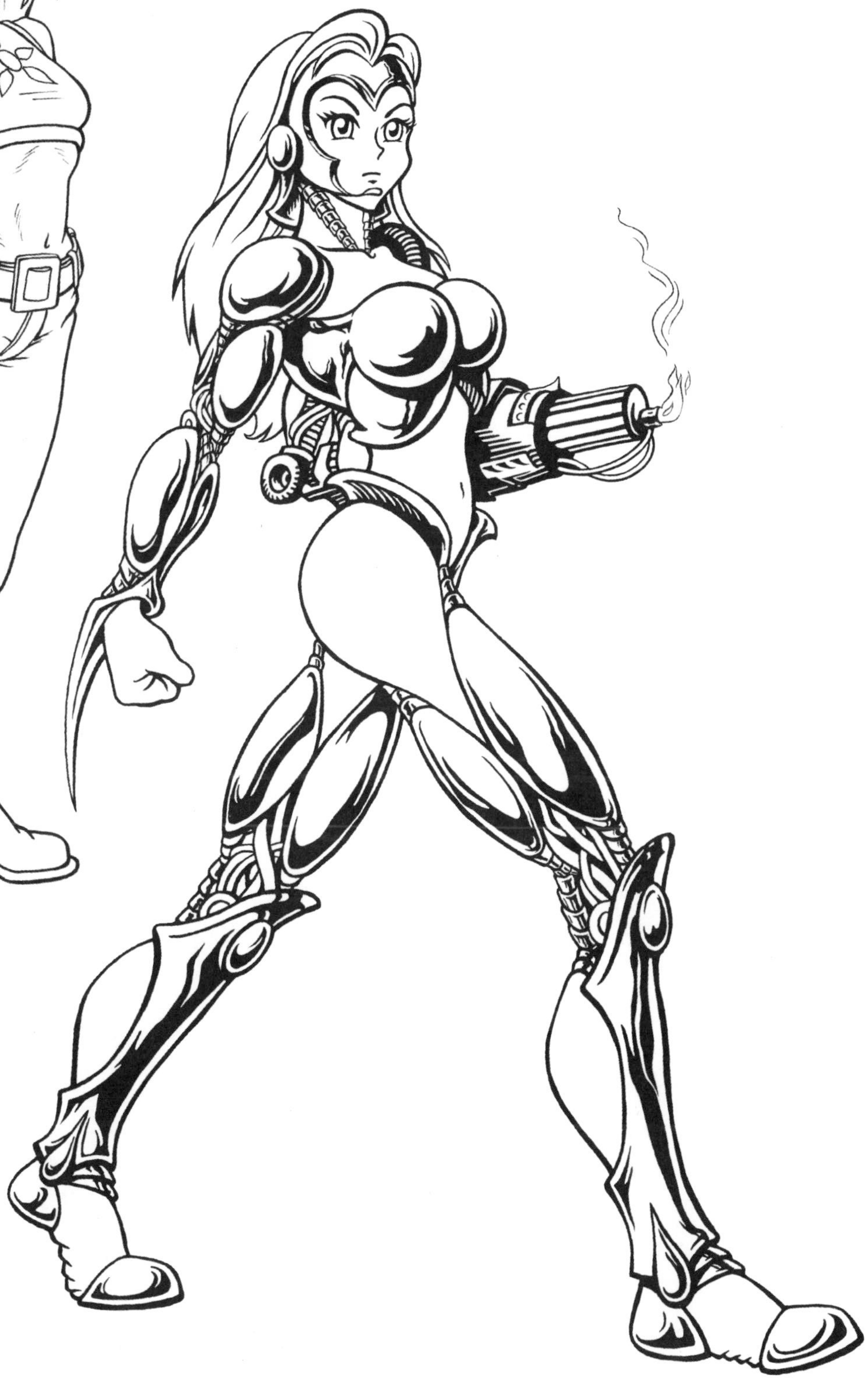

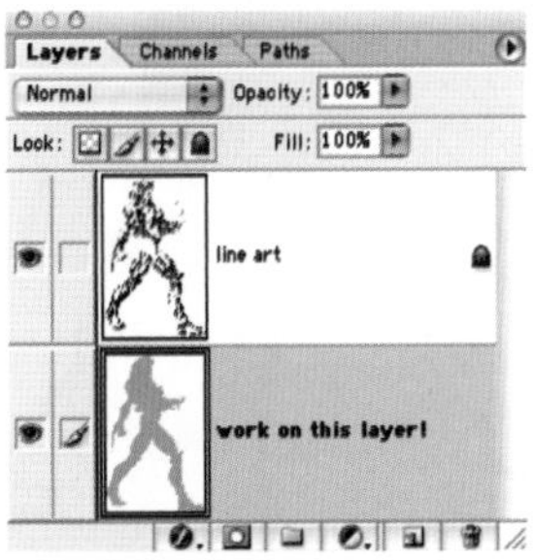
Layers
Channels
Paths
Normal
Opacity: 100%
Lock:
Fill: 100%
line art
work on this layer!

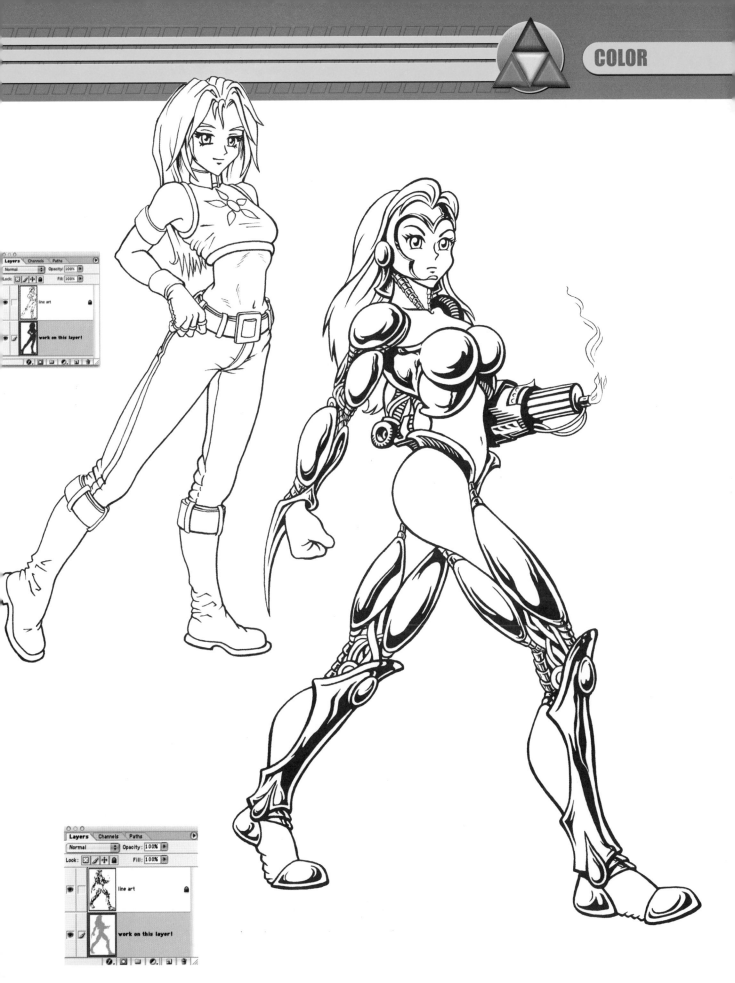

First color

Apply the color (termed Flat Color) on the layer below that of your original line artwork. Begin with the color that covers the largest area of your figure—in our example it's the blue/gray of Duke's and Daisy's pants and the Cybergirl's gray armor. You have to apply this color to your entire figure in order to separate the figure from the background. In further steps we'll change different areas to other colors. To apply the first color, first magnify your image, then use the Polygon Lasso tool to select the area. Now fill up the image using the Bucket tool. Remember to save your work after every stage.

Polygon Lasso

Bucket

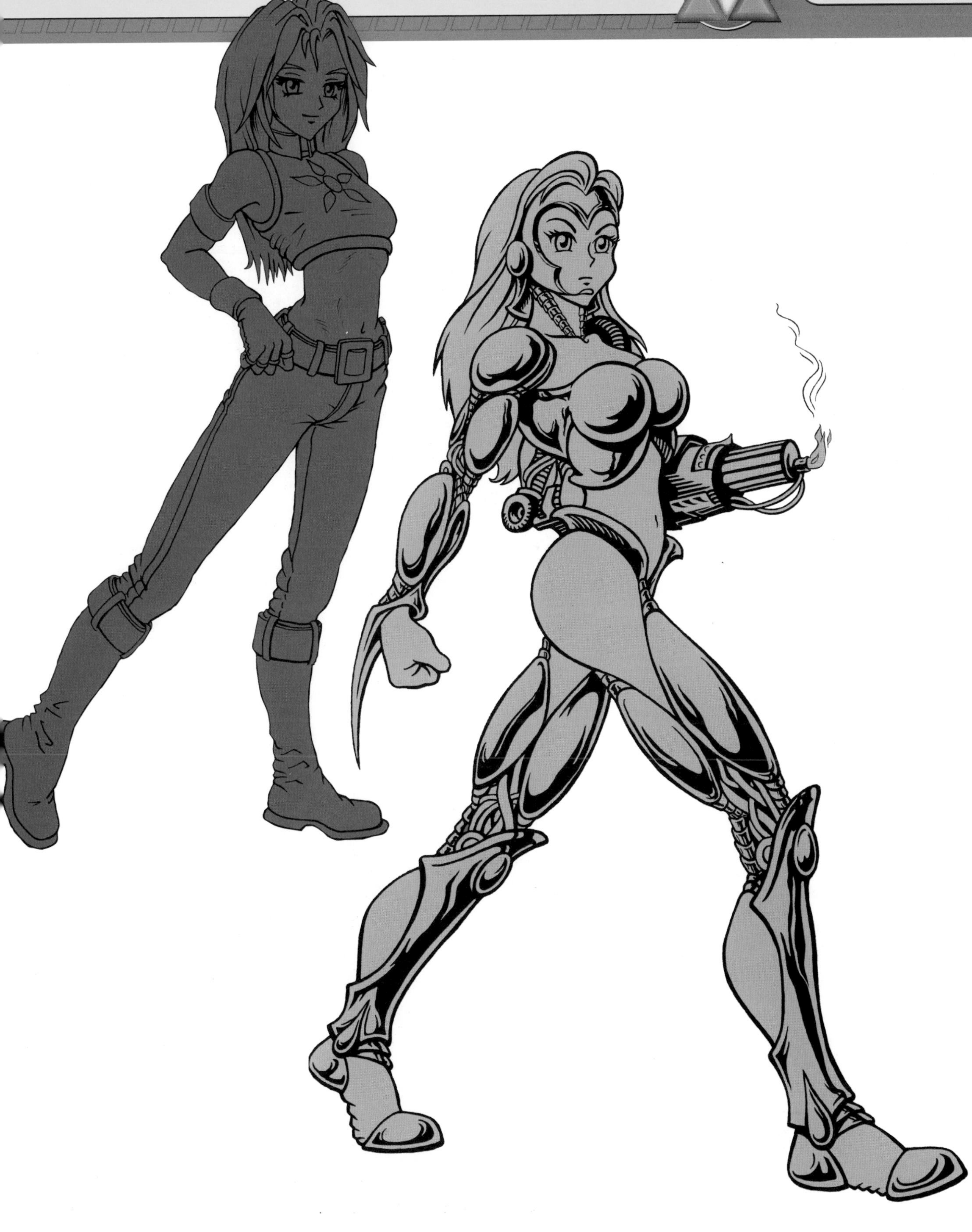

More colors

Now you need to change the parts of your figure that are taken up with other colors. Here, I've selected the same gold for Duke's hair and the details on his tunic and boots. For Daisy and the Cybergirl I worked on the skin tones first. It doesn't matter what order you work in, but complete all areas of the same color at the same time to keep the colors consistent. Once more, use the Polygon Lasso tool, and fill the area using the Bucket. Or, change the color using Image > Adjustments > Hue/Saturation (Apple + U). Repeat this process with the other colors. Hint: Each time you draw out your rough selection area, you can use the Magic Wand with the Alt key pressed down to deselect any differently colored areas that you may have included accidentally.

Magic Wand

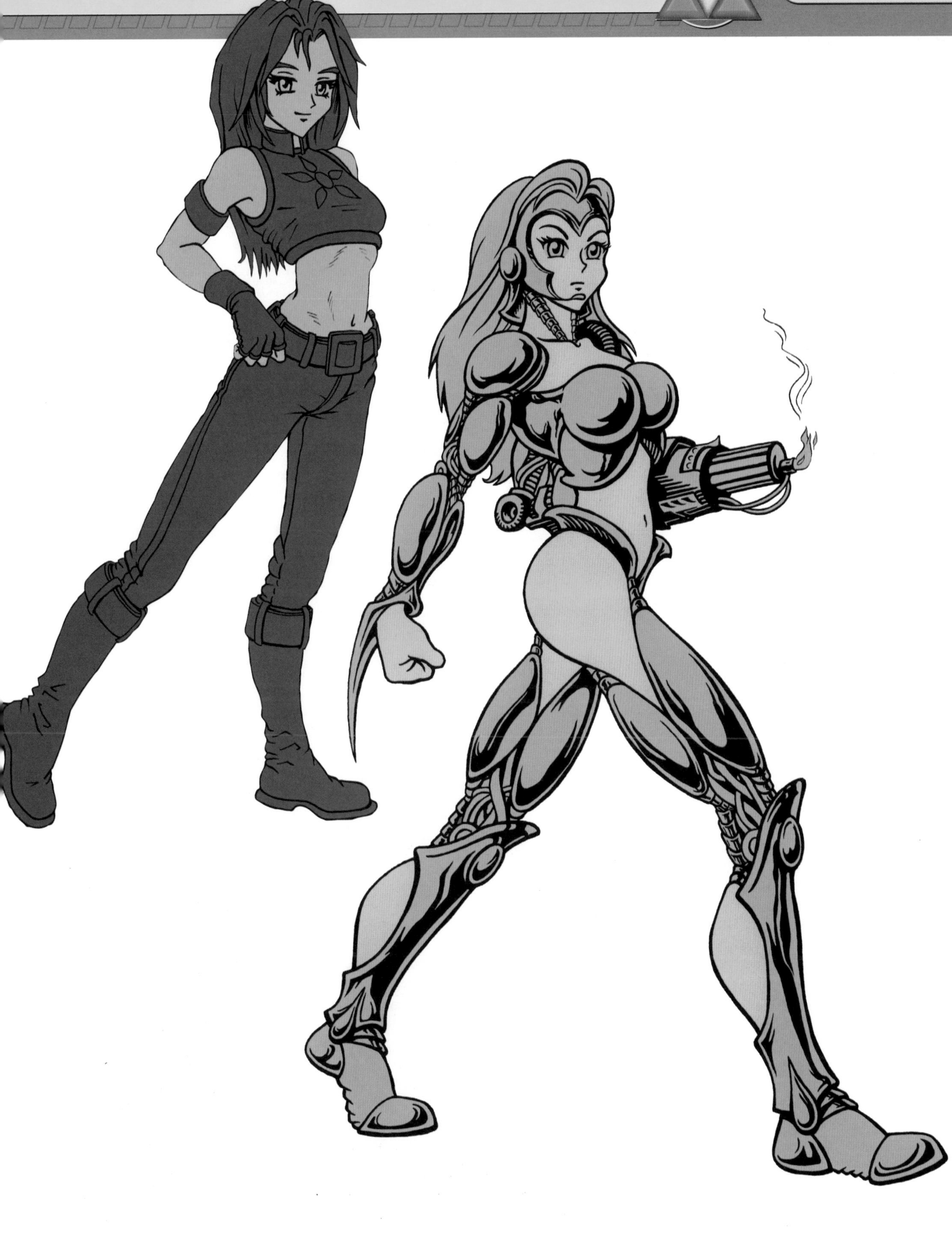

Saving the flat color

Here, I've temporarily hidden the black outlines to clearly show the finished flat colors of each character. You can see how unsophisticated flat color is compared to the final renderings on pages 194–195. Once you've got all the flat color down, select New Layer Via Copy to copy the layer. Name the new copy of the layer (which will appear at the bottom) 'Flat Color', then lock it. You shouldn't need to change this layer again, but it will prove useful when you're working with the Magic Wand tool later. You should have been saving your work regularly, but save now if you haven't already.

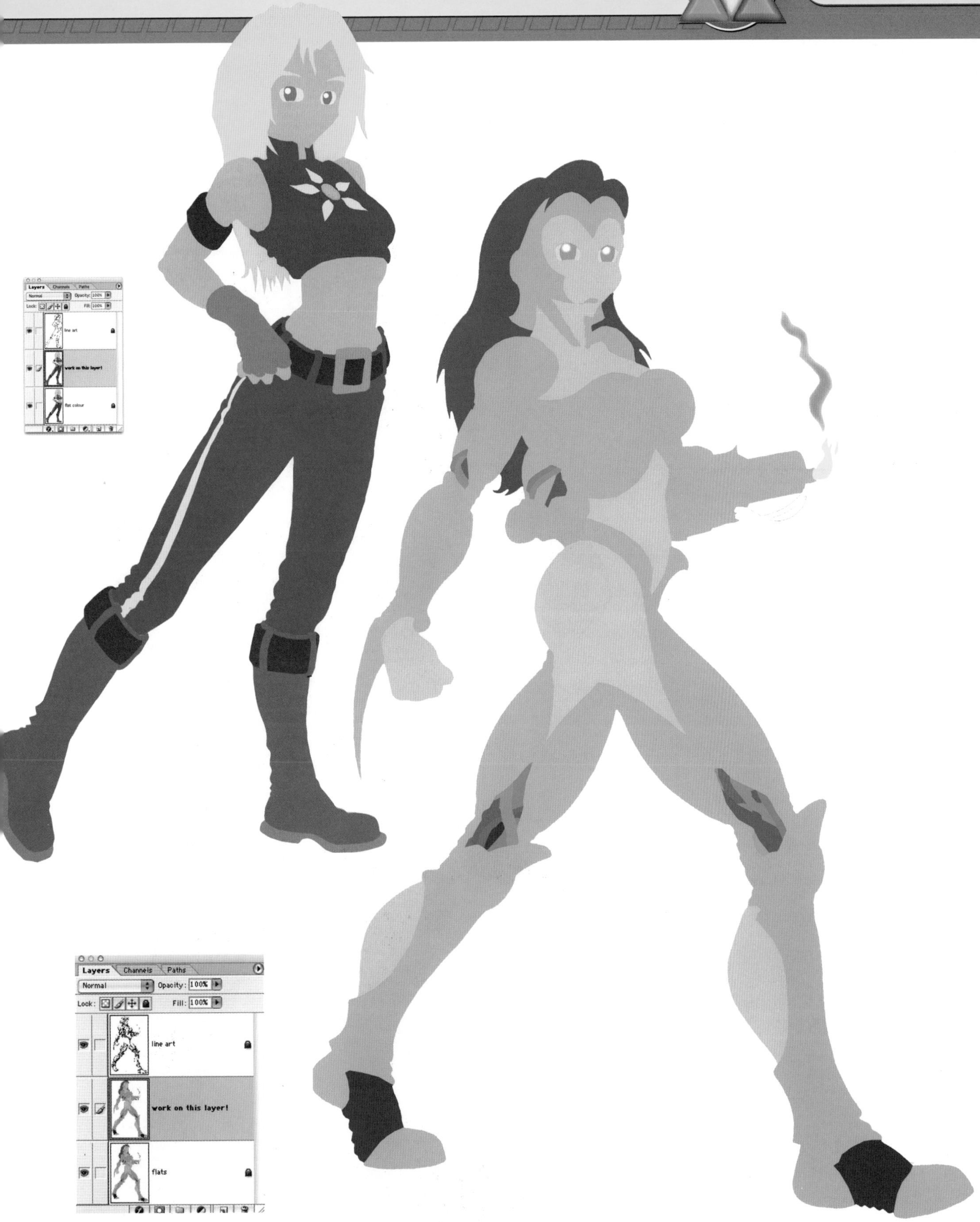
Layers
Channels
Paths
Normal
Opacity: 100%
Lock:
Fill: 100%
line art
work on this layer!
flat colour
Layers
Channels
Paths
Normal
Opacity: 100%
Lock:
Fill: 100%
line art
work on this layer!
flats

Adding shadows

It's time to add the shading and modeling that gives the characters three-dimensional form. For this we'll be using Quick Mask. Click on the Quick Mask icon or press Q. Using the Brush tool, paint an area you want to show in shadow. Don't worry if you go over the lines—we'll tidy up later.

To make Quick Mask easier to use, double-click on the icon in the tool palette to view its Options palette. Check color indicates selected area and choose a dark mask color. To see what you've just done, leave Quick Mask mode (press Q again or the icon in the tool palette). You'll see that you've selected an area of the image. For more feathered selections you can use softer brush tools. Now you can clean up the selection by going to your Flat Color layer and using Alt plus the Magic Wand tool as you did earlier.

Go back to your working layer (the middle one) and use Image > Adjustments > Hue/Saturation to shade to your taste, or just fill it up with the Bucket tool.

Further subtle adjustments can be made by using the Burn tool to selectively deepen shadows.

Quick Mask

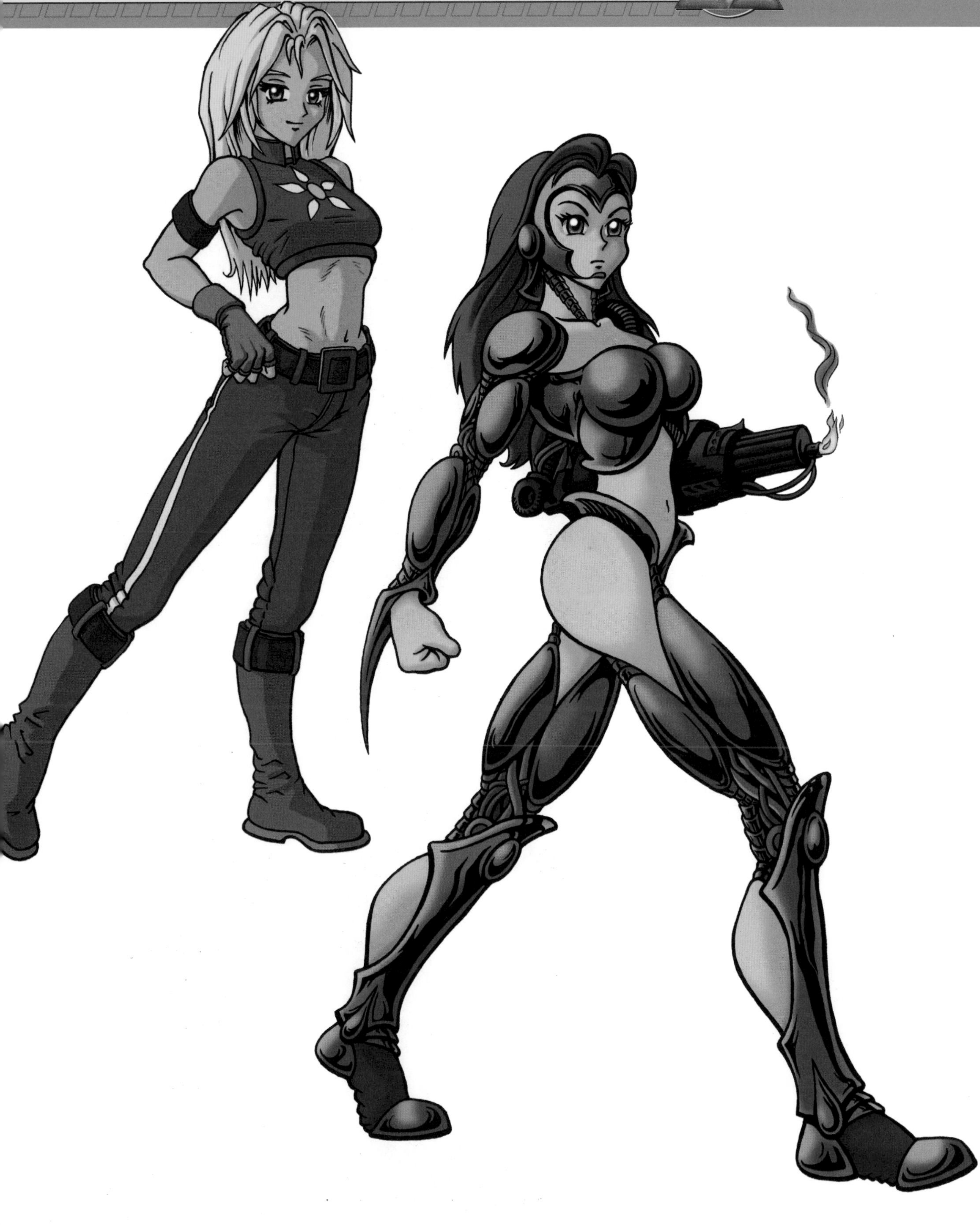

Highlights

Lightening some parts of your figures adds to the illusion of solidity. Bright highlights suggest the sparkle of shiny surfaces and bring your pictures to life. You can use the same technique you used for the shading to make well-defined areas of light. This is how I worked on Duke's and Daisy's hair.

Hint: If you would like precise control over the area of highlight, you can instead magnify the image and use the Lasso tool to select the shapes you want.

If you prefer a more painterly style of highlighting, you can use the Dodge tool, which softly lightens colors wherever it is applied. The Magic Wand will mask off the areas you're working on. Less subtle highlights can be drawn on with the Eraser tool, set to varying degrees of opacity.

At this stage you could also add some colored reflections like the earth color reflected in the Cybergirl's armor. It's not too late to make any adjustments to the shading or color. The beauty of computers is that you can change things over and over without harming the artwork.

Dodge

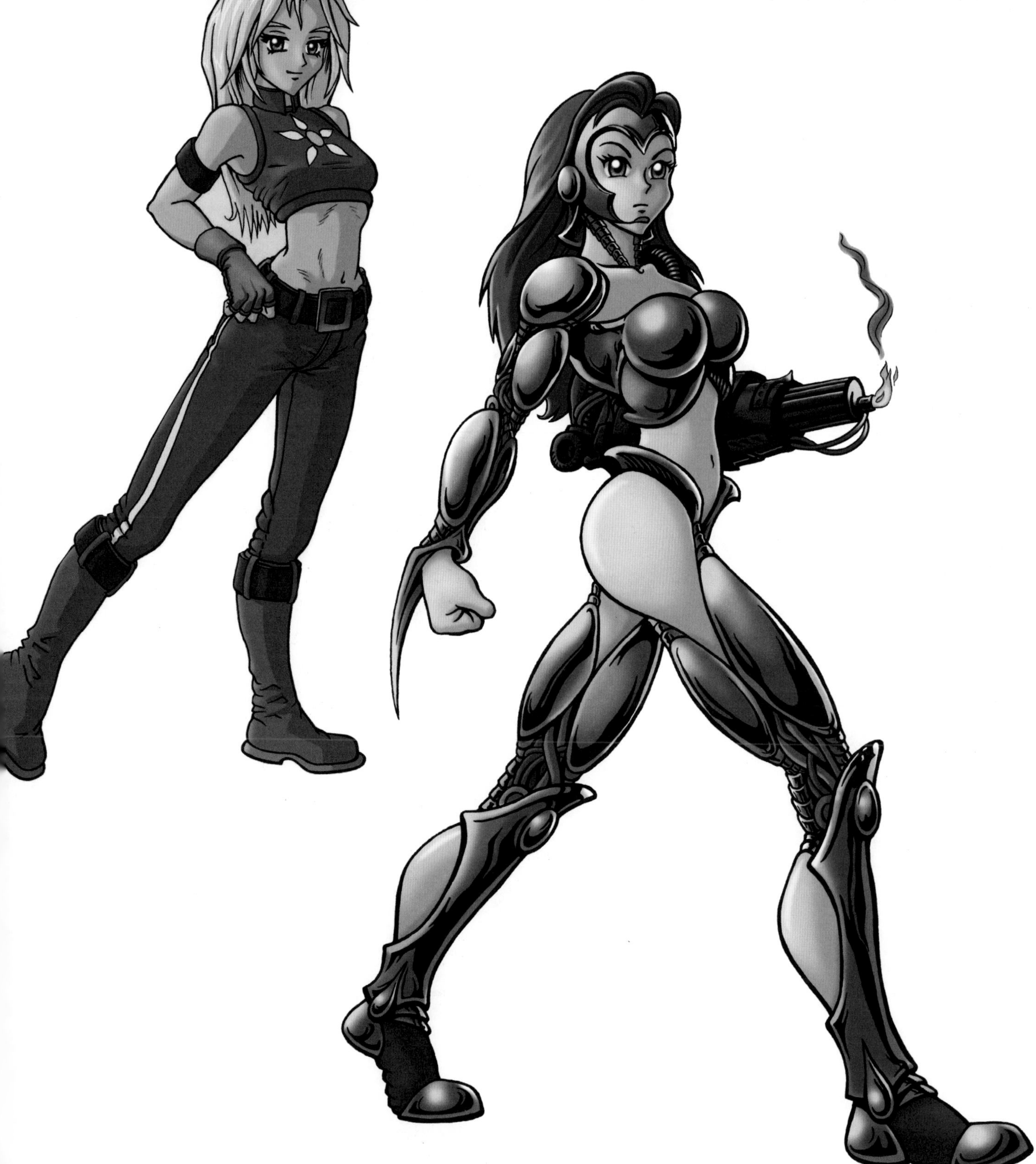

ACTION

Drawing action figures that look really convincing is all about capturing the shape and movement of the character's body.

To get these right, you will need to increase your awareness of the body and how it behaves, so to help you do this, we'll be studying some new poses and we'll take a look at perspective. I'll also introduce you to the technique of foreshortening, which you'll find a useful skill for enhancing your pictures, and making them look more realistic.

There are plenty of opportunities in this section for you to put theory into practise to create some great action characters, male and female. To draw them, it is more important than ever that you start with light pencil lines. If you do this you'll be able to keep resketching until you get them absolutely right—don't be afraid to keep changing your lines until they look accurate.

Persistence does pay off in the world of manga, as the characters you'll be meeting next will demonstrate. If you want results, you have to get going, so let's move it!

ACTION
ACTION
ACTION
ACTION
ACTION
ACTION
ACTION
ACTION
ACTION
ACTION
ACTION
ACTION
ACTION
ACTION
ACTION
ACTION
ACTION

Body Language & Movement

Everyone displays body language in everything they do throughout the day. Often this can be quite subtle, but in manga, there's no place for subtlety! In each of these rough sketches, the character has no facial features, but she is still showing a lot of emotion through her pose. Try copying some of the poses, or choose one of the poses to apply to your own manga character.

The pose of the body doesn't just convey the mood of a character—it can also be used to show movement and action. There's a whole range of poses you can devise for manga figures, but to make the figures look realistic, they should only bend in the same way that a real person's body bends. Shoulders, wrists and ankles can swivel in many directions, for instance, but knees and elbows can't bend backward or sideways. Use your own body to try making a pose you want to draw to see if it's really possible!

Invent a different character for each of these poses. Make each new character's build, hairstyle and facial features as different as possible from the last.

Flirting

In manga, poses are often exaggerated for dramatic effect and the following drawing is no exception. Tellima is standing sideways on but she has turned around to face us, so her body is twisting.

Step 1

Draw a long vertical line, then copy the angle and position of the ovals for the head, chest, and hips, noting where each one crosses the vertical line—the oval for the hips is farther to the left than the top two ovals. Because each part of the body is at a different angle, the vertical guide-line on each oval is positioned differently. Now for the limbs. Because of the angle of the hips, you'll have to just imagine where the far leg joins the hips. The positions of the shoulders are quite difficult to work out too, so copy the picture as carefully as possible. The feet should be angled so that it's clear Tellima is standing on tiptoes.

Step 2

Since you've already had some practise at drawing manga bodies, you should now be ready to draw the outline of Tellima's flesh in one stage. Copy the red lines.

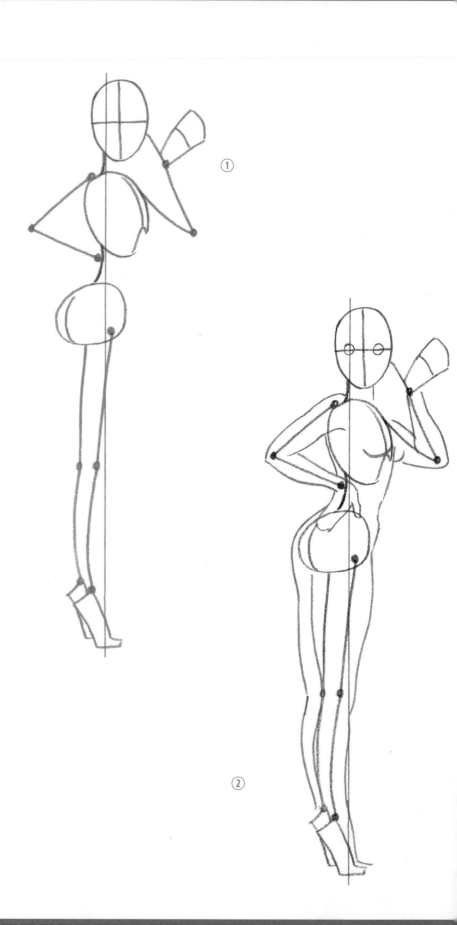

Step 3

Map in the basic shapes of the clothing and hair. Notice how the sleeves finish just below the elbows. The outline of the skirt is almost triangular in shape. Give the hands and feet some more attention, shaping the fingers and toes. Work on the chin and some of the facial features. Add the basic outline of the hair.

Step 4

To draw clothing convincingly, you need to capture the direction of the folds—just as drawing hair convincingly means capturing the way it flows. Add some curved lines to both the skirt and hair, as shown, to give the impression of movement. Draw some crease lines inside the elbows, under the armpit, and on the socks.

‹‹
Step 5

Now you can enjoy establishing the final drawing using a black ballpoint or felt-tip pen. Finish off the eyes and hair. There are all sorts of details you can add to your picture here—try drawing a bracelet on Tellima's wrist to add to the sense of movement. Work on the folds of the skirt, drawing some curves along its hem. Add more detail to the socks too to show their loose-fitting shape.

Step 6

Once you're sure the ink is dry, erase all the pencil guidelines to reveal your finished line drawing.

⑤

⑥

Step 7

You could copy this color scheme to complete your drawing or design your own. Look back at the Color section to help you get started.

⑦

Triumphant Warrior

In this exercise, we're going to draw a fully clothed, dramatically posed action character named Treen. The drawing involves a lot of the aspects we've covered so far, like expression, pose, muscle build, and dynamic hands. Take your time with each step.

Step 1

Draw the skeleton framework as shown. Make sure you copy the central lines on the body parts carefully since these will help you get the rest of the detail in the right place. Look at how the position of the arms affects the shape of the shoulders too.

Step 2

Now that you've had some practise drawing Duke's body, you should be able to draw all the shapes of the flesh in one stage. A lot of the body is going to be covered by clothing, but roughing out the shape will help you to draw the clothes. Copy the red lines as accurately as possible. Notice that Treen is much more heavily muscled than Duke.

Step 3

Still using light guidelines, rough in the approximate shapes of the clothing and sword. Do some more work on the hands, then start placing the facial features. When you outline the hair, try to capture the way it looks when it has been caught by a gust of wind. The waistcoat too should be drawn with a similar texture to suggest fur.

Step 4

Now for some of the detail that really makes this triumphant stance. There's a lot to think about here—the facial expression, the rest of the outline for the hair and clothes, and the strapping around the legs and wrist. Notice the fold lines on the pant legs.

>>

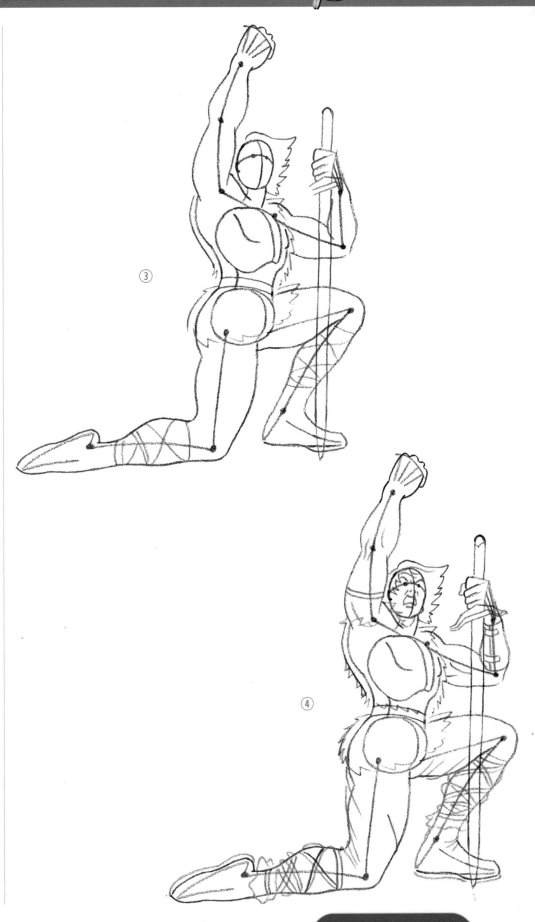

Step 5

Now that all the main guidelines forming your picture are in place, you can enjoy going over all your good lines in ink. There are all sorts of features you can add here—finish off the face and hair, add more detail to the handle of the sword, and work on bringing out the texture of the fur. Copy the fold lines on the boots, and the definition on the backs of the hands.

Step 6

When the ink is dry, erase the rest of your pencil lines to leave a clean picture.

Step 7

You can copy this color scheme to complete your drawing or use different colors and patterns. You might then want to draw the figure again but add different details of your own. The clothing style could change, or you could put a different expression on Treen's face. You could make the arms slimmer or more muscular.

⑦

Action Poses

The pose of the body conveys mood, movement, and personality. All of these examples are based on distinct human emotions and show clearly what each character is feeling despite the absence of the facial features. The figures look realistic because they only bend in the same way that a real person's body bends. Shoulders, wrists, and ankles can swivel in many directions, for instance, but knees and elbows can't bend backward or sideways. Remember this when you create poses.

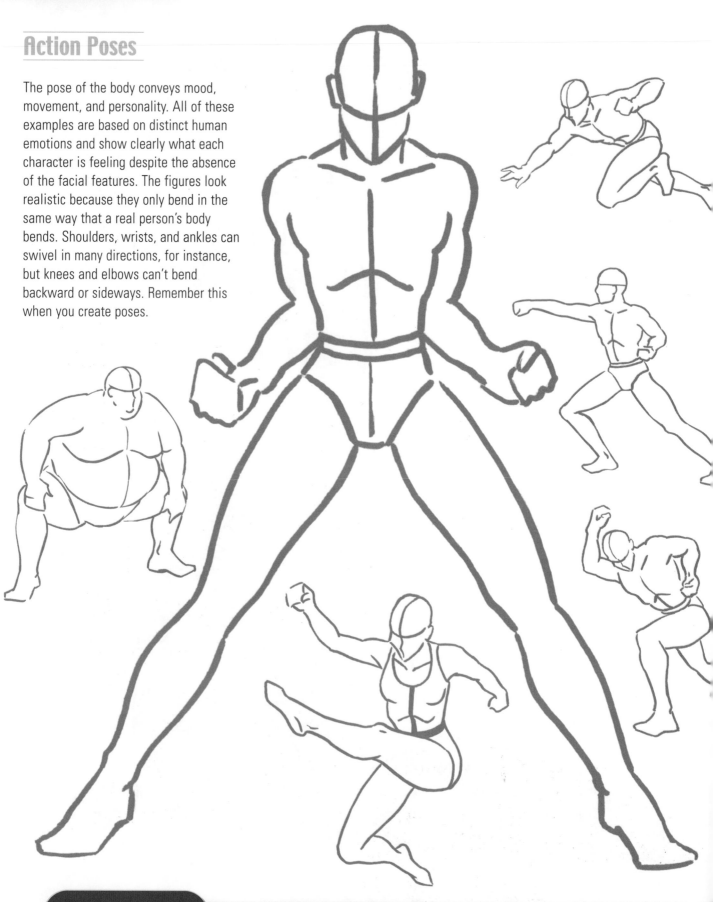

Copy these action stances for practise, then come up with some of your own. Use your own body to try making a pose you want to draw so that you can see if it's really possible!

Running

If you use all the techniques you have learned so far, you'll find this drawing much easier to construct. The main thing about this pose is that it's not balanced—if you tried to stand like this yourself, you would fall over. That imbalance helps give the impression of movement, together with the flowing hair, skirt, and cape.

Step 1

Draw the three main body parts of Lunara's skeleton first. You are drawing her body from the side but with it leaning forward so the body parts follow a diagonal line. Don't make the head too large. Now add the limbs. Lunara is very tall, so her arms and legs are extra long.

Step 2

Draw the outline shape of Lunara's flesh and muscle. Notice how there are strong curves in the shape at the backs of the legs to show Lunara's strong muscles.

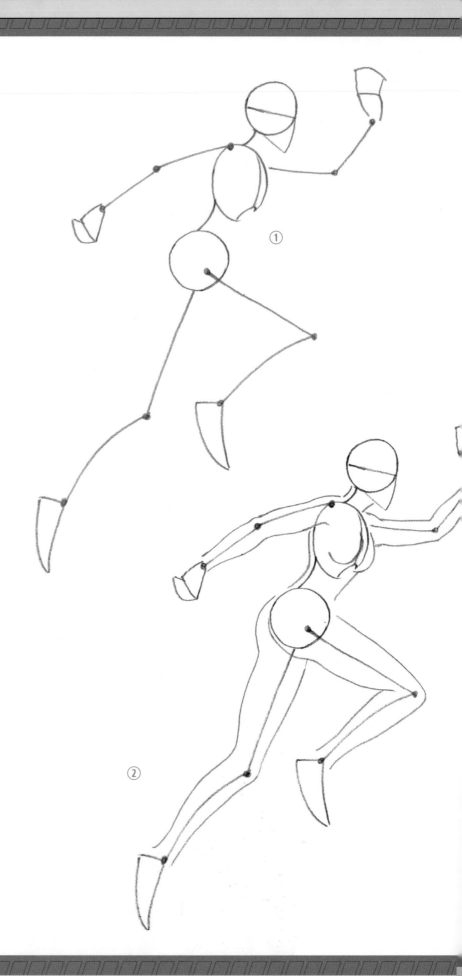

Step 3

Add some basic lines for Lunara's tunic and cloak—study the finished picture on the next page and compare it with this one so you are clear about what you are drawing. Add the main features of the face and some of the curves of the hair. Work on the shape of the feet.

Step 4

Give the clothing more detail—notice the square-shaped neck of the tunic. Add a belt, then draw some lines along the bottom of the skirt and cloak to show the folds. Work on the hands and feet—Lunara is wearing sandals, so you'll still be able to see her toes in the final picture.

»

Step 5

Once you're happy with your drawing, go over your pencil lines in black ballpoint or felt-tip pen. Now add some shading to the hair to give it more depth. Notice how I've created some braids in the hair. I've also worked on the design of the neck of the tunic and secured the cape with a brooch. I've turned the belt into a piece of rope and put a buckle on the outside of one of the sandals. Rather than simply copying this, why not make adaptations of your own—you might even decide to change the clothing to make Lunara look more modern or more futuristic.

Step 6

Leave the ink to dry, then erase all your remaining pencil guidelines.

Step 7

Now you can add some color to your picture. I've given her auburn hair and made the skin fair. Notice how dark the inside of the cloak is, where it is in shadow.

⑦

ACTION LINES

Running through every dynamic figure is an 'action line', a graceful curve around which action drawings are based. These curves concentrate the whole of the body on a certain a pose or action. They are very helpful to the drawing process, and they give your action figures a real sense of force. The action line is usually the first thing a manga artist will draw before adding any other details of a figure.

Action line 1
Action line 2

However a manga action figure moves, even a low creep or a backwards fall, an action line governs their pose. The more dynamic the movement, the longer the line will run smooth and unbroken.

Action line 3

Even in standing, a strong action line lends a figure grace and purpose.

①

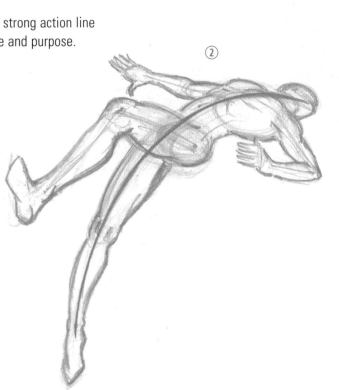

②

③

Action line 4

Where an action line is short or wobbly, the figure lacks dynamic thrust and seems off guard, indecisive or even clumsy.

Action line 5
Action line 6

In manga comics, an action is depicted at the moment of its greatest dynamic impact. For example, throwing something, be it a punch or a spear, is depicted at either end of the action: as the body is fully recoiled in advance of the action, or as the body follows through having completed the action. Note the strong lines of action in both cases.

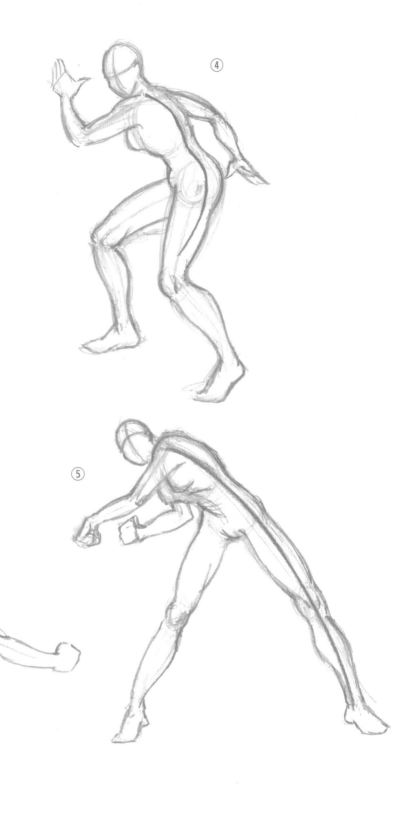

Juni the Sorceress

The main thing to notice about the pose of Juni is that it's not balanced. If you tried to stand like this yourself, you would fall over. That imbalance, as well as her hair and clothing, gives the impression of movement. Take a look at the finished picture of her on the last page of this sequence before you start.

Step 1

The slight twist in Juni's waist affects the positioning and shape of the hips in relation to the head and chest, so copy these parts carefully. Only one foot is lightly touching the floor, while the other is poised to bound forward. Notice the pose of the arms and hands too.

Step 2

Now you need to add the body outline to your skeleton framework. Juni's muscles are toned and taut, but not bulky like a man's. The curves on her raised arm show the softness of her young skin.

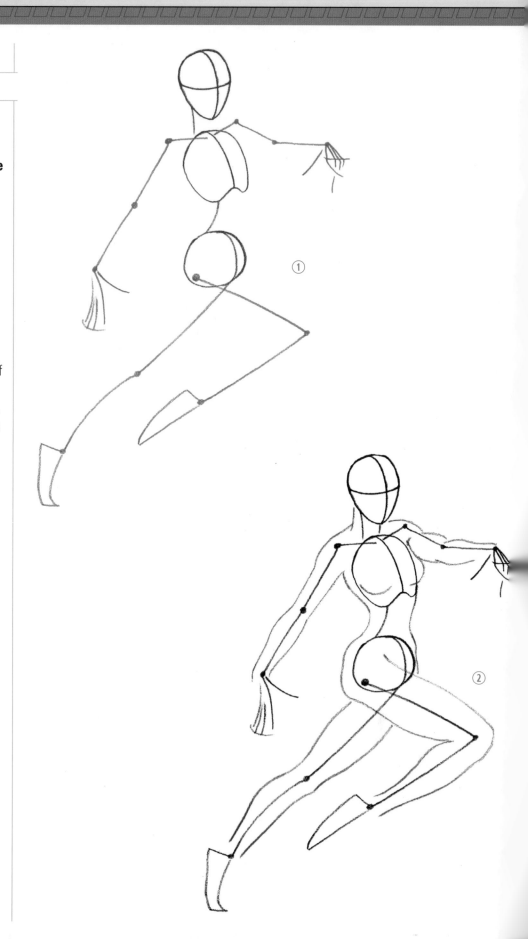

Step 3

Roughly draw in the clothing. The hair and skirt flow backward, adding to the sense of movement. The wavy hair falls away from a center part. The skirt radiates out from a gathered waistband. Work on the fingers of the hands here too and outline the feet of the boots.

Step 4

Now for more detail. Work on the gentle look of the facial features and draw the curls of the hair. Add the tops of the boots, including the crisscross lines of the laces that fasten them. Use the same technique for the front of the bodice. Putting some bangles on one of the wrists as shown will add to the sense of movement.

>>

MANGA

Step 5

Now you should be ready to pick out the final lines of your drawing and go over them in ink. Notice the extra little gather lines I've added around the edge of the collar on the bodice, and the curves I've used to outline the shape of the chest. Draw some short curves along the center part too. Don't forget the belly button.

Step 6

At the last minute, I decided to draw a flame generating from Juni's finger to show that she has special powers—it's not too late to add details like this. When the ink is dry, erase any remaining pencil lines.

Step 7

Adding color will really bring your character to life here. The hair is almost black underneath, where it's in the shadow of the thick locks flowing over it.

⑦

Perspective

When artists talk about perspective, they mean that objects look different according to the angle, the height, and the distance from which we view them. In all the pictures on this page, the figure is holding exactly the same pose.

Figure 1

Notice how when viewed from the front, the figure appears to be resting the box on her foot.

Figure 2

From the side, we can see that the box is actually some distance in front of the figure's feet.

Figures 3 and 4

Looking at our character from behind means the hips are closer to us and so appear wider. Notice how the waistband curves down at the ends—in picture 1, it curves upward.

Figure 5

We are looking down on our figure, so it is below our eye level. This means that all the parts of the picture that look level in picture 1—like the shoulders, the elbows, and the box—now slope up the page, as shown by the blue lines. The farther below our eye level the blue line is, the steeper its slope.

Figures 6 and 7

Here only some parts of the pictures are below our eye level (green line), some are above it, and others are directly at eye level. Some of the blue lines therefore slope up, some slope down, and others are roughly horizontal.

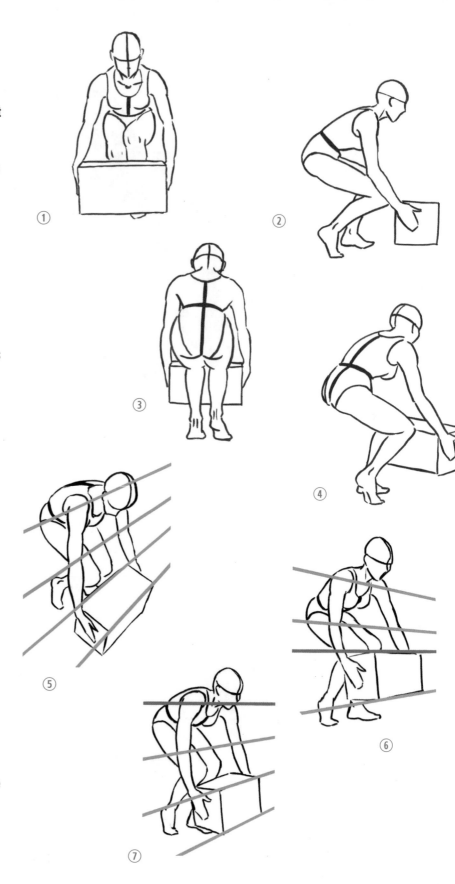

Eye level

This figure is viewed from the level of the hips as shown by the horizontal line in green—this is known as the eye line or horizon. Features above this line, like the elbows and shoulders, appear to slope downward as they get farther away from us, even though they are really level. Features below our eye line, like the knees and ankles, slope the other way. The farther above or below our eye line the features are, the steeper the angle of the slope.

②–③ Changing eye level

In picture 2, our eye line is much higher, whereas in picture 3 it is much lower. Notice how this affects the degree to which different parts of the body slope.

④–⑤ Different views

Here are two sketches of the same figure, seen from different eye levels. You can see that the lower viewpoint can add a sense of drama to a pose.

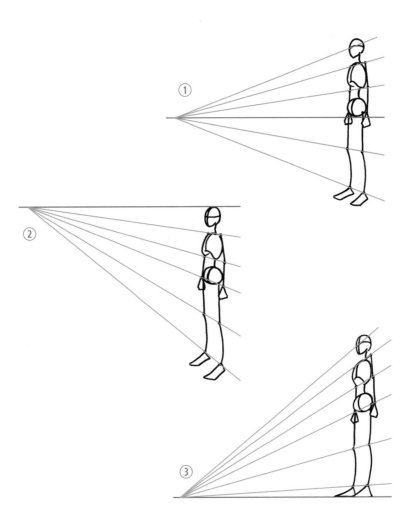

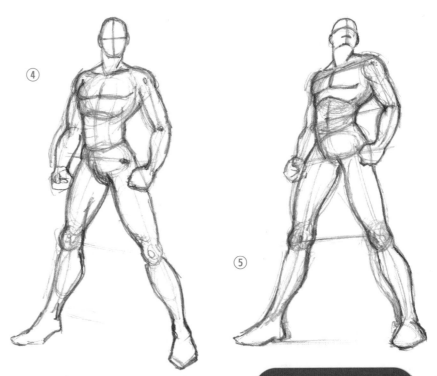

Throwing Boy

Now that you've learned some of the theory about perspective, let's try putting it into practise. Bear in mind that this young character, Kom, is viewed from a very low eye line—level with his ankles.

Step 1

I've drawn on the receding lines to help you with the perspective. Start by drawing the main body parts as shown, then add the limbs. Notice how from this perspective the joints of one arm sit higher than the joints of the opposite arm, as highlighted by the receding lines. When you draw the legs, the ankle joints should line up horizontally. Notice how the knee joints don't both sit on the receding line here since one leg is positioned farther back than the other one. The outlines for the feet should be quite large. Add the ball above Kom's head.

Step 2

If you've drawn your skeleton framework accurately, adding the outline shape for the flesh and muscle here should be easy. Kom is only a boy, so his muscles aren't very well developed yet. You can place the eyes at this stage, too.

tep 3

tart sketching in the clothing.
otice how the legs of the boots are
rge and angular. Remember that
e are looking up at Kom, and he is
so leaning backward slightly, so
e shins and feet are drawn bigger
that they appear closer to us.
ext place the rest of the facial
atures and the hair.

tep 4

ow for more detail. Work on the
air and eyes, then add all the lines
at show the ribbing on Kom's
ace suit and boots.

>>

Step 5

Go over your drawing in pen. By adding some detail to the ball, you can change its texture and turn it from a soccer ball into a lump of rock from outer space. Add some crease lines to the backs of the knees too.

Step 6

When you have erased the remaining pencil lines, your space boy drawing is finished.

Step 7

Use some space-age colors like these to make Kom look really futuristic. You could add a symbol to one of his leg guards, like I have, to show the clan he belongs to. Notice how the space rock casts a glow across the top of Kom's head and the insides of his arms.

Foreshortening

Another technique that is used to make manga figures look more dynamic is foreshortening. This is when the parts of a figure that point toward us look shorter than the parts we see from the side. This can be confusing to draw but can give a picture real impact.

① Side view

Picture 1 shows a flying figure drawn from the side. The lengths of the torso, arm, and leg are all in proportion to each other, but the picture lacks dynamism.

②–④ Changing proportions

If we draw the same pose from a different angle so that it tilts toward us, as in pictures 2, 3, and 4, the figure looks much more dynamic. If you look closely at these pictures, you will see that the proportions of the various body parts have changed. The arms have been shortened, the hands enlarged, and the legs and feet made smaller. Although these proportions aren't really correct, the figure looks normal because the oversized parts just look like they are closer to us and the reduced parts look as if they are farther away. The more the relative proportions are exaggerated, as in figure 2, the closer the figure will seem to us. The less the distinction between the large and small features, as in picture 4, the farther away the figure will seem.

Figure 1

Although the lower legs and feet are missing from this picture, because we know what bodies usually look like, we imagine that from our viewpoint they are hidden behind the thighs.

Figure 2

This figure's upper body has been made shorter to make it look like it is bending forward as the figure runs toward us. The raised shin appears very short, but we accept that both legs are really the same length. We also assume that the figure's hands are equal in size, even though the one pointing toward us is closer and, therefore, larger.

Figure 3

Feet are about as long as the head, but here they are drawn half the size, because they are twice as far away.

If you can't quite make sense of this principle, don't worry—the more you practice drawing figures, the more you'll come to understand it.

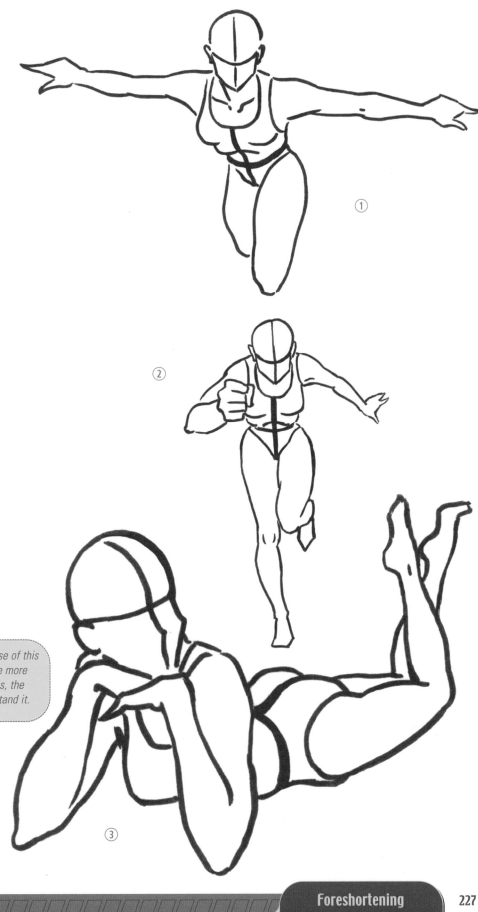

Crouching

This drawing involves foreshortening. Our manga character Elise is crouching down. She has twisted her upper body to lean forward and rested one hand on the ground to help her balance.

Step 1

We are looking at Elise from above and she is leaning toward us. We won't see much of her neck and stomach, so make the ovals for her head, chest, and hips overlap each other. When you add the limbs, make sure you slope the collar-bones. The bones of the front arm should be made longer than the ones forming the back arm to make it appear closer to us. The hand on this arm should also be bigger. Copy the leg bones carefully—one calf bone is missing since from this angle, the lower part of the leg is hidden.

Step 2

As you draw the shapes of the flesh and muscle around the skeleton, think about the angle from which you are viewing the different parts of the body and how far away from you they should look. The shoulders are not level, and this affects the way the chest curves. The long front arm appears broader than the back one. Carefully copy the bend in the leg to the left of your picture.

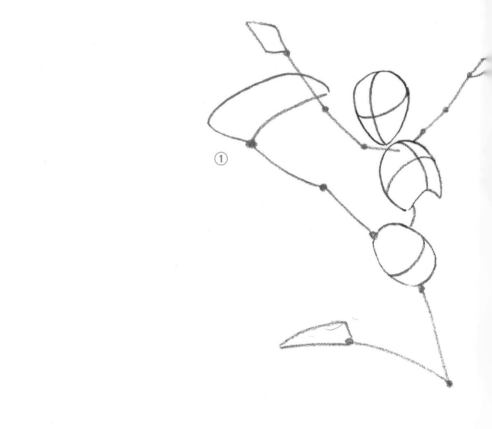

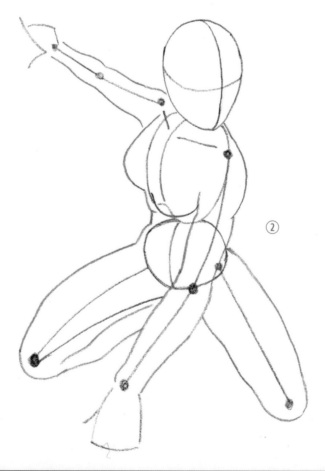

Step 3

Place the facial features—the eyes will not appear level, but your guide-lines will help you to place them correctly. Add some guidelines for the hair. Start to mark the clothing—Elise's suit fits her body closely, so you won't need to draw their whole shape. Add the extra details like the knee pads and belt—study the color picture on the next page to help with this. Draw in the parts of the feet you can see.

Step 4

Add some more detail to the face and hair, then work on the shape of the hands. Now add some crease lines to the clothes and a holster around Elise's leg.
≫

Step 5

Go over your drawing with a black ballpoint or felt-tip pen. Add some extra lines to the hair to give it more definition. Take another look at your picture to see if there's anywhere else you think you need to do this.

Step 6

Wait for the ink to dry, then erase all the remaining pencil lines that formed your skeleton framework. If you get this far and you are happy with your drawing, that's great! Drawing manga women doesn't get much more complicated than this.

Step 7

Now for some color. I've given Elise a futuristic look by making her hair and eyebrows bright blue. I've used a yellow for the parts of her clothing that should appear metallic. To remind yourself about color schemes, look back at the Color section of this book.

Karate Girl

Let's apply the idea of foreshortening to a drawing of manga action girl Jenna, who is practicing karate.

Step 1

Start by drawing the three main body parts. Take the time to position them accurately since everything else hinges on them. Next attach the limbs—copy the proportions of them as they are drawn here. The back arm should be shorter than the front one, with a smaller hand. The front leg will have an oversized foot attached to it.

Step 2

Now draw the outline for the flesh and muscles. Notice how the front leg appears broader than the back one. Place the eyes too—Jenna is looking down toward her front foot.

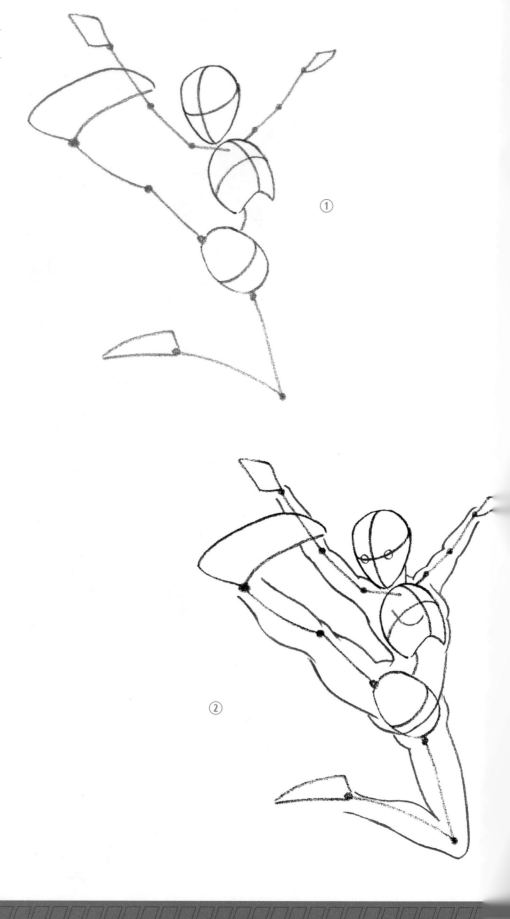

Step 3

Sketching in the clothing won't cause you too much trouble if you follow the outline of the body, but notice that the suit is quite close-fitting so it won't curve in around the joints. Draw the hair flying up behind the head. Place the rest of the facial features too. Spend some time on the hands—try holding your own hands in the same kind of karate pose so you can study the positions of the fingers.

Step 4

From this angle we can see the underside of the shoe on the raised foot—draw some lines across it to show the texture of the rubber sole. Add some crease lines to the clothes—look at your own clothing to see how fabric folds when you bend your arms and legs or twist your body. Work on the hair and eyes as well.

>>

Step 5

Use a pen to go over the lines that form your final drawing. Give the hair and face more detail and add some lines to the palm of the hand. Don't forget to draw around the ankle bones to define these.

Step 6

When the ink is dry, erase all the lines of your skeleton framework to leave a clean picture.

Step 7

In the final color drawing the drama of Jenna's flying leap is underlined by the shadows and highlights. Notice where the light hits her body, and the way the subtle use of lights and darks emphasizes movement just as much as the actual pose.

⑦

Biker Girl

This is biker girl Revvy. You'll see from the sketch I drew when I was working out her pose that I needed to sketch a lot of rough lines to achieve the final result.

Step 1

We are drawing Revvy from a ¾ viewpoint. She is leaning forward, so the head, chest, and hip shapes line up diagonally—the head slightly overlaps the chest. The hips should be relatively small since these are farthest away from us. The lines forming the neck and lower part of the spine curve away from us. Notice the angle of the collarbones—this lifts the shoulders to make the arms stand farther away from the body, creating an active pose. The leg bones cross each other near the top to create a wider stride. The back foot appears much smaller than the one that's raised up in front.

Step 2

Mark the outline shape of Revvy's flesh and muscle. Study this carefully to get the proportions right—she has muscular arms, a curvy chest, and a narrow waist.

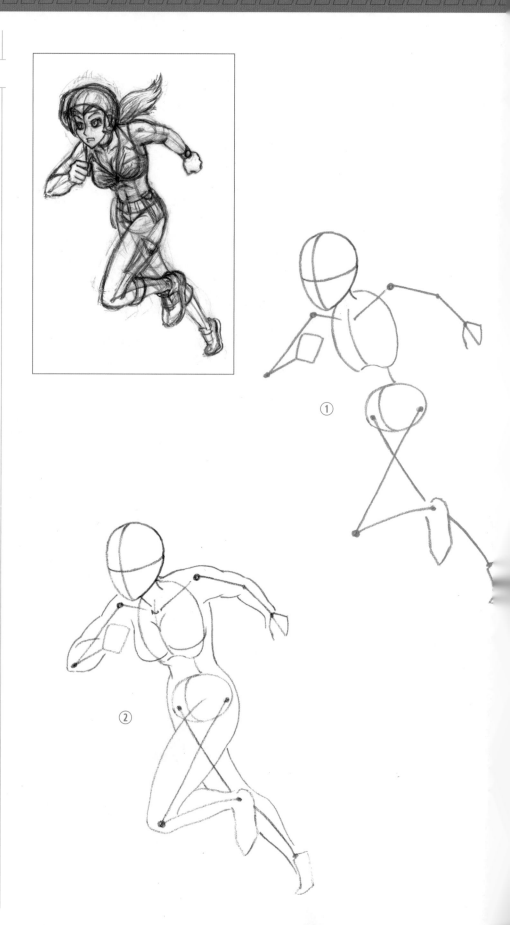

Step 3

Draw the basic outline of Revvy's helmet, sleeveless shirt, pants and running shoes—take a look at the finished picture on the next page to see these items more clearly. Next add the facial features—notice that the mouth is slightly open. Her pony-tail flies up at the back to add to the sense of movement. Work on the hands—spend some time getting the shape of the knuckles and fingers on the front hand right so you capture the tightly clenched fist. Put a choker around the neck and mark the belly button.

Step 4

Draw a visor on Revvy's helmet. Put a collar on her shirt and add the belt and pockets to the pants. Copy all the crease lines on her clothes. Now for the shoes—don't forget that the back one is much smaller because of the perspective. Add some more detail to the hair and give her a wristwatch. Work on the facial features, making the long thin eye-brows sit high above the eyes.

Step 5

Go over the outlines with your fine felt-tip pen, adding extra detail and texture as you go, like the rough edges of the shirt's armholes that make it look like the sleeves have been ripped off. Add extra lines to the upper body to give more definition to the muscle, flesh, and bone. Turn the belly button into a cross shape.

<<

Step 6

Go over some of the lines of your drawing again to vary the weight of the line. Add some shading to the eyes, mouth, choker, watch strap, and belt. Leave the ink to dry, then erase all your pencil guidelines.

Step 7

I've colored my picture using a computer. Look back at the Color section of this book and follow the steps to do this. You'll start by adding the flat color.

Step 8

This is what Revvy looks like after I added some shadows.

Step 9

Here I've added some highlights—notice the glint on the visor and the lighter patches on the hair. The other highlights are more subtle—different surfaces reflect light in different ways.

⑨

MANGA

Fighting Hero

Our hero Rik is set to throw a punch at a villain. It's not just his clenched fist that tells us this—it's his whole pose, including the expression on his face.

Step 1

Rik has swung back his arm, ready to land his punch. As he has done so, his whole torso has twisted. Bear this in mind when you are drawing the body shapes—the head and hips are side on while the large chest is at a ¾ viewpoint. The foreshortening is such that the forearm of the fist pointing toward us is very short, so I won't even draw a bone for this. The hand that's about to throw the punch is much larger than the other one to make it look closer to us and more powerful. Notice that the lines forming the bones of the back leg are slightly shorter than those of the front one to make it look farther away. The back foot is raised to show that Rik is ready to swing forward.

Step 2

Add the body outline. Notice how I've used lots of overlapping curved lines along the arms to emphasize the strong muscles—you can just make out the forearm attached to the clenched fist now. The waist appears very slender, which helps to exaggerate the width of the chest.

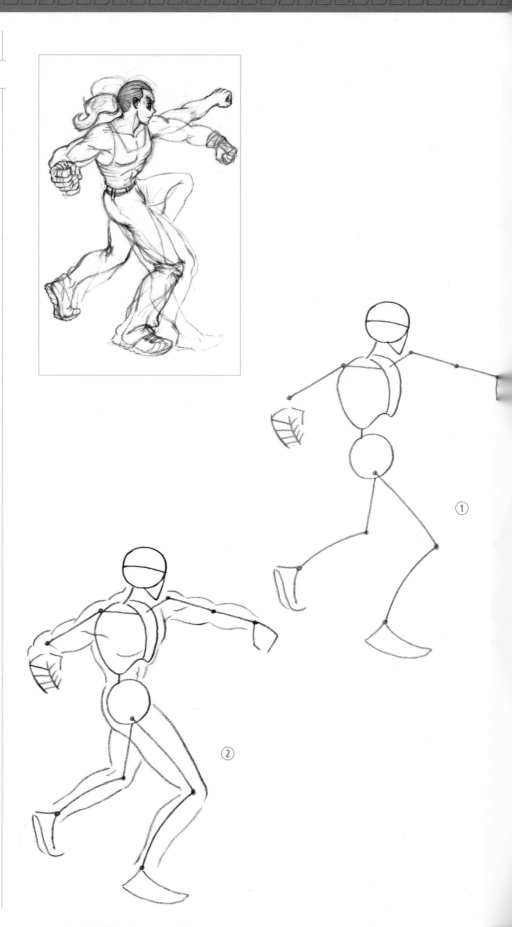

Step 3

Draw on the outline of the undershirt, belt, and sneakers. It might help you to study the final picture on the next page as you do this. Next add the outline for the hair and work on the facial features. Shape the hands—see if you can capture the drama of the clenched fist.

Step 4

Add some more lines to the hair to emphasize the way it flies up at the back. Draw on the taut neck muscles. Now work on the clothes again—notice how I've added some fold lines to the back of the undershirt and where the jeans bunch up over the sneakers. Copy how the jeans are ripped around the bottoms and across the knee. Draw some lines on the hands to show bandages across the fingers.

Step 5

Now go over the final lines of your drawing with a pen. Don't forget all the crease lines on the clothes and the extra little lines on the body that emphasize bone or muscle. Add any other finishing touches like the tread you can see where Rik has started to lift his back foot. Work on the seamlines that run down the sides of the pant legs— notice how they sit differently where the cloth gathers.

«

Step 6

Go over your final drawing in black felt-tip pen. When the ink is dry, erase all the pencil guidelines that formed your original framework.

Step 7

I've added an extra black line around the neck and armhole of the undershirt to create a band that I could make a different color. I've colored Rik digitally, but you can use whatever method you want.

Step 8

I've imagined that Rik is lit from the direction in which he is looking. Notice how this puts some parts of his body in shadow, like the side of his torso and the backs of the legs. The back of his neck and the shoulder nearer us are in the shadow of his hair.

Step 9

Finally, I've added the highlights for full dramatic effect. Putting these in so the final drawing has maximum impact takes a sublety of touch that only experience teaches. The only sure way of achieving it is by repetition—so keep on practicing!

Manga clothes can say a lot about a character's personality and the world they live in.

Falling Villain

This is Steel, the villain who was on the receiving end of the punch being thrown by our hero Rik in the previous exercise. The size of that punch has clearly left him the worse for wear.

Step 1

Start with the three main body parts as usual. Notice how the head is tipped back slightly, making the neck of the spine arch in a different direction from how it does at the waist. Add the limbs—the outstretched hand and foot have been exaggerated in size to show that these are nearer to us and to make the pose more dramatic. You won't need to draw the back foot since this will be tucked under the outstretched leg. The bones that make the framework for the hand will form a wide span.

Step 2

Add the outline of the flesh and muscle. Getting this right will help you place the clothes accurately.

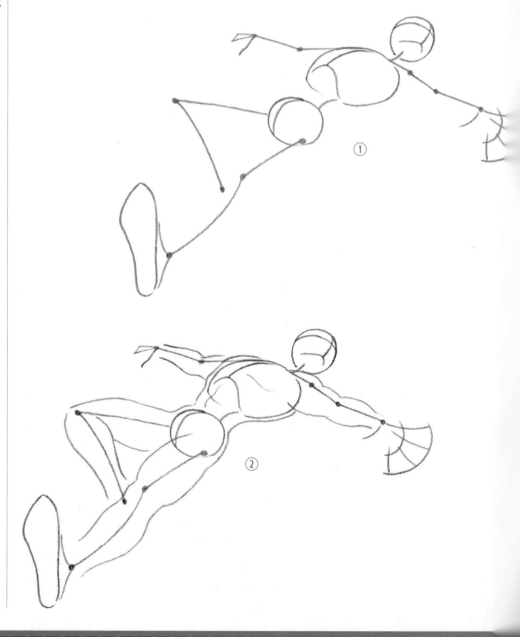

Step 3

Now for the basic outline of the clothes. Copy the curves of Steel's coat to show the way it has fallen open. Outline the bottom of the pants and the shoe. Next work on the hands. Add the outline shape for the hair and facial features—we're looking at the face from underneath, so we can see only the bottom of the nose. The eyes and mouth must show that our villain is in great pain.

Step 4

Add more detail to the coat—copy the way the collar is partly turned up. Fill in the missing parts of the outline for the pants—draw plenty of fold lines where the back leg is bent. Sketch the jagged outline of the hair, then draw some curved guidelines to the right of the head to mark the position for some blood spouting from Steel's mouth.

Step 5

Go over the best lines of your figure. Add the droplets of blood. Work on the shirt buttons and finish off the belt. Make sure you haven't missed anything, like the detail on the shoe.
>>

Step 6

When the ink is dry, erase all the lines of your basic skeleton and any other pencil lines you still need to get rid of.

Step 7

Now put in some color to add even more drama to your picture. I've done this digitally, but you can do it by hand, if you choose. If you have drawn Steel and Rik on the same piece of paper, make sure you use the same coloring materials for both figures to create a unified image. Think too about how the colors of their clothing and skin work together.

Step 8

With the flat color in place we can look at adding in the shadows and how light and dark tones can be used to emphasize the pose, underlining Steel's discomfort.

ACTION

Step 9

The addition of the highlights focuses our attention on the impact of Rik's punch. Look especially at the areas of highlighting on the face, and the hands, reflecting the visual contortions. Ouch! That punch sure did hurt!

Step-by-Step   247

Warrior Queen

While you work through this final exercise, think about the character you're drawing. What's her name? Where's she from? Does she have special powers? Working out what you are trying to convey through your characters will make your drawings much more believable and interesting. As you can see from my original sketch, I changed my mind about this picture a few times before I decided on the final pose.

Step 1

Carefully copy the ovals for the three main body parts. Study the oval forming the chest—instead of being upright, it's almost lying on its side. This creates the extreme arch of the back. The hips are thrust forward while the head twists in a different direction and tilts down slightly. The joint at the top of the back leg sits partway across the hips to make this leg stretch farther back. Both feet are sharply angled so the warrior almost appears to be flying.

Step 2

Draw on the body outline. Overlap the curves on the outstretched arm to give the muscle more definition. Make the waist narrow to emphasize the broadness of the upper body.

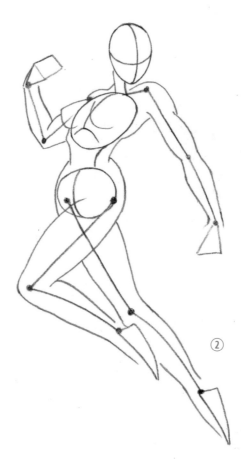

Step 3

Map in the basic shapes of the clothing and hair. Copy the shape of the skirt to capture the flimsy, floaty look. Work on the dagger and the hand holding it. Place the facial features, making the eyes small.

Step 4

Draw around the tops of the boots to show their shaggy texture. Add some guidelines to the hair and make the eyebrows extremely angular. Draw the irises and pupils low down in the sockets. Add two large loops for earrings.

Step 5

Once all your guidelines are in place, you can enjoy establishing the final drawing with a pen. Add a few more details as you go, like the curves on the armulets to help show they are metallic and the fold lines of the fabric at the back of the ankles.

>>

When you are creating your own character, try copying a friend's hairstyle and look in a catalogue for clothing ideas. Borrow bits from manga characters on TV too.

❮❮
Step 6

Now vary the weight of the ink lines to accentuate the curves and lend the figure a sense of solidity. I've also added a thin strip of hair down either side of the face. Look carefully at the small lines I've sketched on the upper body here—this technique really accentuates the warrior's muscular shape. When you work on the leopard-skin pattern of the skirt, notice how the black shapes run into each other where the skirt folds.

Step 7

I colored my picture by computer—there is more information on this in the Color section of this book. You start by adding flat colors like I've done here.

Step 8

Next I added some shadows. I also made some parts of the picture, like the hair and the waistband of the skirt, a deeper shade.

Step 9

Our warrior queen is at the peak of her power. Note the additional enhancements: the glinting steel of her dagger, the armlet and headband, and the burnished, smooth tones of her skin. Compare this picture with the previous one so you can see exactly how I've enhanced it.

⑨

BACKGROUNDS

There are no end of backgrounds that you could create for the characters you draw.

In this section, we'll be looking at abstract backgrounds that work to exaggerate the features of your characters. We'll also look at the creation of full background scenes that you can use to place your character in a particular setting. These scenes range from the kinds of settings you might be familiar with from the world around you, to original futuristic environments.

Although you'll have plenty of opportunity to use your imagination and create some weird and wonderful worlds, there are still some rules you will need to follow, so here you'll find out how to make all these scenes have a convincing feel.

A good background should be able to more than double the impact that your character would make on its own, so I'll give you some tips on getting the characters and backgrounds to work well together.

Successfully combining these is partly down to use of color so we'll need to look at this too.

You can apply the techniques you learn here to create backgrounds for some of your own characters.

BACKGROUNDS

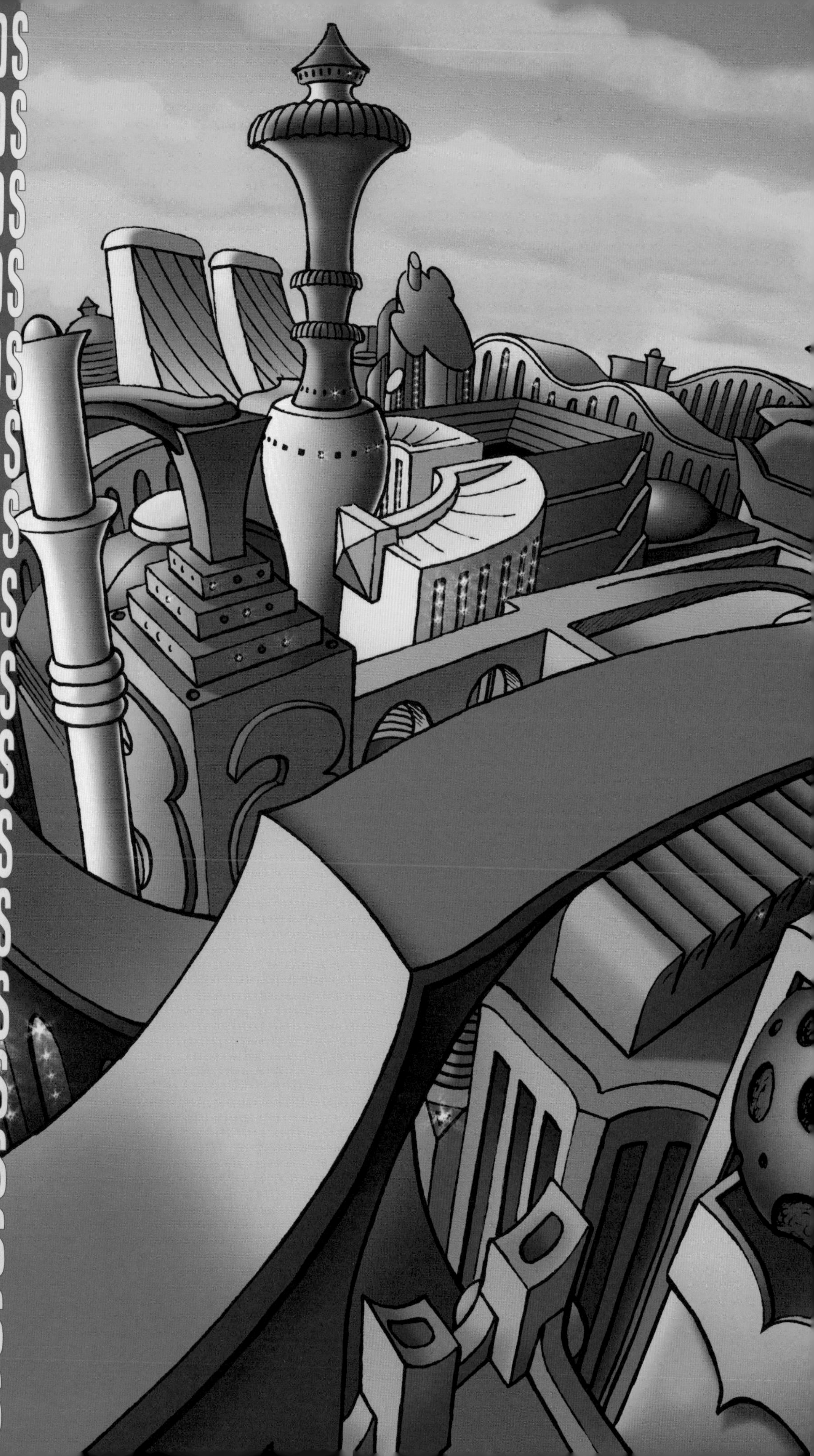

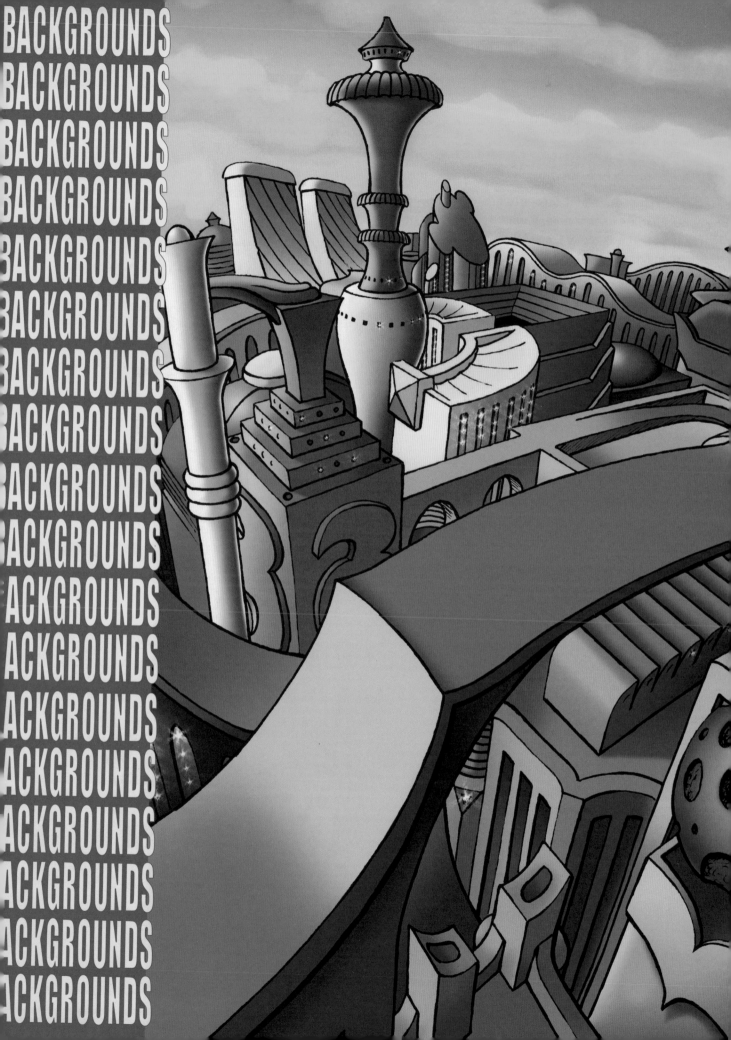

Abstract Backgrounds

A recurring feature of manga artwork is the abstract background. A whole range of textures, colors, and tones (light and dark areas) are used to help show how characters are feeling or how we, the viewers, are invited to feel about them. Daisy is going to model some of the more commonly used types of abstract background.

① No background

Without adding any kind of background to this picture, you can see that there is very little here to indicate any kind of mood or sensation. The picture looks bland and doesn't have the impact of professional manga artwork.

② Contented feel

A little splash of color and some simple cloud shapes instantly convey a feeling of contentment. These are bright, fresh colors that we associate with warm, sunny days.

①

②

③–④ Evil look

Abstract backgrounds don't just work to convey the mood of a character—they can also help to show the personality. In the picture, Daisy's evil twin, Detta, is enhanced by manga-style lightning bolts and flame designs. Color is also important here—the deep reds and purples express rage and vindictiveness.
»

A great deal of expression can be achieved without you having to draw anything difficult. The whole purpose of any kind of art is to communicate, and if you can say what you want with simple effects, there's no point in complicating things.

《

⑤–⑥ **Speed lines**

This is a device that manga artists use regularly. Lines of varying number and thickness radiate from a character to emphasize a range of emotions—their meaning will depend on the story they are used in and the expression on the character's face. They may suggest anything from a sudden realization or shock to determination or excitement. The background color can also enhance the desired effect.

⑤

⑥

⑦

⑦–⑧ Other effects

In addition to stressing a character's personality and expression, background effects can also help to make a gesture more powerful—a raised finger can be imbued with magical qualities, while a clenched fist can be made more triumphant.

⑧

When you read comics or watch animations, look for the abstract effects that are used, then try to emulate these in your own artwork. You can make up your own effects, but they have to work—make sure they mean what you want them to.

Composition

Composition is one of the first things to consider when making a picture. It's all about the elements you want to include in your picture and where you place them. This may sound simple, but good composition takes some thought.

Basic rules

Here we're going to look at the most basic compositional rules. Knowing these will help you to make decisions about your own pictures. Bear in mind that no two pictures are the same and that it's sometimes necessary to break rules—but rules can only be successfully broken when you know what they are!

Portrait format

A picture that is taller than it is wide is known as portrait format. The two pictures on this page show Magnus in a portrait-shaped frame.

① Bad placement

When people are taking photographs, you'd be surprised how often they make the mistake of automatically placing the focal point of the picture—in this case, Magnus's head—smack in the middle of the frame. The same thing can happen when someone draws a picture. Here Magnus is placed too low. His head sits halfway down the frame, as

marked by the green line. There is too much empty space above his head and he looks like he's going to drop out of the bottom of the picture.

② Vertical placement

The height of an object within the frame is known as the vertical placement. This picture shows good vertical placement. Magnus fills the frame nicely, without too much empty space and without having any of his body parts cropped off.

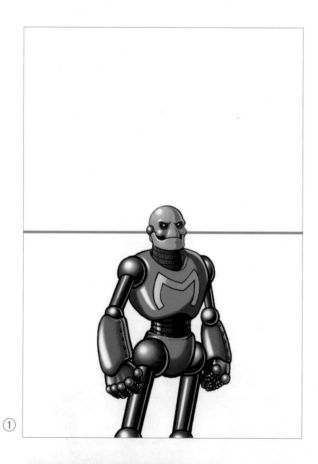

①

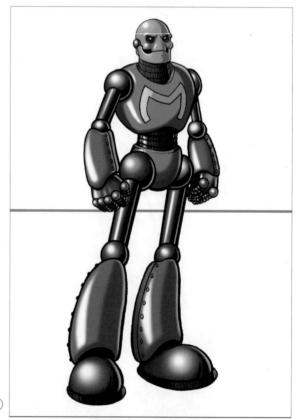

②

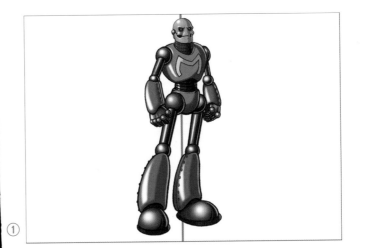

①

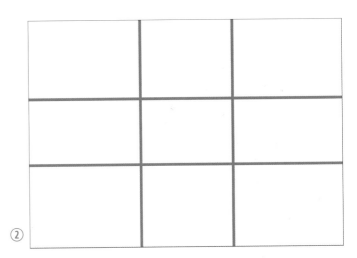

②

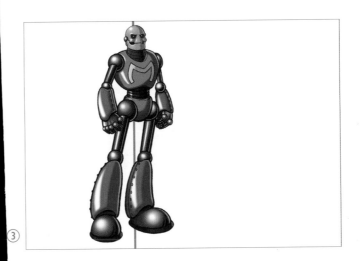

③

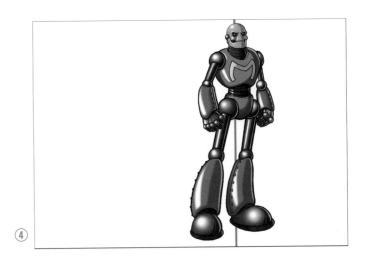

④

Landscape format

The pictures in these frames are wider than they are tall. Called landscape format, it is normally used by photographers and artists when they want to capture a wide expanse of scenery.

① Horizontal placement

The position of an object along the width of the frame is known as the horizontal placement. Here Magnus has been placed centrally. Although this can sometimes work well, depending on the other elements, more often than not it looks boring and should be avoided.

② Golden section

It is generally accepted that pictures work better when the objects are placed to the left or right of center. Artists living in ancient Greece worked out a complicated geometrical equation known as the golden section, and today's artists still follow this rule. In simple terms, it states that objects should be placed just over a third of the way in from the picture's edges.

③–④ Moving left or right

Moving Magnus to the left or right and placing him roughly on the lines of the golden section divisions immediately makes for a more interesting picture. The angle of his body also changes his relationship with the rest of the picture space. In 3, he's facing into the picture, suggesting involvement with any background we might add. Picture 4 suggests the opposite because Magnus is angled away from the main area of the picture.

①

②

③

Love at First Sight

Let's start with a simple, static figure. A lonesome Romeo has just set eyes on Tellima for the first time and is instantly sure that she is the girl of his dreams. At this moment, nothing else exists for him. We are going to create a background that aims to express his emotion. We need to produce the effect of everything pulling toward the girl, yet at the same time, she should be radiating out of the picture. The format I've chosen is a precise square. Next we need to decide how to place Tellima in the square.

① Figure—too small

Here, Tellima is really too small—she doesn't fill much of the space, so she is in danger of being swamped by the background.

② Figure—too big

Tellima certainly isn't going to get lost in this picture, but she doesn't leave much room for adding an effective background. Although we want her to attract our Romeo's attention, she's now too close for there to be any kind of mystery attaching to her.

③ Good-size figure

This is a much better size. The legs will be cropped off, but they're not important to the overall feel. For this picture positioning Tellima centrally would be a good idea. By doing this I'm breaking the golden section rule (see page 258–259) but for a good reason—since I want the figure to be the sole focus of interest.

④ Bad gradients

Here I've tried to use the tone of the background to focus attention on the girl, but it isn't quite producing the desired effect—it seems to be pushing the figure forward.

⑤ Good gradients

This is more like it. The background tone gives the figure an appealing halo effect—it almost seems like we're looking into a tunnel with a light at the end of it.

⑥ Bad radials

To exaggerate the effect of the background, I'm going to add lines

radiating from behind the girl. Here though the lines don't quite work because they are too haphazard.

⑦ Good radials

Drawing all of the lines radiating from a single point makes them look more orderly and elegant.

⑧ Color rough

A color you want can often be made by applying one color felt-tip pen over another. But if you want to use pure bright colors, you'll be limited by the range of colors those pens come in. They're fine, though, for dashing off a quick color rough to help you

visualize your ideas and make sure they work. For the background, I've drawn a series of concentric heart shapes around Tellima, and starting in the center, I've colored them using increasingly darker pinks. For my final artwork I'll use only one pink and make different tints and shades of it by adding white or black. Instead of making my radiating lines black—like they often are in manga comics—I'll use diluted white ink to create the effect of shafts of light. I'll also add some spots of white ink to provide a bit of sparkle.

»

⑤

⑥

⑦

⑧

⑨

⑨ Final color background

On a computer I can easily replicate my color rough and produce a very polished look. Similar effects could be achieved with traditional materials, although it would take a lot longer, and every color would have to be meticulously applied.

Completed artwork

With Tellima in place the picture is finished. I slightly blurred her for a soft-focus effect, and partially erased her legs so as to keep the attention on the top half of the picture.

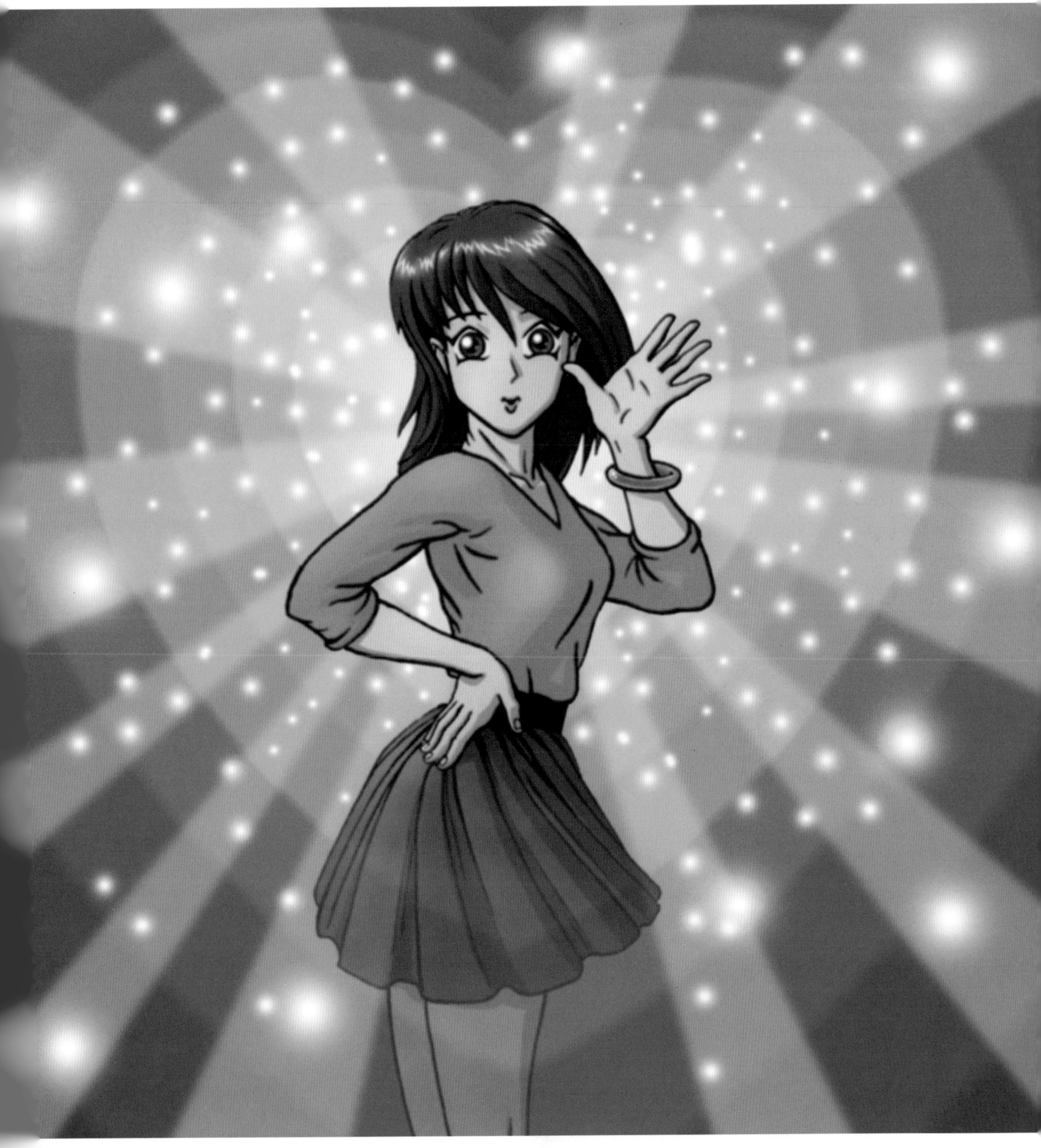

Warrior Woman

Compared to Tellima, this pose has more dynamism and drama; you can tell that the character has plenty of attitude. The challenge this time is not so much to seduce the viewers, but to send shivers down their spines! The background needs to convey movement as well as power and attitude. I also want to capture something of this character's wild spirit—she is one feisty manga babe.

① Figure—too big

Here, our warrior woman is too large to convey movement. A moving figure needs space within a picture.

② Bad placement

This is a better size for the figure and she is at a good height, but the central positioning along the horizontal axis is not right—it's far too static for our requirements.

①

②

(4)

(5)

(6)

③ Using the golden section

Here I've moved the warrior away from the center of the picture by applying the golden section, as explained earlier, on page 258–259. This is better, but her face is turned to the bottom right here, which means that whatever she is looking at is off the edge of the picture, so the picture isn't quite right.

④ Good placement

Placing the figure at the top left conveys the sense that she has reached the peak of her movement and is looking back toward where

she leapt from. Instinctively, I think this position works well.

⑤ Adding a background

The background for this picture needs to be suitably dramatic. The first things to consider are the broad shapes and tones. To create these, I usually sketch out little pictures that are just a couple of inches high, on a single piece of paper, to try out different combinations of lines and shadings. You can work out a lot of things with simple pencil sketches like these. Artists call them thumbnails. At this early stage of a

new design, these pictures don't need to be very big or complicated. This picture shows the effect I arrived at with my thumbnails. The basic tones and shapes give the thrust and mood I'm after.

⑥ The detail

Working up the detail gradually as I went along, I refined the shapes and added a light source. Even at this stage, I'm already thinking about the textures and elements that the finished picture might consist of.
>>

⑦

«

⑦ Color rough

In some manga stories, characters are imbued with the spirits of wild animals. This seems appropriate for our warrior woman. I'm imagining a snake coiling up through the picture around the figure—this could look dramatic and also reinforce the movement. Taking the rough design I came up with for a background, I then dashed off a quick sketch and added color to the tones that I had decided on in the last picture. The colors should be as bold as possible —clashing, even. Since this is not intended to be a subtle picture, I've actually used all the colors of the spectrum: warm colors—reds, yellows, and oranges—for the figure and snake, leaving the cool colors—greens and blues—in the background. This separates the warrior and her snake spirit from the rest of the picture, distancing them from the area below. Since this was only a rough sketch, the lines of my snake are very scratchy, but I like the effect—they add a little raggedness and swirl to the creature. They could work well in my final artwork.

⑧ **Line drawing of background**

Before computers were invented, an artist would draw an entire picture (objects plus background) all at once, then color it by hand using watercolors, colored inks, or a mixture of different media. But now that we have computers, there's no need for me to draw and color the warrior woman that I've already created. I'll finish the background first, then drop her on later. For my precise drawing of the background here, I started with a pencil sketch, then went over it in black line.
»

⑧

⑨

⟪

⑨ Color background

I scanned in my black line drawing and then erased any grubby marks before applying the color and digital effects. (There's a lesson in computer coloring on pages 184–195.)

Completed artwork

When adding the figure I had to erase parts of her body so that she appears to be encircled by the snake. Compare the finish of this computer-colored picture to my color rough.

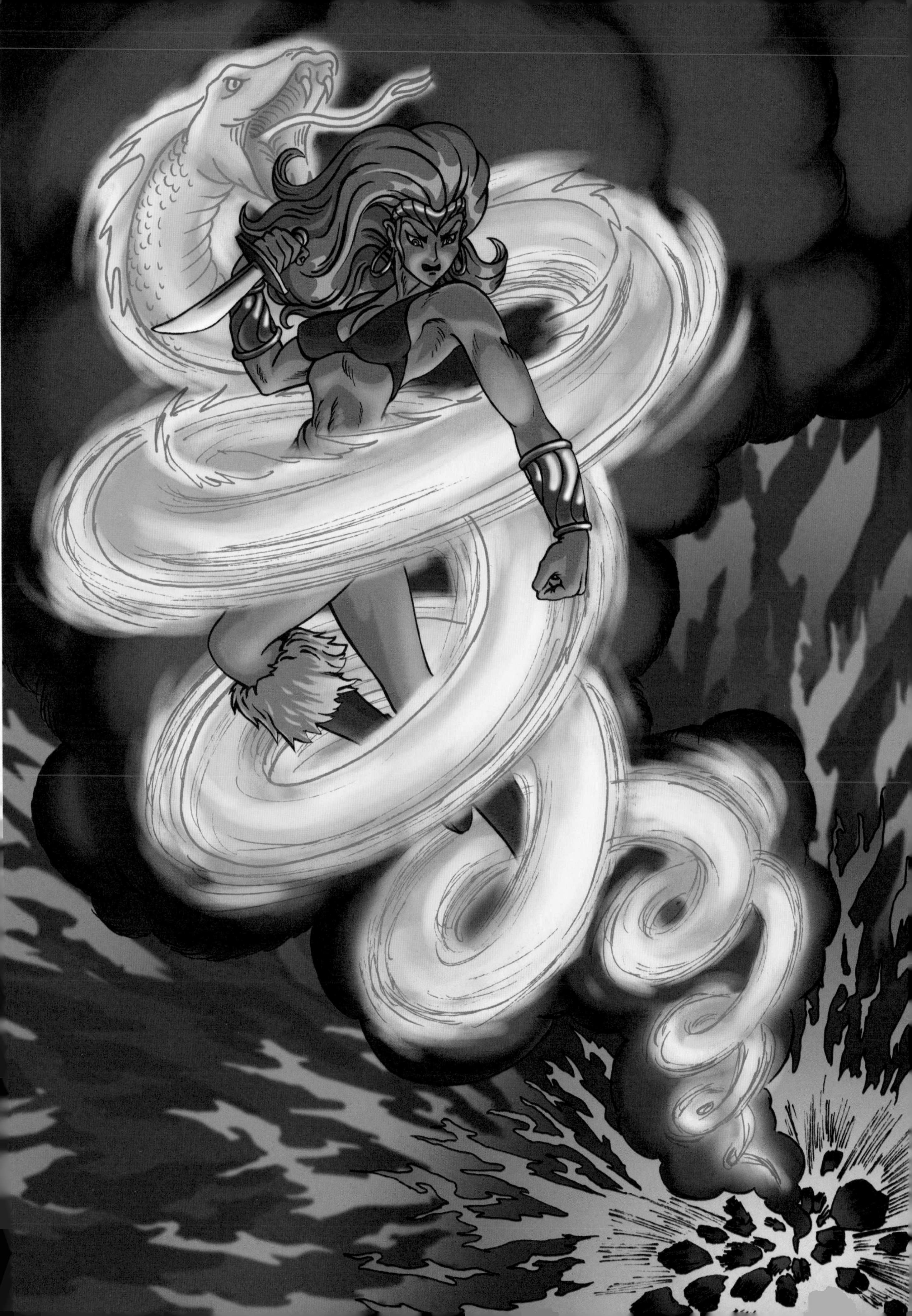

Horizons

When you look out over a flat landscape, there will always be a line where the land meets the sky—this is the horizon. Understanding a little about how the horizon works in relation to pictures will help you design convincing background scenes and place your characters against them accurately.

① **Eye level**

The horizon of a picture represents the eye level of the viewer. In this diagram, we (the viewers) are exactly level with Duke—his eye level is at the same height as ours so it rests on the horizon line. No matter how near or far from us Duke may be, his eye level remains the same—level with the horizon.

② **Low eye level**

Now imagine that you are lying on the floor looking up at Duke. Because your eye level is lower, Duke is no longer level, but towering above you. The horizon here runs level with his ankles, and once again, this remains constant no matter how far or near he may be.

③ **Different characters**

Your manga characters are not, of course, all going to be the same height. Here we're back level with Duke, but as you can see, Magnus is taller and so is higher than our eye level or the horizon. Since Daisy is shorter than Duke, she is lower than our eye level or the horizon.

①

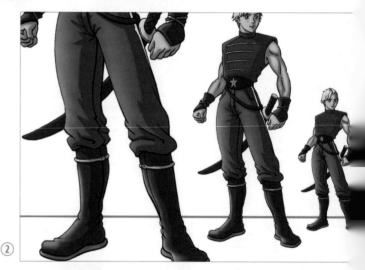

②

③

④ **Distance**

As before, the distance of these characters from the viewer doesn't affect their height above or below the horizon. The horizon still runs through Magnus's chest and near the top of Daisy's head, just as it did in the previous diagram.

The team

Here's the team again but this time seen from a lower eye level, as if the viewer is sitting on the floor.

⑤

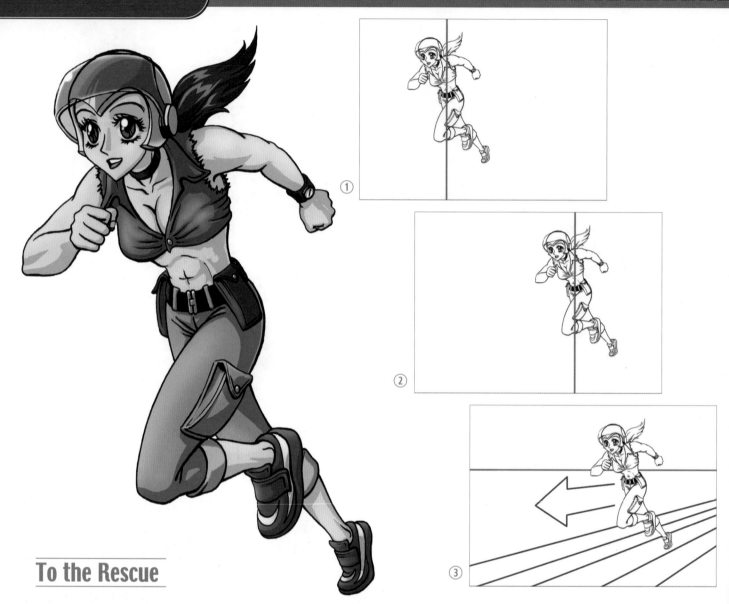

①

②

③

To the Rescue

Our biker girl, Revvy, is clearly running along a ground plane. This gives us the opportunity to put into practise some of what we've already learnt about horizons. The background should be based on the real world and set in the sort of place where danger is never far away. There should be enough in the scene to inspire the viewer to imagine what sort of action is about to occur.

From the way Revvy is dressed, she's obviously somewhere warm. She clearly travels by motorcycle, which would allow her to cover a lot of ground, so I'm going to set the picture in a desert region.

① **Bad placement**
Placing the figure here is not quite right for this scene—the large space to the right of the figure implies that she is running away from something, which isn't the impression we are trying to give.

② **Good placement**
With more space to the left of the figure, there's room for her to move into, suggesting that she's running toward something.

③ **Direction**
I've opted for quite a high horizon and placed the horizon line just over a third of the way down the page. This allows space to show the ground and rocks. The direction lines, marked in blue, show the route Revvy is going to take as she runs through the picture, so I'll be thinking about that direction as I continue to sketch the background.

Background tones

After trying out different options on scrap paper, I arrived at this rough arrangement for the background shapes. The girl has a clear route through the scene but there is also a clear view of the horizon behind her, giving the setting depth and interest. I've been careful not to clutter the area around the figure.

Color rough

Armed with some photographs of desert scenes, I've added some color and detail to my rough design. The color scheme is harmonious, with mainly yellows and blues, and mixtures of them to make green for some parts. Other colors are in the background too, but nothing so bright that it jars with the overall scheme. I've also added a desert cat at Revvy's side.

⑥ **Line drawing of background**

Now that I know what I want to do, I draw the outline of all the background objects more carefully and go over them in black line. I've created different textures by varying the lines. Rocks are made with rough heavy lines, while the lines of the cacti are more wobbly. In contrast, the skull is smooth and the cat has hints of fur. Objects in the foreground are drawn with heavy lines, which become finer as the features recede into the distance, helping to give the picture depth. »

⑦ Color background

Looking at my color rough, I can see the scene looks quite light and airy. I want a sense of heat and oppressiveness. I decide to leave out the clouds and also make the coloring of the rocks more dense.

Completed artwork

When putting figures into a background it's important to think about the shadows they may cast. I put a dark patch at Revvy's feet to tie her into the picture. The dust kicking up from her heels also helps.

⑦

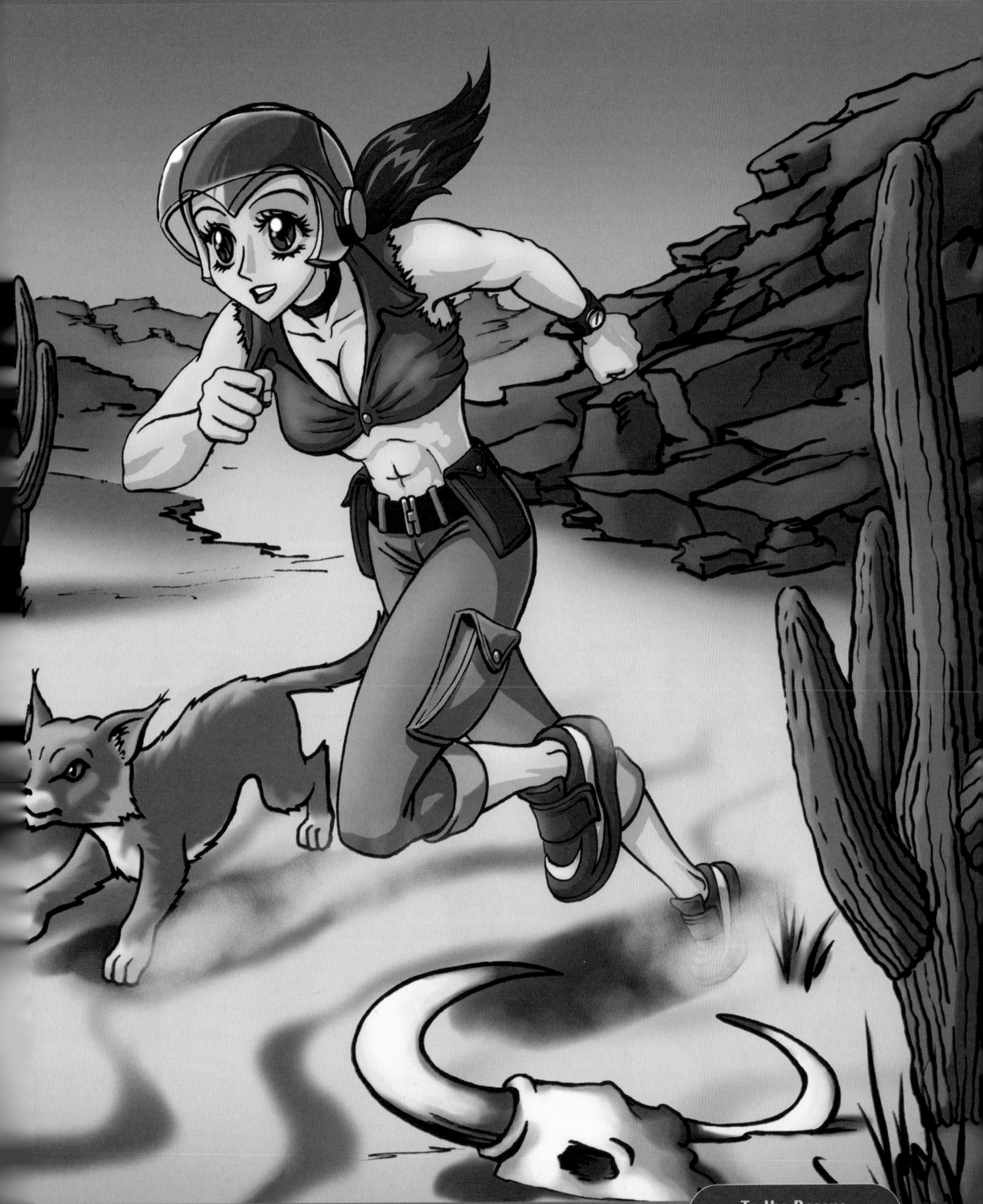

To the Rescue

Gothic Nightmare

To demonstrate the dramatic effects of light and shade in a picture, I am going to use this werewolf. It's the dead of night and something is prowling in the shadows, hungry for the taste of blood. We therefore need a setting that conjures up the gloom and atmosphere of a horror story and shows our werewolf at his most threatening. A graveyard scene fits the bill perfectly.

① Placement

I'm breaking away from convention again by placing the figure in the center of the picture because I want the focal point to be his wild, glowing eye. I've placed this on the intersection of horizontal and vertical golden section divisions (see page 258–259 for an explanation of this). I'm keeping the figure quite small since I want him to blend in with the background and not appear too obvious in the picture.

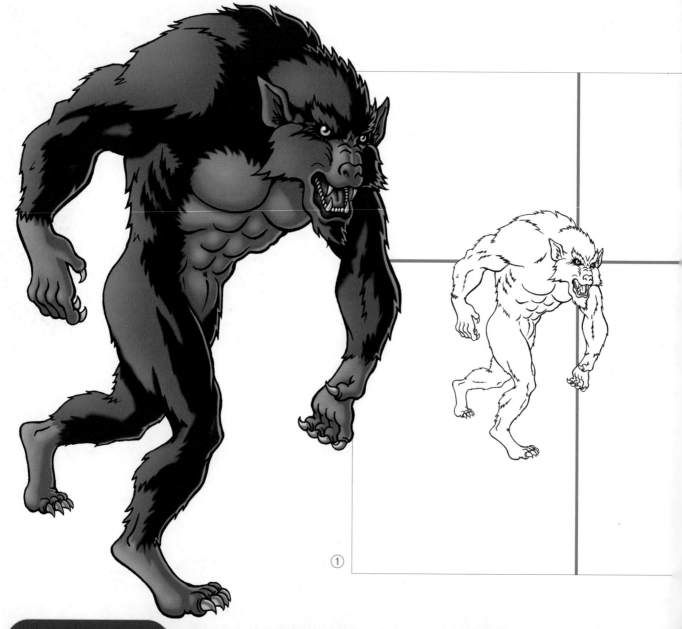

③

② Basic shapes

The lumbering swagger of the werewolf suggests to me that an informal, irregular composition might be appropriate. I'm hoping to envelop the werewolf within the composition, concealing him and hopefully adding to the sinister atmosphere. A curve in the foreground leads the viewer's eye straight to the werewolf's glowing eye. This curve also frames the creature, echoing his hunched stance, and suggests a path for him to follow on his midnight prowl. The rough shape of a building in the background contrasts with the dark curve in the foreground. Without this building, the picture would seem unbalanced and too heavy toward the bottom left.

③ Final tones

I had originally imagined that I'd turn the dark curve of the foreground shape into some kind of foliage. I then decided that such a mass of darkness would be too heavy, and opted instead to include a creepy-looking bare-branched tree. Dotting some rough gravestones around helps me think about how to make the lights and darks work in the middle ground. A darker gravestone in the foreground adds to the feeling of rambling clutter I want to convey. ≫

④

«

④ **Color rough**

The elements of this scene are relatively straightforward to draw—it's all about light and dark masses. With the moon in its current position, the direction of the light should mean that everything is a silhouette. I put the full moon in since it's important to the concept of the werewolf, but I worked taking into account another unspecified light source coming from the upper left and used the moon as a secondary light source. This is technically known as cheating, but it's an effect that you see in manga a great deal—a spot of back lighting like this helps add creepy-looking highlights around the edge of shadowy characters. At night, when the lighting is dull, color becomes very muted and indistinct. For this reason, I've kept the color range very limited, using more black and gray than any other color.

⑤

⑤ Background in black line

There's no point in doing a detailed pencil drawing for this kind of scene. It's as effective—and more fun—to just use a pencil for roughing in the basics of the features, then getting right down to drawing the spindly branches and the blades of grass with brush and ink. I took a little more time over drawing the tomb stones and church, but the great thing about scenes like this is that nothing has to be very precise— wobbly and rough lines help create the look of gnarled wood and old stone.

»

⑥

⟨⟨

⑥ Full color background

Having done all my working out in my color rough, coloring this background was a very simple task. Unfortunately not all my rough marks with felt tips were reproducible by computer.

Completed artwork

The tree overlapping the werewolf and the similarity of coloring serve to unite the werewolf with his environment. Quite simply he belongs in this scene.

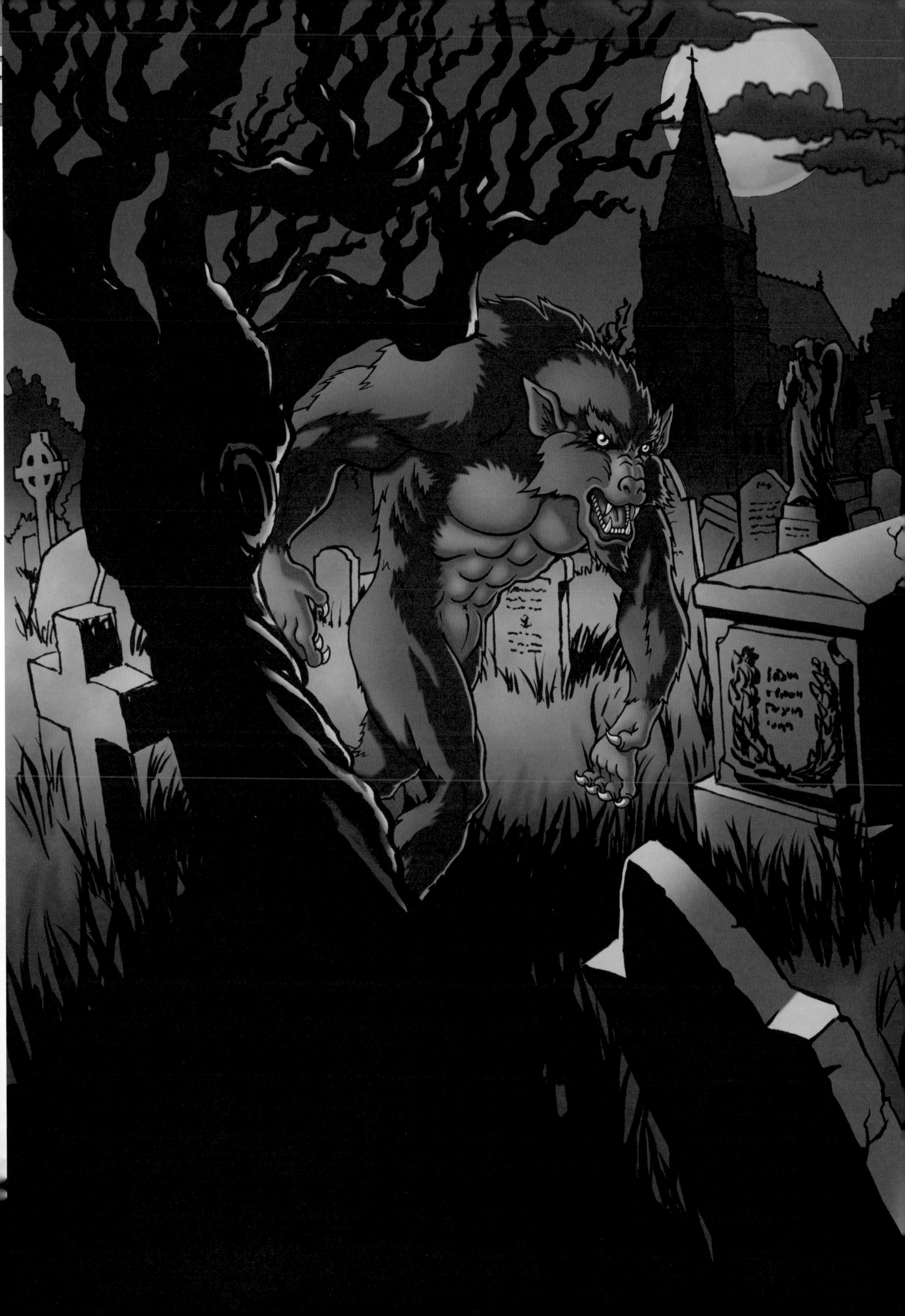

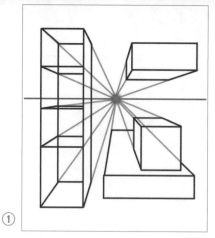

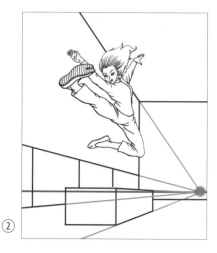

Kung Fu

The setting for this character, Jenna, should be appropriate to her manner of dress, which is traditional Japanese. The composition should also make the most of her dynamic flying kick pose and suit the exaggerated foreshortening.

Perspective

I'm going to set this picture inside a building. I'm hoping this will provide an intriguing contrast to the action of the figure. To make sense of all the angles of a room, we have to know the rules of perspective. We already touched on this when we looked at different levels of horizon, but now we'll take it a stage further and explain what you need to know to draw buildings.

① The setting

Most buildings are constructed of right angles—floors are level, walls strictly vertical. That fact makes the perspective of a building quite simple. Here we see a number of boxes drawn to look three-dimensional, and to show us one-point perspective—all the horizontal lines pointing away from the viewer converge at a single point on the horizon regardless of whether the box is above or below it. The point at which these lines converge is called the vanishing point (marked in red). From this angle, all other lines of the boxes remain vertical or horizontal. Let's see this in practise.

② Rough composition

After trying out a few variations as thumbnails, I arrived at this rough arrangement for the elements of my picture. I'm not too concerned with precise composition at this stage because I want to get the perspecti sorted out first. The idea is to use t perspective of the room to lend direction and impact to the figure. I constructed a room to match the perspective of the girl. To create a sense of her height above the ground, I chose a low horizon and placed an object (just a plain box a this stage) beneath her.

③

⑤

⑥

③ **Refined composition**

Once the environment is established, I can concentrate on making the picture work compositionally. Here I've simply cropped off the right-hand edge—this immediately makes the picture more balanced. I still think it can be improved, though.

④-⑤ **Skewing the picture frame**

A common device used in manga is to skew the frame of a picture. This creates tension and breaks up the monotony of vertical and horizontal lines. By twisting the same picture around within the frame, different compositions arise, each of which affects the dynamics of the picture. Picture 4 is more visually interesting than picture 3, but it still doesn't quite work. The girl seems to be falling rather than leaping upward. My second attempt (picture 5) works much better. Jenna really seems to be exploding across the room.

⑥ **Color rough**

Traditional Japanese interiors are usually quite minimalist. A few simple objects and decorations, and a restrained and harmonious color scheme are all that is needed to conjure up an authentic atmosphere. Against this backdrop, Jenna's vivid red suit makes quite a splash. I deliberately kept the area around her quite empty—to allow space to trail some movement lines behind her. Since the girl is moving in line with the room's perspective, these movement lines should lead to the same vanishing point.
»

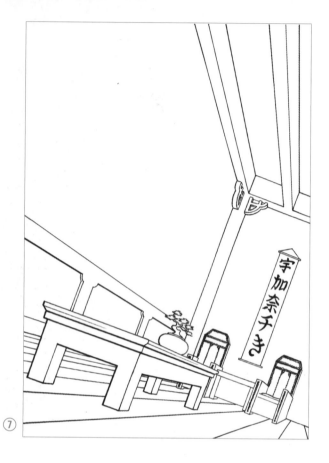

⑦

⑧

«

⑦ Background in black line

This drawing is not quite as simple as it looks. The skewed angle is disorientating when drawing the verticals and horizontals. I used a set square constantly to keep checking right angles, like the ones made by the top and legs of the table. I also used a ruler to ink all the straight lines—appropriate to the clean lines of Japanese interiors. For the kanji script on the wall, I used a Japanese brush pen to create the right feel.

⑧ Color background

Computer coloring is very well suited to the smooth, flat surface of this room. Rooms are usually darker toward the corners, so I've put some shading on the walls. I also decided to break up the plain floor surface with some reflections of the furniture.

Completed artwork

Because of the action of the figure, adding her to the background was quite a complicated job. The speed-lines in front of her show up well against the plain wall. Behind the figure I went for a more sophisticated effect, tracing Jenna's path with diminishing 'ghost' images.

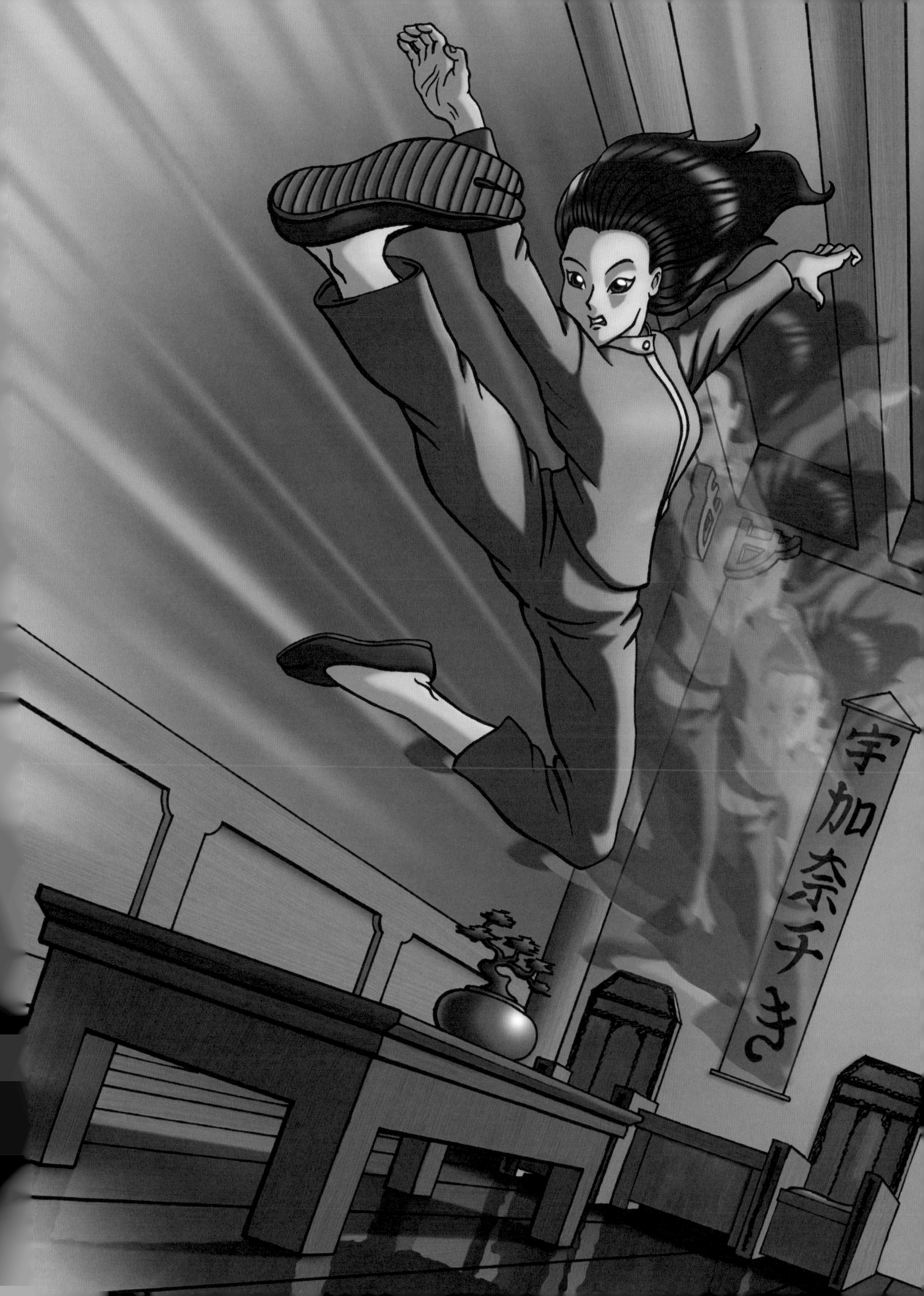
宇加奈チき

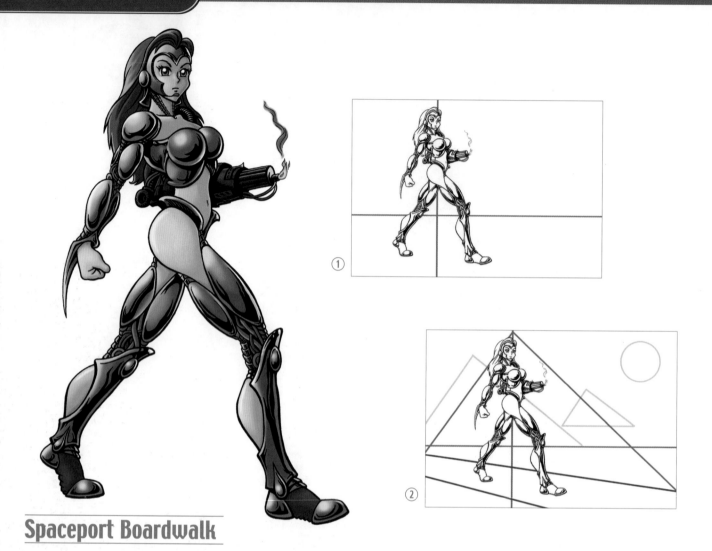

①

②

Spaceport Boardwalk

This cyborg girl is half-human, half-robot. Her character demands a background that echoes the high-tech and organic mix of her styling. She would clearly fit in a future or alien world. She is striding with a purpose but has no sense of urgency, so we need not concern ourselves with conveying too much movement in the background—we can concentrate on creating a backdrop that suits her elegant poise.

① Placement
Like the biker girl on the previous page, this cyborg needs a space to move into. I'm therefore going to place her toward the left of the picture so she has space in front of her. I think a lower horizon than I used for the biker girl would work well here—showing the character from a low eye level will give her an imposing presence in the picture.

② Geometry
The blue lines indicate the route the cyborg will take. I've made a subtle change to the original pose, slightly altering her left leg so it appears she is walking toward the front of the picture, rather than directly across the page. There's something sturdy and triangular about her pose and

position on the page, so I think I could base a strong composition on that idea. Thinking about picture-making in terms of geometrical shapes can often inspire interesting compositions. To enforce the girl's triangular shape, I've added more triangles for background shapes. Although the girl's pose is rigid and upright, her body is quite rounded. A circular sun or moon might work well to soften the angularity of the background. The triangles could be mountains, pyramids, or spacecraft—just about anything. The next step is to decide on a theme.

③ **Color rough**

The cyborg's body suggests the armor of a medieval knight. This made me think of castles and city walls, and gave me the idea of creating a futuristic version of a medieval landscape. But instead of drawing ancient cities surrounded by water-filled moats crossed by drawbridges, I imagined these cities surrounded by the void of space, with jetties stretching out to spaceships. The cyborg is walking along one of these jetties. Although in my scene we do not see where she is crossing from or to, the background features provide enough information for the viewer to imagine the details that lie beyond the edges of our picture.
>>

③

<<

④ Pencil sketch of background

From my rough color composition I decided to move the foreground jetty up slightly so that I can include more of the deep space underneath. It was also clear that the cities needed to be drawn in more detail. I thought about including other medieval features and came up with the idea of using the shapes of chess pieces for the design of some of the buildings. No material can compete with pencil on paper for working up this kind of design. Start with a hard pencil for sketching in the broad shapes, then gradually add the individual features. Switch to a softer pencil as you home in on details. Always keep your eraser handy—you're bound to need it.

④

⑤

⑤ Simple line drawing

All sorts of materials and tools can be used for inking—from fine brushes, flexible-tip dip pens, and felt-tip pens to rulers, compasses, and ellipse templates. Different types of pictures demand different approaches. Here I've used a single, black fine-tipped pen to go over all the features to clarify the rougher pencil lines. Then when the ink was dry, I erased all the scruffy pencil marks to leave a simple black line drawing.

⑥

⑥ Full line drawing

Here I want to demonstrate the difference that careful inking can make. Compare this picture with the previous one. Think of it as consisting of four layers of depth. As in the desert scene, the closer an object is to the foreground, the more dense the line should be. I'm also conscious of the light source. The cyborg is lit from above left, so to reflect this in the background, I've given all the features thicker lines on the side that faces away from the direction of this light source. I chose to draw everything freehand. Precise line work is important for some pictures. For this one, I want to avoid it looking too slick and technical.

⑦ Color background

Consistent with the shading of the figure, I've gone for some fairly high tonal contrasts, as you would expect to see in deep space. The color range is essentially green, blue and yellow with some pink and orange borrowed from the figure to add richness. Shading each of the buildings took hours. Sometimes you have to accept that certain pictures need a lot more time spent on them than others. All that remains now is for the cyborg and her shadow to be put in place.

Turn over to see the completed artwork.

⑦

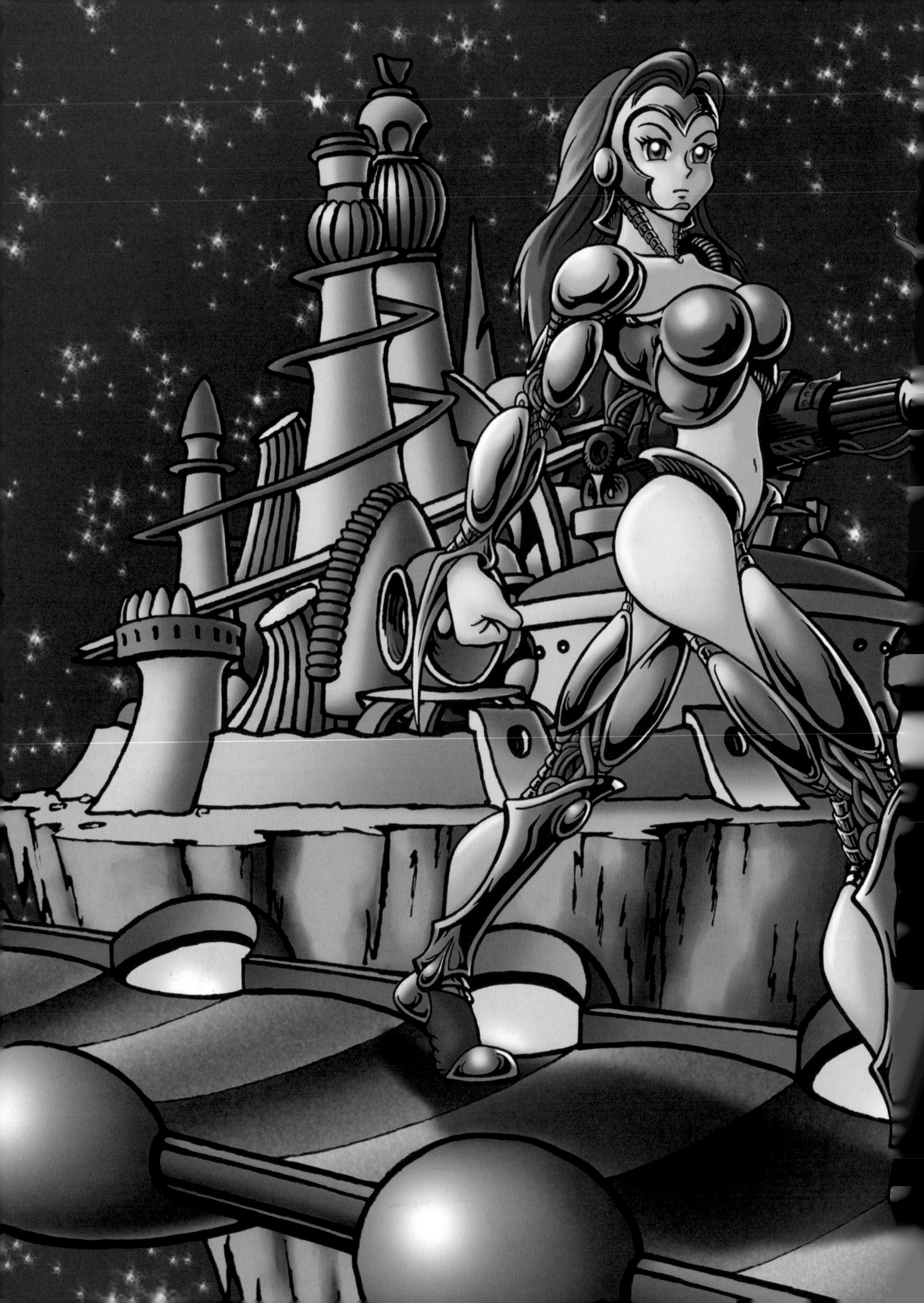

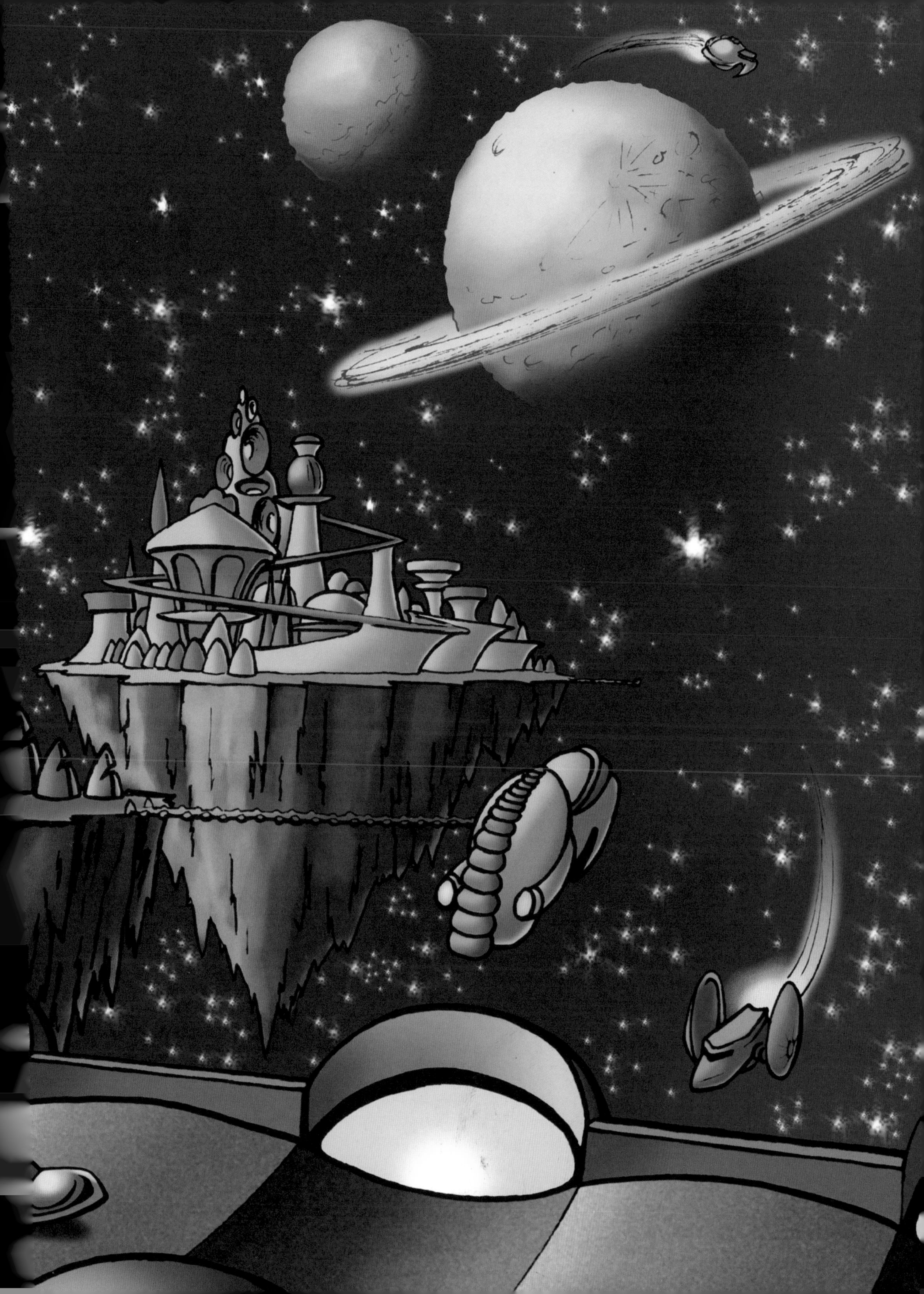

①

Urban Brawl

It's quite obvious what these two are up to, so we need to bring them together in a scene that suits their fist fight. We want a setting that's suitably squalid, like a smoky bar or, even better, a grimy, rat-infested back alley. The composition should complement the action.

① Dynamics

The composition doesn't need to be too elaborate because there's so much dynamism already. Combining figures in close combat means that their bodies may overlap—in our picture Rik's leading fist is in front of Steel's arm and Steel's foot sticks out in front of Rik's right leg. Two distinct motions are at play—Rik is swinging a punch, so all of his movement is in his upper body. His feet are placed firmly on the ground. In compositional terms he is balanced. In contrast, Steel is decidedly unbalanced and falling at quite a steep angle. This immediately suggests a diagonal composition—where the line of Steel's body follows a diagonal division of the picture (shown by blue line). With most of the action in the top part of the picture, it makes sense to leave the bottom half empty as a space for Steel to fall into (shown by blue arrow).

② Composition

Some kind of foreground object is needed in the empty space at the bottom right-hand corner to balance the action in the upper half of the picture. I've put this in as a random dark shape for now. A large solid mass behind the figures, such as a wall, will present a plain surface to place the action against. I intend to add movement lines, which will stand out against the wall, as will the droplets of blood. I've chosen a shallow one-point perspective—there's plenty of drama going on between the characters without needing the extra impact of steep angles in the background. Rik's perspective indicates a high eye level, which we need to be aware of for adding other elements to the background. After drawing this, I decided that the figures would need just a little more room to move, so when I sketch my color rough, I'll draw them at a reduced size.
➤➤

Mise-en-scène

When composing a narrative scene like this, we need to consider what to put in the picture. Each element and its effect on the scene needs to be considered individually—adding one small item can make a huge difference to the impact of a scene and what it communicates. Filmmakers and animators call this mise-en-scène.

Scene 1

All we see here is a fight between two men in an alley. We can guess which one is the bad guy—in manga, purple and green are usually associated with villains—but it's only a guess since there's little other information to go on.

Scene 1

Scene 2

I've brought in the right-hand edge of the building to allow space for a small vignette of life beyond the alley. Adding those few details immediately tells the viewer that the alley is in a big town or city and that it's night-time. These additions also break up that great expanse of brickwork and provide an extra layer of depth to the picture. A few spots of graffiti to the wall helps convey the squalor of the scene, along with some trash scattered about. But the viewer still might want to know more.

Scene 2

Scene 3

Scene 3

The addition of something as simple as a bunch of flowers can completely alter the interpretation of the scene. Now it looks like the guy throwing the punch is the villain, attacking an entirely innocent man.

Scene 4

Introducing another figure can also change our view of things—the fight doesn't seem so serious when it appears it's for a movie.
»

Scene 4

③ Final color rough

Of course, I don't really want flowers or a camera man in the finished picture. A trash bin and debris are much more suitable for breaking up that empty space and also add to the sense of squalor. Putting a knife in place of the flowers removes any doubt as to which of our characters is the bad guy. I like the way it's heading for the bin—just where it belongs! Now for one last manga touch—a sound effect to lend weight to that punch.

④ Line drawing of background

Inking a scene like this is quite straightforward. The lines should be rough and scruffy, so there's no need to use a ruler. All sorts of rough marks on the wall and floor can add interesting textures and scuffing. Some spots of gum and litter can be liberally scattered about.

⑤ Extras

As I'll be coloring my artwork on computer, I've drawn the sound effects and the knife separately; they can be applied as separate layers and positioned precisely once the figures are in place. I'll show you more about lettering effects on pages 324–325.

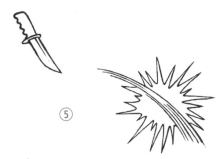

⑤

⑥ Color background

This is quite a sophisticated scene in terms of its coloring. The balance of light and reflections in the wet road surfaces are not easy to achieve. This is one of those instances when having done a rough color version first makes life a lot easier. With the color and tones finally settled, it was rather fun to add the graffiti, trying to emulate different styles.

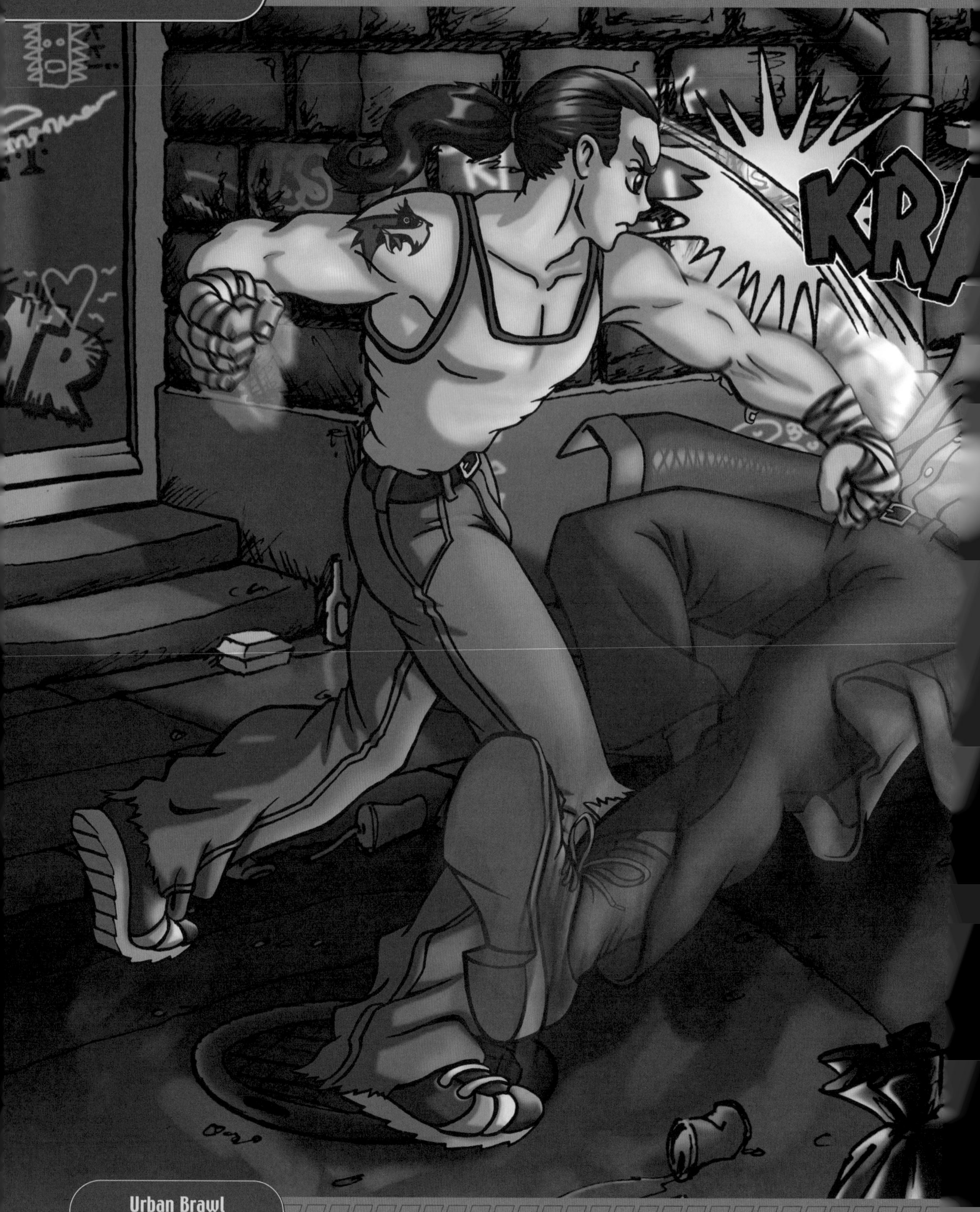
KRA

Completed artwork

Placing the figures and lettering involved a bit of juggling until their positioning looked right. Then I added their shadows and reflections on the ground and experimented with motion blurring effects, so emphasizing the movement. A white line around the lettering makes it clearly visible. I decided against any further highlighting of the figures because they stand out quite well enough.

①

②

Alien Ambush

I don't think we'll ever come across a character like this in real life, so we'll have to use our imagination to conjure up some suitably unwelcoming environment. I want the scene to look hard, like our alien's body surface, and have something of the angularity of his claws—bizarre rock formations might be just the thing. I want the composition to accentuate his posture and threatening gesture. Lastly, I want to see if those interesting highlights on his body can be incorporated in the scene.

① Composition
By trying out some alien landscapes as thumbnails, I gradually arrived at the idea of an underground setting. Here's the composition I came up with. A succession of curves draws the eye into the depths of the picture, toward a light source behind the alien. The shape of these curves acts as a framing device for the figure and also echoes the stoop of his posture. I've placed him low in the frame to stress the weight of rock and stalactites above. He has a clear route through the picture, marked in blue. To make a feature of his clawed hand, I've placed it at the meeting of

two golden section lines (see pages 258–259 for explanation of this theory). Although there's no visible horizon in this scene, we still need to keep the eye line in mind which is shown here as a paler green line.

② Secondary points of interest
After giving this composition more consideration, I decided that although it works well as an arrangement of shapes, as a picture it's not really telling a story. It needs another element—a secondary center of interest. The addition of space boy Kom could be just what's needed to inject some drama into the scene.

③ Adding an extra character

Bringing in Kom has immediately changed the dynamics. Kom is drawn as if we are looking at him from a low eye line, so he needs to be placed high up in the picture—I erased a bit of the rock to fit him in. The curve of the rock formation implies the direction in which he is about to hurl the boulder. Now there's a real sense of a story unfolding—the alien is coming out of the cave after the boy, but has no idea he is about to be ambushed.

④ Rough color sketch

I built up the tones bit by bit. Not only must the cave appear to have depth and solidity, but the lighting must be consistent with the scene. There are two light sources here, like in the earlier graveyard scene: a mysterious light behind the alien casting an orange glow on him and on some parts of the rocks, and a more natural light from top left. When using deep shadows, try to construct your picture so that important features are brightly lit

against dark areas and starkly silhouetted features are lit against very bright areas. Less important elements can be closer in tone. Although I'm happy with the tones, I'm uncertain about the color scheme. I don't want the rocks too dull and gray, and yet I don't want the colored light getting lost among too much other color.
>>

③

④

⑤

⑥

«

⑤ Black line drawing

For this kind of scene, it is not necessary to make a detailed pencil sketch. I drew a few pencil curves to show the basic shapes, then went to ink and brush. Starting with the foreground rocks and working back, I made progressively lighter marks with each layer of depth. I also varied the brush marks to describe different kinds of rock surfaces, and used solid black for places completely shielded from both light sources.

⑥ Color background

This being a very dark picture, I again worked on the light and shade first, darkening the shadow areas bit by bit. Once I was happy with the cave's depth and contrast, I added the colored highlights. Then it was just a case of dabbing on some grays and browns to build up the color and texture of the rock surfaces.

Completed artwork

Because I had kept the colors of the background quite dull, when the figures are added their colors are vibrant in comparison. Against the darkness of the cave interior they really seem to glow, which is an effect I had not predicted. Among the greatest thrills of creating artwork are the happy accidents that can occur along the way—even when using a computer.

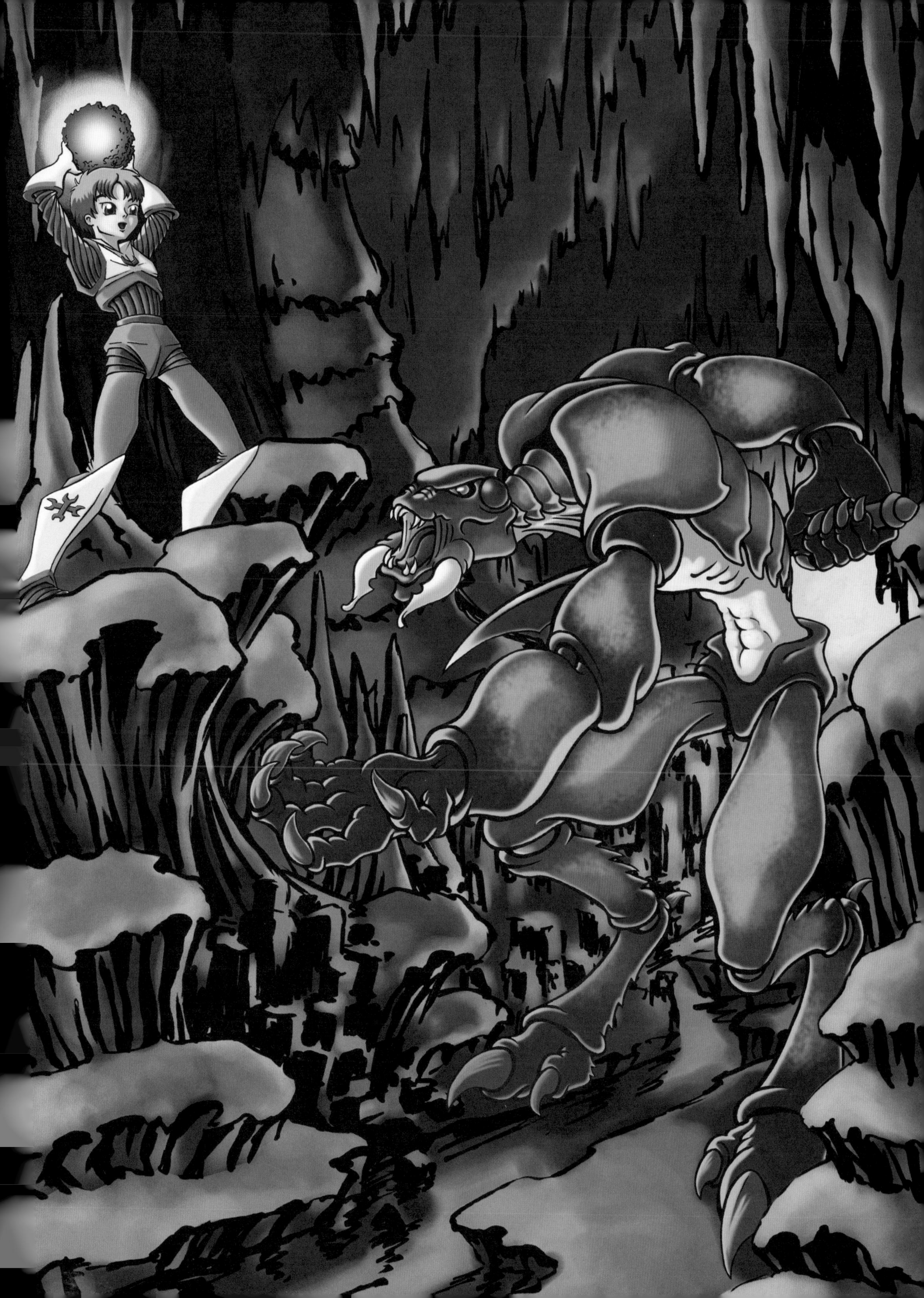

Robot Rampage

A character like our giant robot needs to be placed in a large-scale setting, and to be amongst objects where it looks like he could do some serious damage. A big-city scene would be a good backdrop. The challenge would be to drop him in among the skyscrapers and suggest impending havoc.

① **Composition**
Out of a whole batch of thumbnail drawings, I chose this rough

composition. The perspective of the figure is such that his eyes are level with the viewer's. I've therefore placed the eyes on the top-right golden section division, level with the horizon. This gives the robot plenty of space to swing his mighty arm. I'm treating the perspective of the buildings as simple blocks at this stage. Here I just need to work out the size and placement of the broad masses. I'm imagining the robot hemmed in, as if he's fighting his

way out. In all good stories, there should be tension, so it shouldn't be obvious who is going to win this battle. I want to present the robot as being under heavy attack. The helicopter alone doesn't pose much of a threat, so when I draw the background, I'm going to introduce a couple of fighter planes. I've left space in the composition for them— the blue arrows indicate their direction through this space.

①

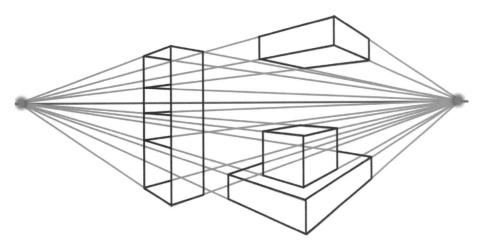

Two-point perspective

Here's the same set of blocks we saw on page 282 from a different angle. In this diagram the lines of the horizontal edges of the blocks now also converge at a second vanishing point farther along the horizon. It helps, though, that all the lines of the vertical edges remain rigidly vertical wherever the blocks are placed in the picture. The best way to understand this principle is to see it in action, so we'll now apply it to drawing a background for our giant robot.

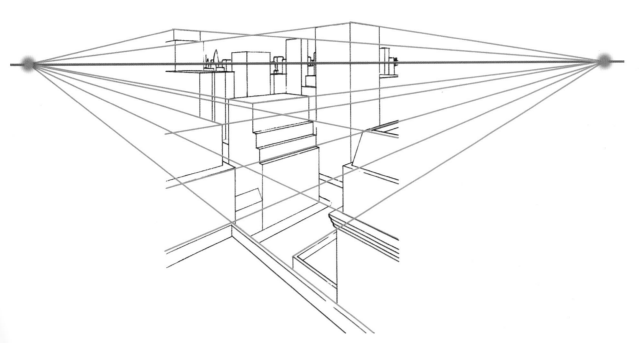

Background in perspective

Working from my rough composition, I have redrawn the main blocks more precisely and in perspective. For a drawing like this you need to mark the horizon (green line) and the vanishing points. The easiest way is to work on a desk and fix the paper with masking tape. Then, using a soft pencil, position the vanishing points off the edges of the

paper, directly on your desk—if you don't press too hard, the pencil marks should rub off easily later. Using a hard pencil, lightly block in the main shapes. When they are close to what you want, take a long ruler and use your softer pencil to line up the edges of the buildings so their lines meet at your vanishing points. I've used two different colors to show these lines. Remember: 1, vertical edges

should remain vertical and parallel to each other; and 2, the horizon is the lowest point of the sky—objects may cross the horizon and reach into the sky, but the sky never falls below the horizon.

Once the main blocks of your drawing are in place, leave your piece of paper where it is—you'll find the vanishing points invaluable for drawing all the tiny details later.

②

② Color rough

I drew this rough sketch straight out of my head. The perspective isn't perfect, but it's close enough for the purpose of trying out my composition. As for the color, I've kept the palette restricted to dull browns, grays, greens and blues to give the scenery a naturalistic feel. The bold red of the robot stands out nicely against them. The tones and colors are stronger in the foreground and become weaker the farther away they are in the distance. The term for this effect is aerial perspective.

>>

③ **Background in black line**

Creating a precise and detailed line drawing takes time—this one took me about 12 hours! There's a lot of careful ruling, measuring and double checking along the way. Make sure you don't completely cover the page in detail—the picture needs some empty space or it will look cluttered.

Ink all the lines with a ruler, still lining them up with those vanishing points, then erase the pencil guidelines that you will have built up.

④ **Line drawings of planes**

These are the line drawings of the airplanes that I will scan into my computer, color separately then place

on top of the background. I haven't included much detail in them, because I plan to blur them for a sense of speed.

③

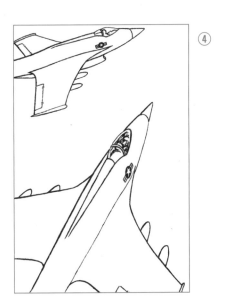

Having the luxury of a computer for the final coloring means I'm free to keep some elements separate from my background artwork. This is absolutely essential for animation but also useful for creating an individual piece. It means that the positioning of all the elements can be adjusted right up to the final stage.

 Full color background

⑤ Full color background

With quite simple shading and coloring, I've gone for broad areas of flat color and tone, enough to show the solidity of the buildings but not to clash with the detail of the linework.

Completed artwork

Having parts of the robot obscured by foreground elements instantly places him in the scene. The planes are rendered in the same simple style as the buildings.

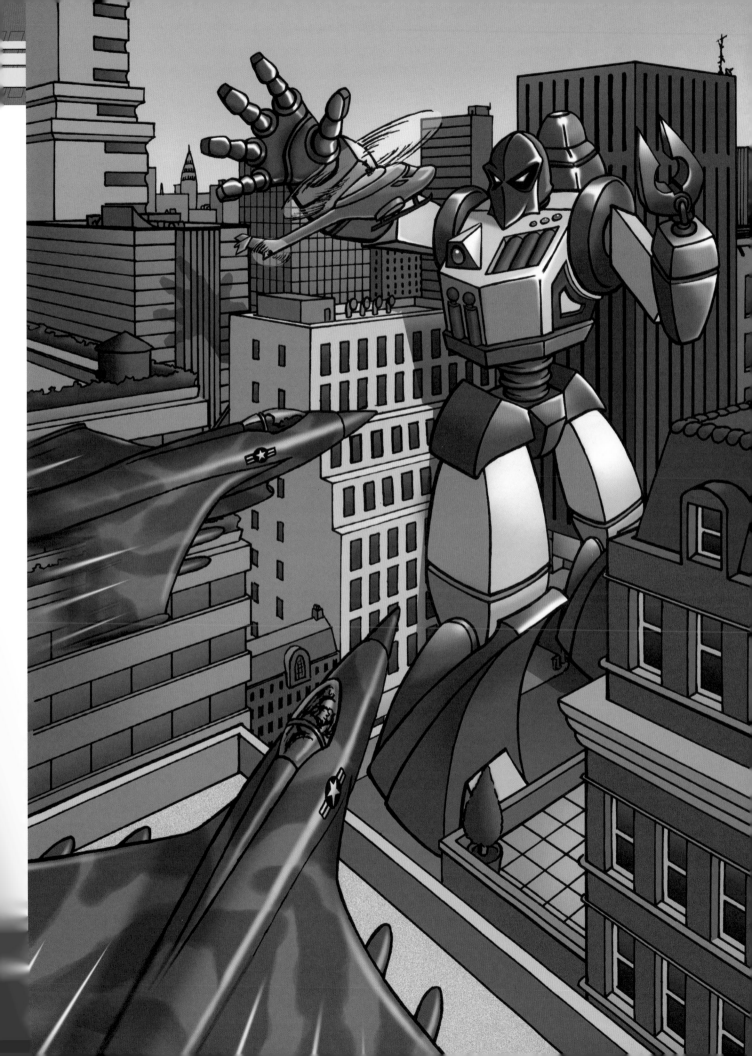

City of the Future

The challenge is to put our character, Elise, in a setting that suits her other-worldly look and makes use of her complicated pose and gesture. I also want to use this picture to demonstrate yet more complex perspective. I'm therefore going to place her above a futuristic cityscape with strange buildings stretching to the horizon.

① Composition

This figure will fit neatly into a composition similar to that of the giant robot picture. But Elise needs a reason to be placed above the scene. Some sort of high-tech hovering surfboard might be fun. I've marked the rough position and scale of this as a dark ellipse.

①

Three-point perspective

One of the defining characteristics of manga is impressive perspective drawing. So far, we've looked at one- and two-point perspective and also touched on aerial perspective. Now we'll look at three-point perspective.

When a picture features objects that sit far above or below the viewer, an extra vanishing point is needed. In this diagram all the lines that remained vertical in the two-point perspective diagram (see page 305) now slope and converge on a higher vanishing point. This creates the impression that we are close to the boxes and looking steeply up at them from a low viewpoint.

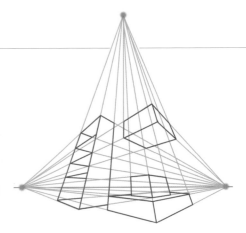

② Background in perspective

Here's a pencil drawing of the background I came up with—I'll show you this in more detail on the next page. This drawing shows the main blocks of the buildings. I had in mind the concept of a world where every bit of land is built on, rising ever higher to accommodate an escalating population. To convey this idea of a small planet I want to show the curvature of the surface so I made the horizon curve, as shown by the green line. This means that all the lines of perspective running to either of the horizon's vanishing points have to bend too (blue and purple lines). This also has the effect of emphasizing the depth of the third perspective point—this is deep below the horizon because we are looking down on the scene. All 'verticals' converge on the third perspective point (orange lines). There is only one vertical line in the whole picture, running directly up from the vanishing point. The tallest tower sits directly on this vertical line for maximum impact.

>>

②

③

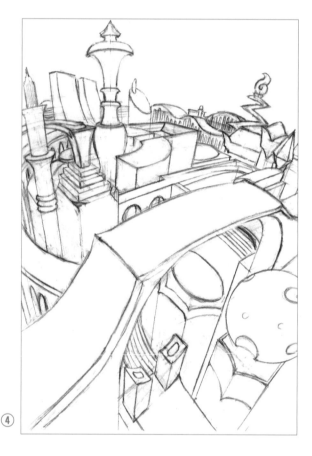

④

③ Rough color sketch

Rough color sketches can be very helpful to find out which elements do and don't work in a composition. I can now see that my original idea for the girl to be crouched on a hovering vehicle doesn't work—the space bike gets lost amongst the chaotic colors and shapes of the background and it does not completely suit the girl's pose. This calls for a rethink. Some things did work well, though. I've used a whole range of clashing colors to add to the sense of new buildings being squeezed into this city at random over the years. Cropping off the edges of the picture to make a taller format suits the nature of the buildings and emphasizes their height. There is no doubt about the focus of the girl's interest—she is pointing to a mysterious tower.

④ Pencil sketch of background

Before you apply color, a scene like this must stand up as a line drawing. Referring to my color rough, I have redrafted my picture in pencil on decent paper, keeping the elements I liked and changing those that I was less pleased with. The flying surfboard has been replaced with a bridge structure between two buildings. The building forms here have come straight out of my head. I'm redesigning them because those of the color rough appear too bland and blocky, and I need to accommodate the new bridge. Even though I expect to crop the edges, I include detail at the sides so that I can decide on the eventual format later on.

⑤ **Simple black line**

Once I worked out the basic shapes and perspective in pencil, I went over my final pencil lines in black ink to make a simple line drawing. I added some bits of detail as I went, then erased all my rough pencil lines.

⑥ **Final inking**

Next I added the last details to my picture. I then worked over the line, smoothing out the curves and increasing the weight of the line work in the foreground. Finally I took another look at all the parts of the picture to make sure that all the buildings were clearly defined, strengthening the lines where necessary.
»

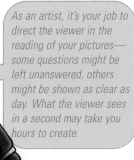

As an artist, it's your job to direct the viewer in the reading of your pictures— some questions might be left unanswered, others might be shown as clear as day. What the viewer sees in a second may take you hours to create.

⑥

<<

⑦ Full color background

Before applying any color, I worked on the tones of the buildings, keeping each one clearly defined and the lighting consistent. The tones were also important for capturing the eerie twilight feel I wanted.

Completed artwork

With Elise in place, and a shadow put in underneath her, I decided not to crop the sides of the picture. This change of mind ensured that the chaotic sprawl of the cityscape could be retained.

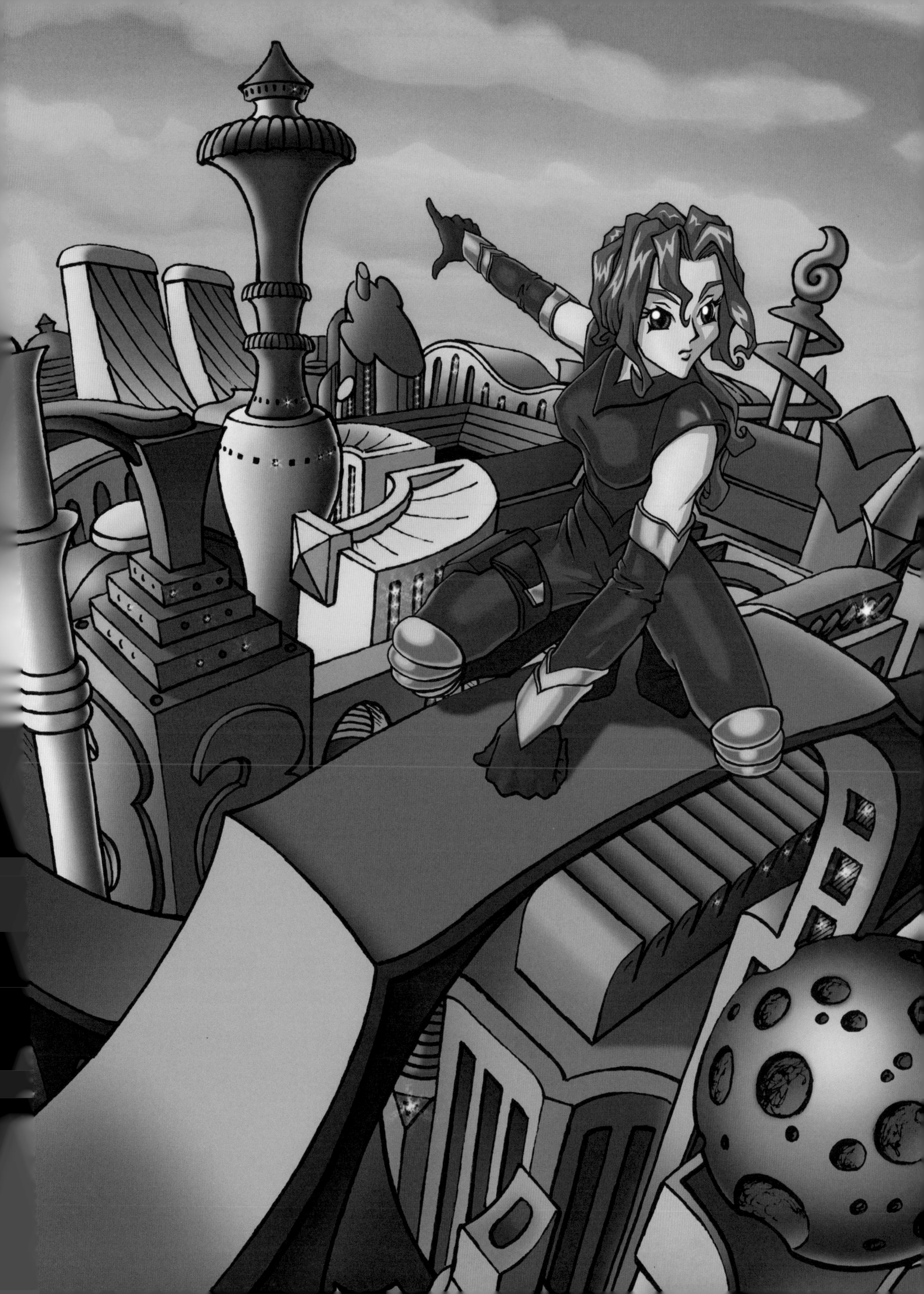

So far, we've covered a wide variety of manga genres and looked at lots of ways in which single pictures can be constructed to suggest a narrative. Here, we are going to examine how individual pictures can be assembled to tell an extended and carefully orchestrated story—in other words, we're going to create parts of a comic book.

I'll start by taking you through the stages of designing the first page of a comic book and then show you how to create a title page. To show you the power of images alone, we won't be adding any dialogue.

Most stories essentially begin with a state of equilibrium, or calm, and then some event occurs to break that calm. The remainder of the story is a series of efforts to overcome the upset and restore equilibrium.

But before even picking up a pencil, we'll need a scenario and a rough script to work to ...

THE BRIEF

Daisy and Duke have gone away to a mountain retreat, so that they can work on their latest manga story. Their log cabin is out in the wilderness, miles from the nearest town. Duke has gone out to get some supplies, leaving Daisy all alone —and there's something lurking in the forest. In a few pictures—or as they are called in comics, panels—the aim is to convey where the story is set along with a sense that something is about to happen, culminating in a disturbance that intrigues the reader enough to turn over the page.

COMIC STRIP

COMIC STRIP
COMIC STRIP
COMIC STRIP
COMIC STRIP
COMIC STRIP
COMIC STRIP
COMIC STRIP
COMIC STRIP
COMIC STRIP
COMIC STRIP
COMIC STRIP
COMIC STRIP
COMIC STRIP
COMIC STRIP
COMIC STRIP
COMIC STRIP

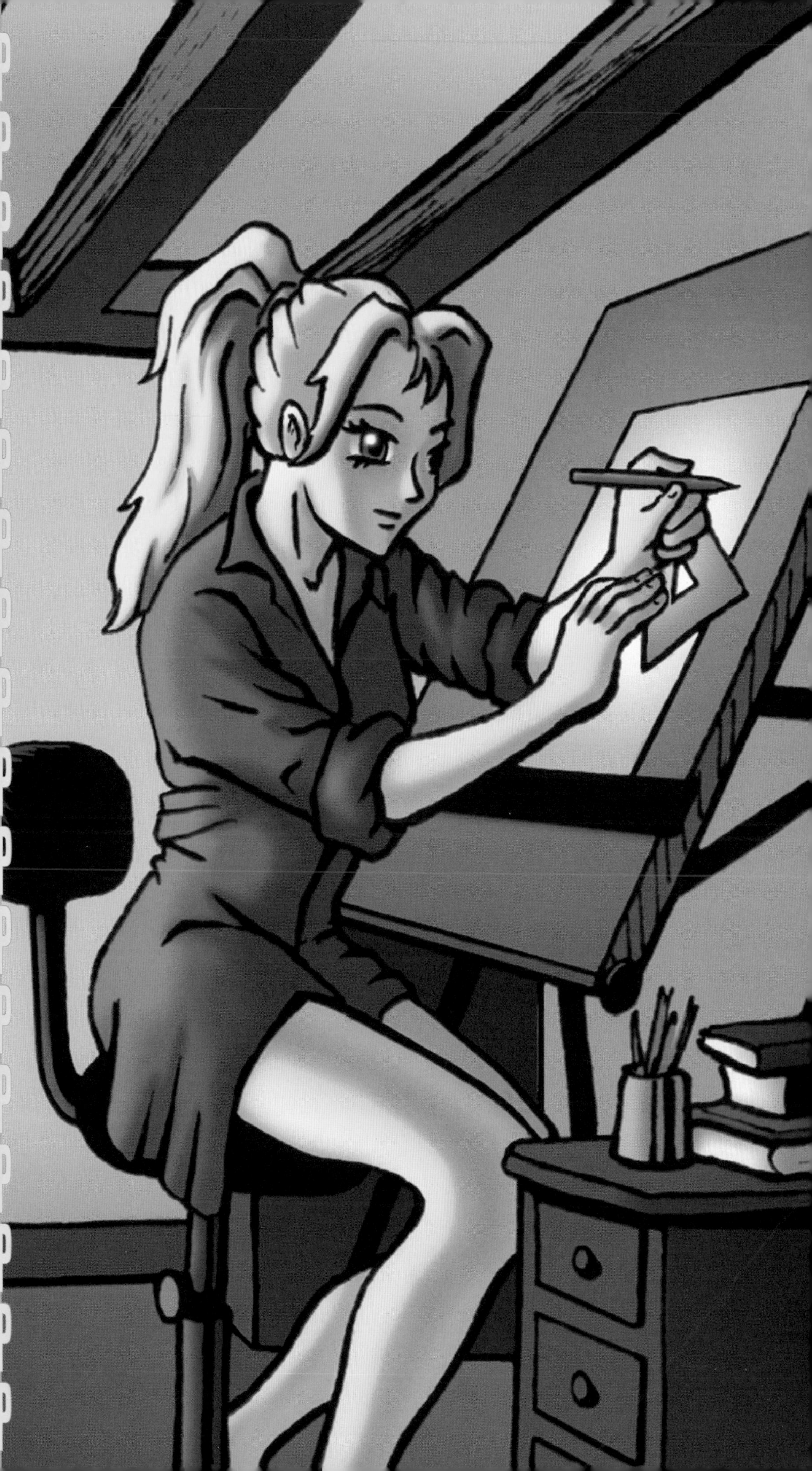

Creating a Comic Strip

The first stage of designing a comic strip layout is to work out what each panel should contain and decide on the order in which the panels should run. This is known as story-boarding. These drawings should be simple and quick—no one else will ever need to see them, so they only have to make sense to you.

Step 1

Panels 1, 2, and 3 show the environment—they gradually tell us what's going on through the window of the cabin. In panel 4, we find out that we aren't the only observers of the scene—and then realize that the previous three panels are what this mysterious figure is seeing as he approaches the cabin. Panel 5 reinforces the equilibrium hinted at in panel 3 and shows more detail of Daisy—what she's doing and the fact that she's alone. In panel 6 the mystery character gives away his presence. Daisy reacts. Her expression then turns to horror. In Panel 9 we see what she is horrified by. The fact that we still don't see the intruder keeps us intrigued.

Step 2

Now we need to choose the best shape, size, and composition for each individual panel. Your ideal pictures are unlikely to fit together perfectly—compromises have to be made to get each panel to work in its own right and to fit within an overall page design. There is clearly more work to be done.

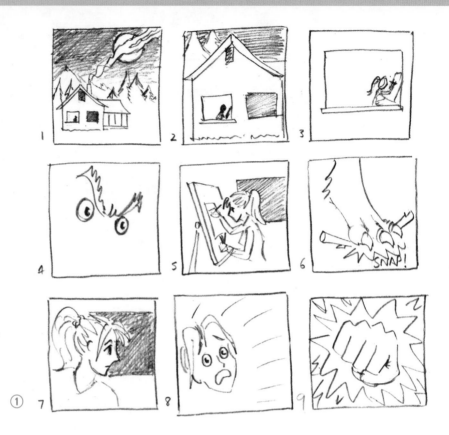

Step 3

The panels can be made to fit together by adjusting their shapes, sizes and positions. This looks pretty good as a rough layout.

Step 4

All the while you have to bear in mind what the color and tone of the panels will look like in the final artwork. In this story, half the panels are set outside and half inside. The outdoor pictures will be inked and colored much more heavily than the others. This gives us a problem—all the dark pictures are together in one corner of the page.

Step 5

In order to balance the tones on the page, I've had to change the format of some of the panels.

Step 6

By shading the panels again, we can see that these further adjustments have led to a much more balanced page. Just as we saw with single pictures, the overall composition is essential to a quality piece of work.
»

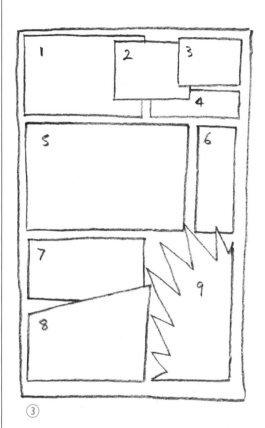

③

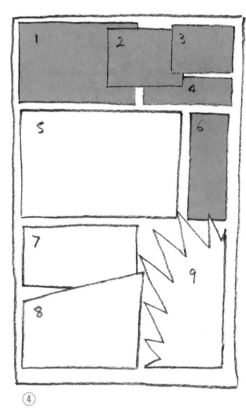

④

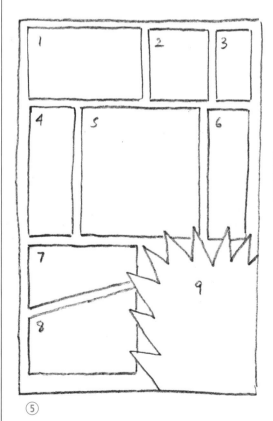

⑤

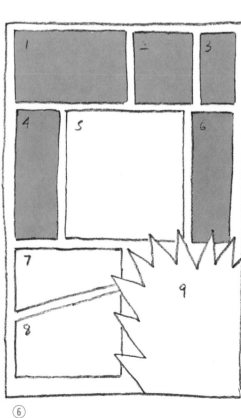

⑥

Step 7

Before I started making a pencil sketch of my storyboard idea, I decided that I would make a couple of additional changes to the panels. I started the page with an extra panel showing a full moon to hint that something spooky might be about to happen. For the final panel, I thought that an open hand might look more threatening than a fist, and that a sound effect would add impact to the action.

I mapped out this page roughly with a hard pencil then worked up the details with a softer one.

⑦

Step 8

I'm going to use a lot of solid black on this page. If you do this, you need to think carefully about it since it's easy to get carried away when you open the bottle of ink! First I go over the lines of my pencil sketch with a black fine-tipped pen, using a ruler for the panel edges. Then I can erase all my pencil marks. Compare this page to the following one to see the difference made by darker inking.

≫

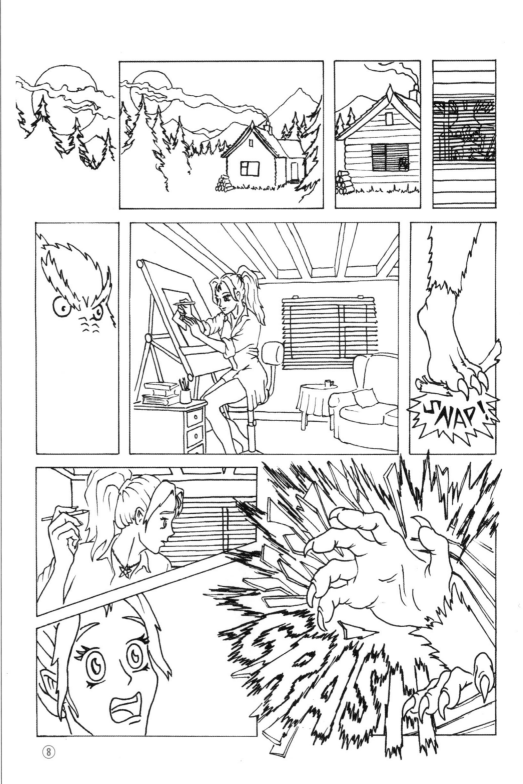

«

Step 9

Fleshing out some lines with a thicker pen and adding solid black to the panels that are set outdoors gives the drawing a real lift. I also used the black for the spaces between the panels to give the page a unified design. I haven't ruled off the first panel of the moon, and I've allowed the sound effects to break out of their panels. Simple tricks like these add variety and interest to the page.

Finished artwork

In a sense, a lot of the coloring decisions were made when I refined the inking at the previous stage. The main thing here is to retain the distinction between the outdoor panels and those set indoors. Cool, dark shades as opposed to warm, bright colors.

So that's the introductory page of my story finished. Now it needs a title page to really grab the reader's attention. Before we look at the titling I devised, let's look first at the kinds of effects which can be achieved by adding words to your pictures.

⑨

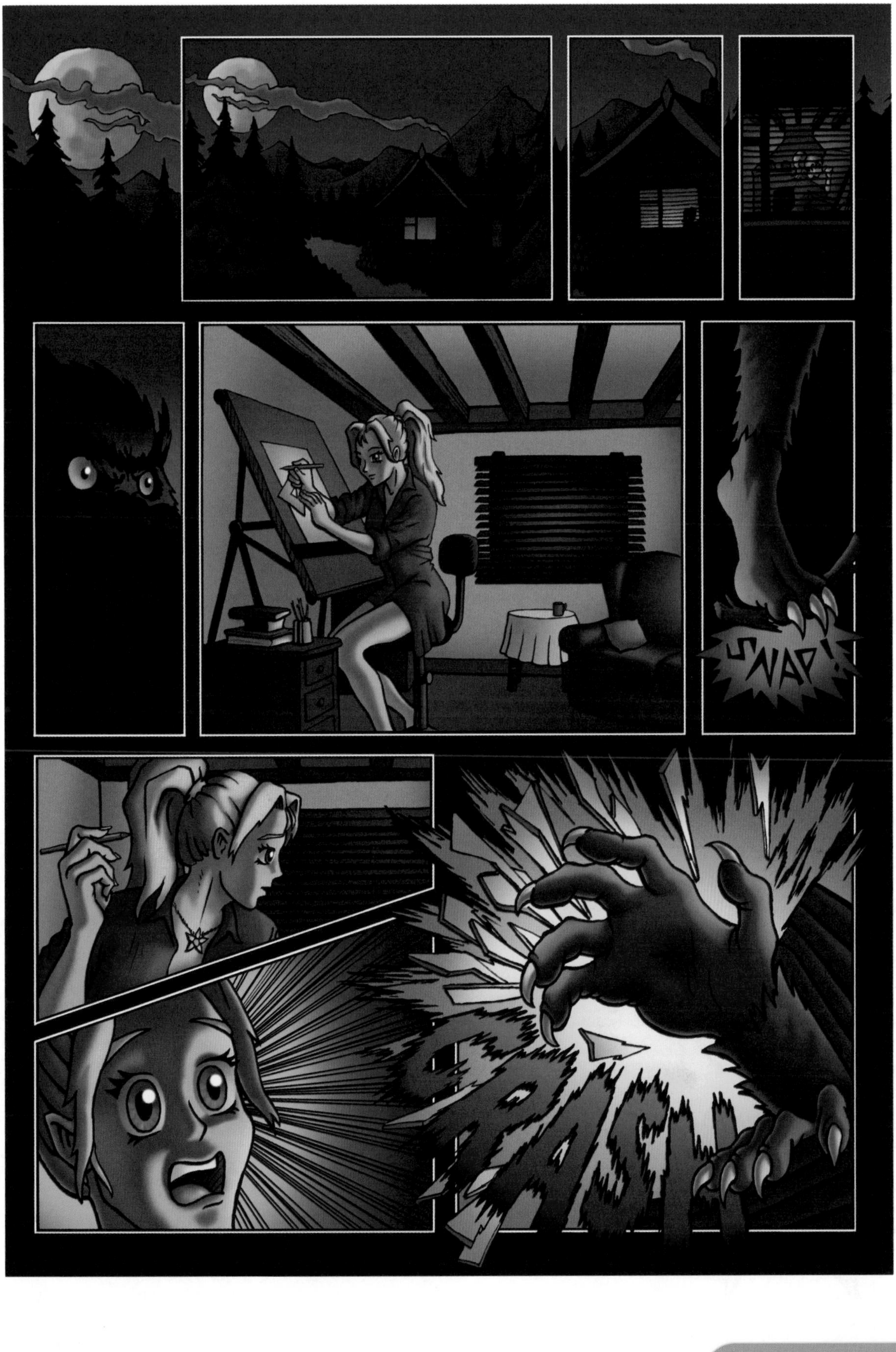
SNAP!
CRASH!

Creating Lettering and Sound Effects

On page 296 the addition of a single word to the fight scene had the effect of exaggerating the impact of the punch. Such devices are known as sound effects and are used extensively in manga, in some manga comics in nearly every panel. Here's a very brief look at the kinds of effects you can achieve with the design and placement of words in your manga pictures.

Bang 1, Bang 2

Bang is typical of the kinds of words used in manga. It's one of those words that sounds like its meaning. But the word alone is not enough for a dramatic manga effect. For a start, it needs to be written, or rather, drawn in an appropriate style. Precisely designed and spaced lettering is not as effective as roughly proportioned letters, skewed and overlapping. In these cases an exclamation mark is often a good idea.

The meaning of the word can take on different associations depending on the context and the way the word is presented. In these examples, exactly the same lettering seems to make a different sound. In the first, the sound appears to be muffled by the cloud design and suggests a dull explosion. In the other, the shape of the outline suggests a sharper sound, such as a heavy blow or objects striking against each other.

Arrrghh! 1

Here are more examples where roughly drawn lettering is more effective than neatness. Duke's clearly in pain judging by the look on his face so, one could argue that the lettering is unnecessary. But this is manga, where drama is all-important. The lettering reinforces Duke's emotion with its angular shape and increasing size, as well as the meaning of the word itself.

Arrrghh! 2

Same word, different emotion. With a more wobbly shape to the letters and a change of expression on Duke's face, Arrrghh! becomes a cry of fear rather than pain.

Using symbols

Lettering is not only used for sound effects, more subtle expressions can be drawn out of the considered use of letters and symbols. Here, Duke's quizzical expression can be read in three different ways. The implication in each of these is not of noise, but of thought.

①

②

③

Designing a Logo

Now that we've looked at what can be achieved with simply drawn sound effects, let's consider applications where you'll need to spend more time designing the lettering.

① Logo line

Here's a logo I've been working on for Daisy's comic. It had to go through several stages of development to realize my idea of Daisy's character: gentle and rounded and yet also angular and dynamic.

② Logo outline

Once a logo is designed, there are many decisions yet to be made about it's final rendering. In this trial I've coloured it in flat red and added an outline—very manga. To do it yourself make sure that the outline is the same width all the way around the letters and don't forget the areas inside and between the letters.

③ Logo shadow

Another common manga lettering device is known as drop shadow. To achieve this effect you need two versions of the lettering, exactly the same shape in outline. One is offset from the other and when coloured or shaded in a darker tone, it gives the impression of a shadow underneath raised lettering. In this example, I've also added a few basic highlights to increase the suggestion of light and shade.

To see the final rendering of Daisy's logo, turn to the 'title page' section on page 333.

Creating a Title Page

In the previous exercise, we set the scene with the first page of our comic strip story. Now I'll show you how to design the title page of the story. Just like in movies and television dramas, the tension in a comic is often built up before the title is introduced.

The brief

This picture should be the revealing moment—when we see the intruder for the first time. It's effectively the next panel of our story. It should convey Daisy's plight and the impending danger. First I need to decide on the composition of our picture, which I've done by making some rough sketches.

Rough 1

I want to show the difference in scale between the two characters, but here the beast takes up too much space in the picture. This kind of composition would work well for a smaller panel, but not here.

Rough 2

This could work better because the mass of the beast's body serves as a fairly plain background to the lettering. Daisy looks suitably cornered, but I think we ought to see more of the beast's face.

①

②

Rough 3

Shadows are great for creating mystery but I don't think this approach will work for the title page. I like Daisy's pose, though, so let's look at the scene from the other way around.

Rough 4

This is much better. The beast and Daisy are both in full view. The size of the beast is apparent, and there's space around them to show some background detail and the disarray of the room.

>>

③

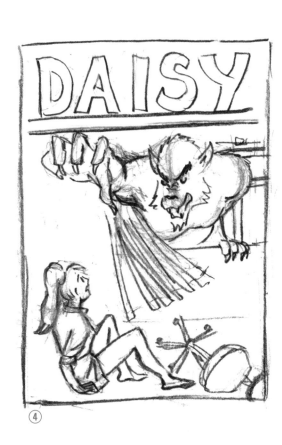

④

When you are creating your own character, try copying a friend's hairstyle and look in a catalogue for clothing ideas. Borrow bits from manga characters on TV too.

« Pencil drawing

Once I had worked out where to put the figures, I decided to skew the picture to add to the impact—this changes the perspective, making the beast tower over Daisy even more as she cowers in the corner. At this stage I'm only concerned with the basic shapes and perspective which I've roughly sketched in with a hard pencil.

Adding detail

The expressions of Daisy and the beast are crucial to the impact of the picture, so I've spent some time on them. I've added the furniture and the slats of the broken blind the beast has burst its way through. These details are added with a softer pencil over very rough guidelines.

Simple ink line

Once I was satisfied with my pencil sketch, I carefully inked over all my final lines with a black felt-tip pen. When the ink was dry, I erased all my pencil marks.

Finished ink line

Now I strengthen the line and add a few areas of black, especially around the beast's eyes. Now the picture is ready to be colored. I'll break down the computer coloring into simple stages so that you can produce similar results with your own pictures.

Scanning and preparation

Once you have your final ink drawing, you are ready to scan it in. It's best to scan at a high resolution —say 500 dpi—and as grayscale. This gives crisper lines later on and eliminates the risk of a color cast from your scanner. When you are in Photoshop, reduce the resolution to about 300 dpi. That's about the maximum you'll need to print with, and larger sizes will only slow your computer down. Convert the image (In Image>Mode>) to RGB. This is a good time to look at your work close up and clean any large blotches and imperfections. Use the Eraser tool for this. Making sure your background color is white, Select All (Apple + A) and make New Layer Via Cut (Apple + Shift + J). Set the Blending Mode of this layer to Multiply, name it 'Line Art' and then lock it. You shouldn't need to touch your original artwork again.
➤

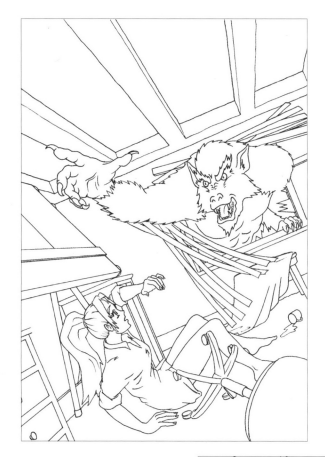

« First color

On a layer below your black and white drawing, start putting down the flat colors. You have to get rid of the white areas first. In our first illustration you can see that the main color used is the warm brown of the cabin walls. I used the Lasso and Bucket and Magic Wand tools to put down this broadest area of color. In the second picture I used a dark brown to roughly cover the area of the floor. Select this area with the Lasso tool. You'll find it easier if you magnify the image quite a lot and use the Polygon Lasso tool to make your selections. Fill it up using the Bucket tool.

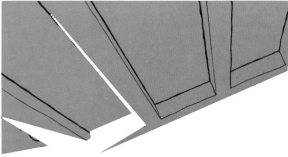

Second color

Select what will be the next largest area of color. You can fill it with the Bucket, or alternatively change the color using Image > Adjustments > Hue/Saturation (Apple + U). I decided to mark out the dark color of the wolf-creature's furry coat.
Hint: After drawing out your rough selection area, you can use the Magic Wand with the Alt key pressed down to deselect any different-colored areas you may have accidentally included.

Flat color

Once you've got all the areas of flat color down, merge these color layers, name it 'Flat Color' and Lock it. You shouldn't need to change it again, but it will prove useful with the Magic Wand tool later on. Make a new layer. We'll be working on this new layer from now on. Save your work. (You have been saving regularly, haven't you?)
>>

«
Shading

Time to put on some shadows. For this we'll be using Quick Mask. Click on the Quick mask icon, or just press Q. Using the Brush tool, paint an area you want to be in shadow. Don't worry about going over the lines—we'll be fixing that shortly.

To check what you've just done, leave Quick Mask mode (again Q or the icon in the tool palette). You'll see that you've actually selected an area of the image. For a more feathered selection you can use a softer brush. Now you can clean up the selection by going to your 'Flat Color' layer and using Alt + the Magic Wand tool just as you did earlier. Go back to your working layer and use Image > Adjustments > Hue/Saturation to shade to your taste, or just fill it up with the Bucket tool.

Highlights

If you would like exact control over the area of highlight, you can magnify the image and use the Lasso tool to select the shapes you want, then lighten them with the Hue/Saturation command. This is the way I worked on Daisy's hair. For most of the images in this book I used the Dodge tool, which softly lightens colors wherever it is applied. If you prefer a more painterly style of shading, you can use it and the Magic Wand to mask off the areas you're working on.

Your finished artwork is now ready to print out.

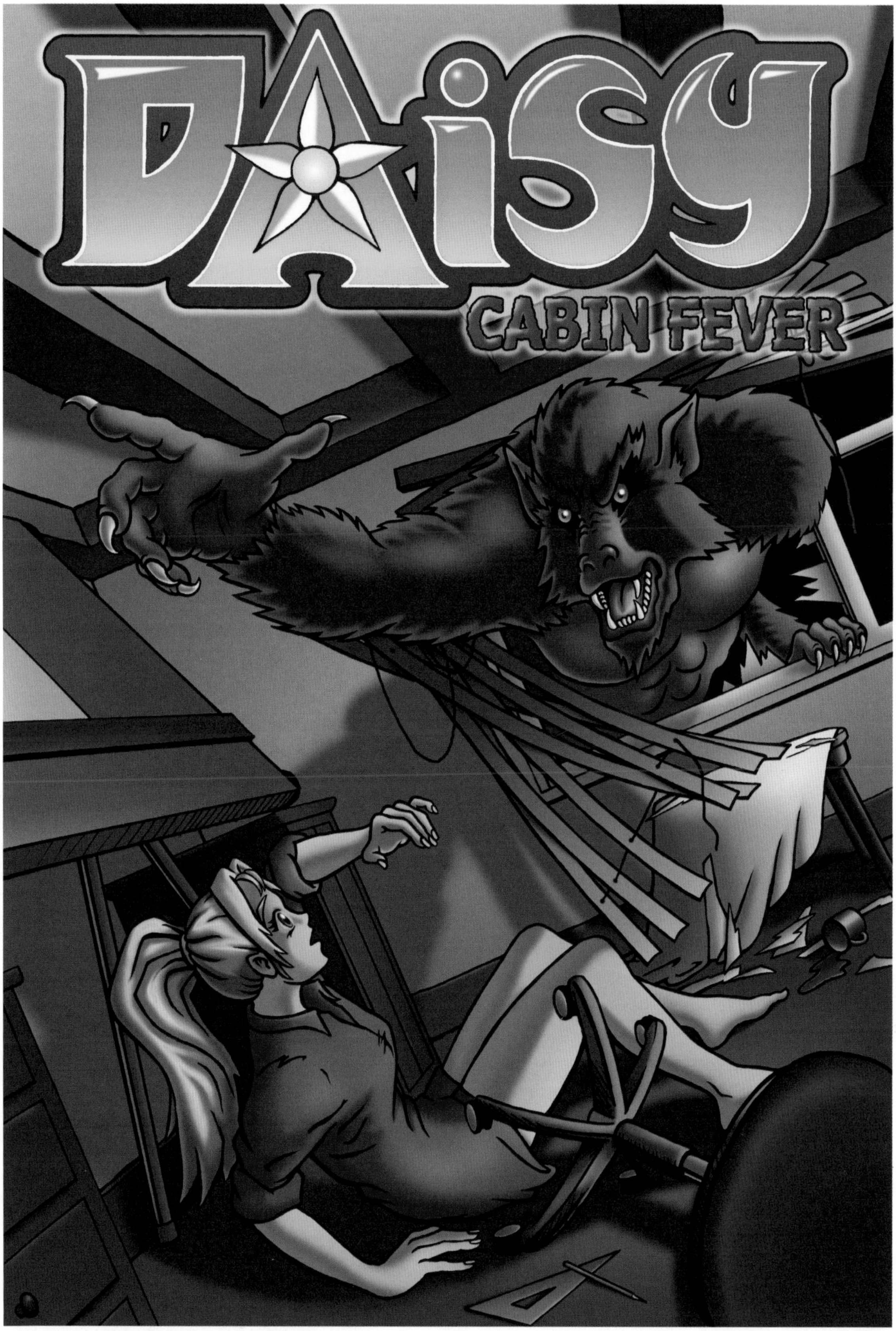
DAiSY
CABIN FEVER

CONCL

So that's it—except that you can always do more to improve your manga drawings. All the scenes in this book need to be complemented by well-drawn figures, so practicing character drawing is crucial. This book can help you get better day by day if you follow the step-by-step instructions to drawing manga males, females, mechas, and monsters in action. Now that you've taken a stab at starting a comic strip, you could storyboard what might happen next—or create storyboards for adventures you think up yourself. For this you'll need inspiration which you'll find in the world around you. You can base your ideas on real news stories and your characters might be people you know. Any time an idea strikes you, jot it down or sketch it. Even if you can't think what to do with it immediately, you might find a place for it once you have a batch of ideas to thread together.

Duke, Daisy and Magnus have given you all the help they can. Now it's down to you to become a master of your manga destiny. Enjoy the journey!

USION

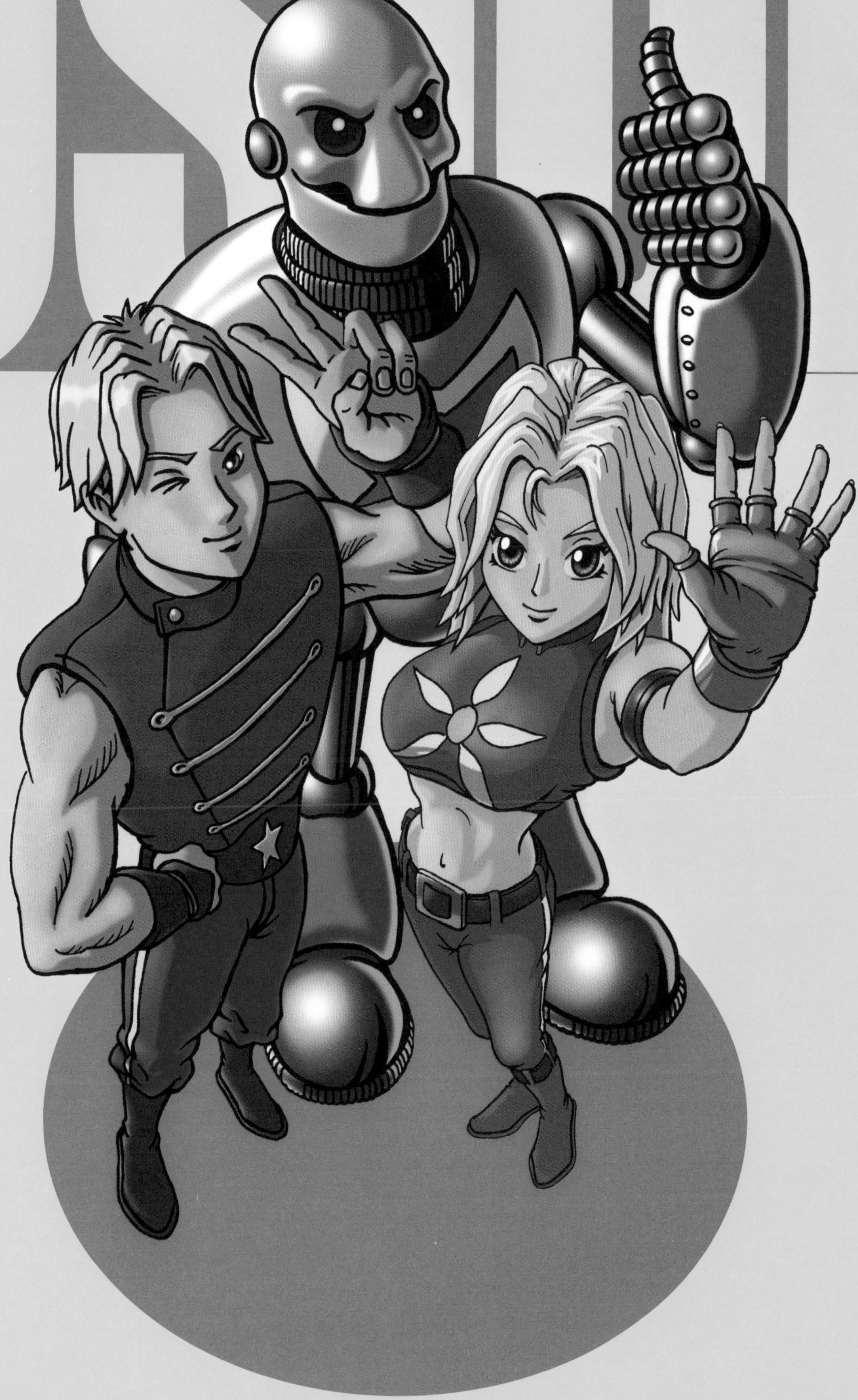

MANGA

INDEX OF CONTENTS